REPRINTS OF ECONOMIC CLASSICS

ADAM SMITH, 1776-1926

ADAM SMITH, 1776-1926

LECTURES TO COMMEMORATE THE SESQUI-CENTENNIAL OF THE PUBLICATION OF "THE WEALTH OF NATIONS"

BY

JOHN MAURICE CLARK

PAUL H. DOUGLAS

JACOB H. HOLLANDER

GLENN R. MORROW

MELCHIOR PALYI

JACOB VINER

REPRINTS OF ECONOMIC CLASSICS

AUGUSTUS M. KELLEY · PUBLISHERS

First edition 1928
(Chicago: University of Chicago Press, 1928)

Reprinted 1989 by
AUGUSTUS M. KELLEY, PUBLISHERS
Fairfield NJ 07006-0008

Library of Congress Cataloging-in-Publication Data

Adam Smith, 1776-1929 : lectures to commemorate the sesquicentennial of the publication of "the Wealth of nations."

(Reprints of Economic Classics)
Reprint. originally published: Chicago : University of Chicago Press, 1928.
Includes index.
1. Smith, Adam, 1723-1790. 2. Free enterprise.
I. Clark, John Maurice, 1884- . II. Series.
HB103.S6A6225 1989 330.15'3 88-32065
ISBN 0-678-00138-3

Manufactured in the United States of America

PREFACE

The lectures which are contained in the present volume were delivered at the University of Chicago during the months of December, 1926—February, 1927 in a series designed to commemorate the sesquicentennial of the publication of the *Wealth of Nations*. The influence of Adam Smith upon economic thought and practice has been so pronounced that it was thought worth while to trace some of the more prominent features of his teachings and to indicate some of the main channels of his influence. Grateful acknowledgment is made to the scholars who delivered the lectures in the series and also to The Robert Brookings Graduate School of Economics and Government for permission to include in the present volume the lecture by Professor Clark, part of which was delivered in a series of lectures sponsored by that institution as well as in the series at the University of Chicago.

TABLE OF CONTENTS

CHAPTER I

THE DAWN OF A SCIENCE

JACOB H. HOLLANDER

"In every department of human affairs," declared John Stuart Mill sonorously in the opening paragraph of his *Principles of Political Economy,* "Practice long precedes Science: systematic enquiry into the modes of action of the powers of nature, is the tardy product of a long course of efforts to use those powers for practical ends."[1]

Historians of thought, going beyond Mill's generalization, agree in recognizing two distinct stages in the evolution of a social science. There is first a period of specific and detached discussion of particular incidents, ordinarily evoked by association with practical affairs. There is later a systematic inquiry, inspired by philosophic interest, into the structure and sequence of the general subject matter.

In the history of English economic thought, the year 1750 serves as a convenient dividing line for this transition. Much was written upon economic matters before that date. An eighteenth-century bibliographer lists some twenty-three hundred such publications, issued in Great Britain from 1557 to 1764,[2] and the catalogue is far from complete. Ranging from mere broadsides to stout volumes, the bulk of this literature figures in the history of economic writing as ephemeral and local. But an appreciable part of it is significant. The tracts of John Wheeler,

[1] "Preliminary Remarks," *op. cit.* (London, 1848), I, 1.

[2] Joseph Massie; cf. *infra.*

Gerard de Malynes, Edward Misselden, Thomas Mun, Lewis Roberts, Henry Parker, Dudley North, Josiah Child, Joshua Gee upon commerce; of Sir Isaac Newton, John Locke, Nicholas Barbon upon money; and of Sir Charles Davenant, Sir William Petty, Sir William Temple, Francis Fauquier, Joseph Massie upon taxation not only discussed contemporary episodes, but in casting about for theoretical warrant for specific proposals often phrased scientific truths to an extent that has won the admiration of later students. Sometimes an unusual contact with affairs, as in the case of Jacob Vanderlint, or a larger social vision, as with Bishop Berkeley, inspired a more ambitious contribution. But even in such cases, the inception and issue were associated with specific events. We owe *Money Answers All Things* to Walpole's excise scheme, and *The Querist* was suggested by the economic distress of Ireland.

In the middle of the eighteenth century, however, economic thinking entered upon a more deliberate and systematic phase. The Peace of Aix-la-Chapelle in releasing England from continental entanglement, and the battle of Culloden Moor in establishing the Hanoverian succession, gave impetus to commercial and industrial growth.[4] The religious revival identified with the spread of Methodism directed attention to neglected social conditions and foreshadowed the advent of a new humanitarianism. In the philosophical world Francis Hutcheson replaced the old Calvinism by eighteenth-century rationalism,[5] and Montesquieu proclaimed to Europe that political and social institutions were the reflex of material environment and national character.

A series of events followed whose cumulative significance is

[4] George Chalmers, *An Estimate of the Comparative Strength of Great Britain* (new ed.; London, 1804), p. 123.

[5] Leslie Stephen, *History of English Thought in the Eighteenth Century* (3d ed.; London, 1902), II, 56.

unmistakable. In 1748 Joseph Massie began his famous collection of economic literature as the basis for an inductive study of the elements of commerce. In 1749 Adam Smith organized a public class for instruction in political economy in Edinburgh and paved the way to professorial appointment in Glasgow. In 1750 Robert and Andrew Foulis commenced to reprint important economic texts—Child, Gee, Petty, Law, Berkeley—in sympathy with the awakened interest in the principles of trade and commerce. David Hume's *Political Discourses,* destined to attain a vogue unequaled by any other economic writing, appeared in 1752. Cantillon's *Essai sur le Commerce,* written a generation before, and Francis Hutcheson's posthumous *System of Moral Philosophy,* containing the substance of his lectures upon natural jurisprudence, became accessible in 1755. In the same year Josiah Tucker published the outline, actually projected several years before, of a general treatise on *The Moral and Political Theory of Trade and Taxes,* and made substantial beginning in his *Elements of Commerce.*[6] Quesnay's first economic article, marking the beginning of the Physiocratic movement in France, saw light in 1756; Harris' *Essay on Money and Coins* followed close in 1757–58, and in 1760 Joseph Massie addressed a formal representation to the commissioner of the treasury "to be employed in forming for public Service *the Elements of Commerce,* and *an historical account of the British Manufacturies and trade.*"[7]

Examined more closely, this development of economic writing shows a distinct bifurcation traceable as far back as the point of initiation and conveniently distinguished as "political arithmetic" and "political economy." Having for a common purpose the discovery of the principles whereby national wealth

[6] Walter Ernest Clark, *Josiah Tucker: Economist* (New York, 1903), p. 62 n.

[7] *Representation concerning the Knowledge of Commerce as a National Concern* (London, 1760), p. 25.

was amassed, the rival methods foreshadowed the methodological issue of a century later.[8]

Of the two, political arithmetic represented the main current. Sir William Petty, under the spell of the Baconian philosophy,[9] introduced the term in 1674 and gave consciousness to the use of this "geometrical justice" in economic discussion in lieu of "grandisonous or euphonical nonsense farded with formality."[10] Two decades later Sir Charles Davenant presented a formal definition: "By Political Arithmetick, we mean the Art of Reasoning, by Figures, upon Things relating to Government,"[11] and more fully:

> A great Statesman, by consulting all sort of Men, and by contemplating the universal Posture of the Nation, its Power, Strength, Trade, Wealth and Revenues, in any Council he is to offer, by summing up the Difficulties on either Side, and by computing upon the whole, shall be able to form a sound Judgement, and to give a right Advice: and this is what we mean by Political Arithmetick.[12]

Thereafter argument "in terms of number, weight, or measure" became an accredited mode of economic exposition. The economic superiority of Britain was the favorite theme—this, in turn, being resolved into discussion of population, area, and productivity of land, volume and direction of commerce, sometimes for expository purposes, more often for comparison with reported conditions in other lands with an eye to legislative or administrative change.

[8] Dugald Stewart distinguished the devotees of the two modes of inquiry as "political arithmeticians, or statistical collectors," and "political economists, or political philosophers" (*Collected Works* [ed. Hamilton], III, 33).

[9] Charles H. Hull (ed.), Introduction, *Economic Writings of Sir William Petty* (Cambridge, 1899), I, lxiv–lxv.

[10] Stephen Bauer, "Arithmetic, Political, History of," in Palgrave (ed.), *Dictionary of Political Economy, sub nom.*

[11] *Discourses on the Publick Revenues, and on the Trade of England* (London, 1698), Part I, p. 2.

[12] *Ibid.*, p. 15.

Petty, Graunt, Halley, Derham, and De Moivre used the bills of mortality to arrive at estimates of population and vital phenomena. Gregory King, Charles Davenant, and Erasmus Philips inquired into the wealth of the nation, using the returns of the poll and excise taxes as bases. Less qualified writers assumed the validity of a method which they were incompetent to employ. The very term became the earmark of a craft, used as lightly and as uninformedly as Carlyle's epithet of a later day.

> Moral arithmetick to him was known
> And ev'ry statesman's merit, but his own,

sang Pope of Roscommon, with echo a century later by Chalmers[13] of Gregory King. "Political arithmetic, an art of greater use than entertainment," was the *Spectator's* tribute in 1711,[14] and as though despairing of finding readers with so forbidding a caption, a later editor—perhaps anticipating Emerson's conviction that we shall never understand political economy until we get Beranger or Burns or some poet to teach it in songs[15]—countenanced a typographical lapse of the title into "poetical arithmetic."[16]

When in the middle of the century Montesquieu's *De l'Esprit des Lois,* promptly translated into English, suggested the systematization of economic uniformities, political arithmetic by right of origin and by avowal of purpose seemed the appropriate device whereby "not so perfect Demonstrations as are required in pure Mathematicks; but . . . . such as our Superiors may work with, as well as Wheelwrights and Clockmakers do work without the Quadrature of a Circle."[17] This conception that economic principles must rest upon economic induction marked an unrealized purpose of Joseph Massie.

[13] *Op. cit.*, p. xvi. [14] No. 200 (October 19, 1711).

[15] *Journals, 1849–1855* (Cambridge, 1912), VIII, 389.

[16] Table of Contents, *British Essayists* (ed. Berguer; London, 1823), Vol. IX.

[17] Sir William Petty, "A Treatise of Ireland, 1687," *Works* (ed. Hull), II, 611.

The circumstances of Massie's life are hidden in the same irritating obscurity that enshrouds other important English economic writers—Vanderlint, Harris—of the middle eighteenth century.[18] We know only of his astonishing productivity as pamphleteer in the period from 1750 to 1765, and of his death in 1784. It is as bibliographer rather than as author that Massie has figured largest in the history of economic thought. The "Fifteen Hundred, or more, Books and Pamphlets" concerning "the *Commerce, Coin,* and *Colonies* of *Great Britain*" which he had been "above Twelve Years in Making," though he "resided in *London,* and was not sparing of either Time or Money to enlarge it," were sold in 1760, and thereafter dispersed, lost, or hidden—how and in what manner we have no knowledge. But Massie left a monument to his zeal in an admirably compiled finding list which he continued to revise and extend even after he had disposed of the actual collection, and this "Alphabetical and Chronological Index of Commercial Books and Pamphlets,"[19] which by December, 1764, had grown to 2,377 items, still serves as a helpful guide to English economic literature before Adam Smith.

Massie's interest in economic literature was not, however, merely as bibliographer or collector. If not present from the first, the intention soon developed of utilizing the materials that he had gathered for two works, a "commercial history of Great Britain" and a treatise upon the "elements of commerce illustrated by Applications." In 1760 Massie submitted the desirability of their preparation to the commissioners of the treasury and of the exchequer and sought public employment. Nothing

[18] See Introduction to reprint (ed. Hollander; Baltimore, 1912) of Massie, *An Essay on the Governing Causes of the Natural Rate of Interest* (London, 1750).

[19] British Museum, Lansdowne MSS 1049; lettered "Massie's Catalogue of Commercial Tracts."

seems to have come of the proposal; but the tract in which it was urged, "A Representation concerning the Knowledge of Commerce as a National Concern," remains of interest as suggesting an early and vivid conception that economic principles must rest upon economic facts.

While a few thinkers like Massie and Tucker cherished the larger purpose of an inductive economics, political arithmetic in the older and narrower sense continued to claim its devotees. The controversy as to "the populousness of ancient nations"—that "happy hunting-ground for learned antiquarian essay writers"[20]—initiated by Montesquieu, Hume, and Wallace, and revived with local applications during the war of 1756 by Bell, Brackenridge, and Forster, was continued up to the very close of the century by Price, Young, Chalmers, Eden, Wales, and Howlet.[21] Resistance to new commercial policies evoked discussion by Chalmers and Clarke as to the comparative strength and prosperity of Great Britain at successive periods of national life, based largely upon estimates of the volume and direction of exports and imports.[22] The encyclopedic spirit of the day appeared in antiquarian "annals of commerce" of Macpherson, in a descriptive "state of the poor" of Eden, and in agricultural "tours" and "surveys" of Arthur Young, John Sinclair, and James Anderson—all with political arithmetic serving as an overburdened handmaid. The pressure of war budgets induced Richard Price to apply his studies of probability to proving "by irrefutable arithmetic" that a sinking fund honestly administered must ultimately extinguish the largest debt that can be conceived.[23] The agricultural reformers, hard put to it to find secure footing

[20] James Bonar, *Malthus and His Work* (reprint; New York, 1924), p. 31.

[21] George Chalmers, *op. cit.*, pp. 193–94.

[22] *Ibid.*, p. viii.

[23] Cf. J. Holland Rose, *William Pitt and National Revival* (London, 1912), p. 189.

against the rising tide of economic liberalism, elaborated their pleas in a form suggested by the very title of Arthur Young's long-forgotten work, published two years before the appearance of the *Wealth of Nations, Political Arithmetic containing Observations on the Present State of Great Britain; and the Principles of her Policy in the Encouragement of Agriculture.* As late as 1785, James Laffan reviewed the "political arithmetic of the population, commerce and manufactures of Ireland";[24] in 1798 Joseph Priestley "first broke his silence [in America] on subjects of political controversy with a paper entitled *Maxims of Political Arithmetic"*; and in 1799 Thomas Cooper incorporated economic discussion in his *Political Essays* under the caption "Political Arithmetic."[25]

But whether pursued in the traditional way as the fanciful elaboration of fragmentary and imperfect data of population, trade, and agriculture into general propositions of national wealth, or elevated into a Baconian endeavor to obtain a body of economic principles by systematic induction from the facts of record, political arithmetic led nowhere. This barrenness of result, aggravated by frequent extravagances of method, probably induced Adam Smith's verdict: "I have no great faith in political arithmetic, and I mean not to warrant the exactness of either of these computations";[26] to which a discriminating expositor, Dugald Stewart, added: "In general, as Mr. Smith remarks, little stress ought to be laid on the results of what is commonly called Political Arithmetic."[27] Thereafter none too unworthy to cast a stone.

[24] Dublin, 1785.

[25] Dumas Malone, *Public Life of Thomas Cooper, 1783–1839* (New Haven, 1926), pp. 91, 98–99.

[26] *Wealth of Nations,* Book IV, chap. v; *ibid.* (ed. Cannan; London, 1904), II, 36.

[27] *Collected Works* (ed. Hamilton; Edinburgh, 1756), IX, 48.

Hail! most prudent Politicians!
Hail! correct Arithmeticians!
Hail! vast exhaustless source of Irish Propositions,

jeered the *Rolliad*.[28]

In 1787, the "new-coined name" of statistics crept unobtrusively into England in the writings of Zimmerman and Sinclair, with the credential of having then already been formed into "a separate science" and having become "a favorite study" in Germany.[29] But as used both by German writers of the eighteenth century and by the English writers whom they directly influenced, statistics was far less ambitious as "a species of political enquiry" than political arithmetic, and meant simply "the exposition of the noteworthy characteristics of a state, the mode of exposition being—almost inevitably at that time—preponderantly verbal."[30]

The bare possibility of political arithmetic conceived as a technical economic method came to an end in 1801 with the definite returns of the first census, and of the newly imposed income tax. A few years later, Dugald Stewart pronounced the obituary:

> The facts accumulated by the statistical collector are merely *particular results*, which other men have seldom an opportunity of verifying or of disproving; and which, to those who consider them in an insulated state, can never afford any important information. . . . . If these observations be

[28] Rose, *op. cit.*, p. 263.

[29] G. Udny Yule, *An Introduction to the Theory of Statistics* (London, 1911), pp. 1–2. Professor W. F. Wilcox has called attention to the fact that "the earliest occurrence of *statistics* in English was in 1770 and thus more than fifteen years before Sinclair, when Dr. Hooker published a translation of Bielfeld's *Elements of Universal Erudition*. One of its chapters is entitled Statistics, and contains a definition of the subject as 'the science that teaches us what is the political arrangement of all modern states of the known world' " (*Pub. Amer. Statis. Assoc.*, December, 1914, p. 287).

[30] Yule, *op. cit.*, p. 2. "A descriptive political science almost devoid of figures but systematic and suitable for presentation in academic lectures or treatises" is Professor Wilcox's definition (p. 286).

just, instead of appealing to political arithmetic as a check on the conclusions of political economy, it would often be more reasonable to have recourse to political economy as a check on the extravagancies of political arithmetic.[31]

While political arithmetic thus straggled on its devious, purposeless course, the main stream of economic thought and writing was taking direction and volume with the extension of philosophical speculation into the domain of economic relations.

The traditional exposition of moral philosophy from classical times had been a review in succession of man's relations to God, to the state, and to society. When in 1727 Gershom Carmichael, after a generation of junior service, was designated professor of moral philosophy at the University of Glasgow, and philosophical studies formally entered the Scotch universities—where alone in Great Britain they were to be pursued with any vigor throughout the eighteenth century—politico-economic speculation had already won recognition. Carmichael was a disciple of Hobbes and Grotius; he had edited Pufendorf's *De Officio Hominis et Civis,* and his lectures appear to have included an intelligent commentary. Carmichael died in 1729, and Francis Hutcheson, a former pupil, was elected to the vacant professorship. Basing his early teaching upon Pufendorf and the "compend" of his predecessor Carmichael, Hutcheson later developed a course of "constant lectures five days of the week on Natural Religion, Morals, Jurisprudence, and Government,"[32] repeated session after session with many digressions and additions, but not issued in printed form until years later.

Hutcheson accepted "the celebrated division of philosophy among the ancients" into "the rational or logical, the natural,

[31] *Elements of the Philosophy of the Human Mind* (1792–1827), Part II, chap. iv, sec. 5, in *Collected Works,* III, 331–32.

[32] Leechman's memoir, prefixed to *System of Moral Philosophy* (Glasgow, 1755), p. xxxvi.

and the moral." Restricted to the area of "moral philosophy," he expounded in turn the elements of ethics, the law of nature or the doctrine of private rights, and "the principles of œconomicks and politicks."[33] It was under the last head that opportunity was afforded for the discussion of economic principles.[34]

There is little evidence of any direct impress exerted upon economic thought by Hutcheson's opinions. His lectures were well attended, but apparently lacked the distinguished quality that marked the philosophical course of the Scotch universities of a later day. His message filtered through to the public mind for years only by the medium of student shorthand reports and epitomized "compends." The *Introduction to Moral Philosophy* was published in Latin in 1742, the English translation appearing only in 1747. The more formal *System of Moral Philosophy* saw light as a posthumous work in 1755.[35] An earnest and devoted teacher, Hutcheson's largest influence as an economic thinker was exerted through his two great pupils, David Hume and Adam Smith.

In 1737 Hume, then twenty-six years of age, had returned from France to London with the manuscript of the first two parts of his *Treatise on Human Nature.* The work was published in 1739, and, to Hume's great grief, "fell dead born from the press, without reaching such distinction as even to excite a murmur among the zealots."[36] Returning to Scotland, Hume soon came within the range of Hutcheson's influence. It was to Hutcheson that the manuscript of Part III of the *Treatise on*

[33] Preface, *Introduction to Moral Philosophy* (Glasgow, 1747).

[34] W. R. Scott, *Francis Hutcheson* (Cambridge, 1900), Part II, chap. xi; Adam Smith, *Lectures on Justice, Police, Revenue and Arms* (ed. Cannan; Oxford, 1896), pp. xxiv–xxvi.

[35] W. R. Scott, *op. cit.*, p. 144.

[36] *Essays: Moral, Political and Literary* (ed. Green and Grose; London, 1875), p. 33.

Human Nature was submitted for criticism, and thereafter the two men continued in active correspondence, and doubtless in personal contact. Indeed, it was out of this relation that Hume's memorable acquaintance with Adam Smith sprang.

It is not altogether fanciful to ascribe to the association with Hutcheson a politico-economic bent to Hume's hitherto exclusively philosophical studies. In the advertisement to the first volume of his *Treatise* (1739), Hume had announced that he would "proceed to the examination of Morals, Politics and Criticism."[37] The third volume of the *Treatise,* published in 1740, treated of "Morals," and the remaining tasks awaited performance. It was in possible preparation for the politico-economic part that his reading and note-taking at this time included the texts of Josiah Child, Marshall Vauban, and Michael Geddes.

The actual outcome was a series of essays "wrote with a view of being published as weekly papers" after the manner of the *Spectator* and the *Craftsman,* but actually issued "partly from laziness, partly from want of leisure" in 1741–42 in two little volumes of *Essays, Moral and Political.* The division was as equitable as the title indicated, the political discourses forming almost one-half of the original fifteen papers, and more than one-third of the full two-volume edition. They constituted, moreover, the most valuable part of the publication. Without attempting to found a system, they dealt with the topics of the day in the light of general principles, and with a fund of historical illustration.

Curiously enough, no strictly economic topic figured in these causerie-like performances. Hume's reading and reflection may not have proceeded far enough to justify economic composition. More probably the indifferent reception accorded the *Treatise* made Hume reluctant to discuss economic issues at an appar-

[37] *Ibid.,* p. 44.

ently inopportune moment. The frenzy into which the public mind had lashed itself over Walpole's excise scheme had subsided, and the economic revival of the midcentury, with its stimulating effect upon economic thought and writing, had not yet developed.

A decade later all of this had changed. Montesquieu's *De l'Esprit des Lois* had appeared, and Hume, who had been in correspondence with Montesquieu from 1749, was instrumental in securing an Edinburgh reprint. Hutcheson's *Introduction to Moral Philosophy* had been published in English translation, and Adam Smith's first lecture course on political economy in Edinburgh had been delivered. Moreover, in economic matters "the new light was thus breaking in on groups of inquirers in Scotland as well as elsewhere," and Hume, like Smith, "was from its earliest days within its play."[38]

Significant in this connection was Hume's intimacy with James Oswald, of Dunnikier, then a member of Parliament from Kirkcaldy and a commissioner of the navy, and later commissioner of trade and plantations, lord of the treasury, and vice-treasurer of Ireland. Oswald "had made his mark largely by his mastery of economic subjects," and Hume had years before (1744) described him in this connection as a "great genius."[39] It was now with Oswald that he conferred and to him that he submitted the draft of his new essays. Even the scant evidence extant as to this contact suggests that Hume was indebted to Oswald for some part of what has been regarded as one of his most characteristic doctrines—the stimulating effect of a gradual increase in the money of a country. In much the same manner Dugald Stewart records that, as "appears from a manuscript of Mr. Smith's now in my possession," the analysis of "price"

[38] John Rae, *Adam Smith* (London, 1895), p. 38.

[39] *Ibid.*, p. 37.

into its component parts which figures in the *Wealth of Nations* was suggested by Oswald.[40]

The collection of essays upon which Hume's fame as an economist rests actually appeared early in 1752 in a small octavo volume under the title of *Political Discourses*. It is doubtful whether any economic composition, with the possible exception of Henry George's *Progress and Poverty*, has ever enjoyed a greater vogue. Such subjects as "Commerce," "Luxury," "Money," "Interest," "Balance of Trade," "Taxes," and "Public Credit"—the very matters as to which current developments in public and private affairs were running afoul of traditional misconception and unenlightenment—were discussed by Hume with an acuteness of reasoning, a soundness of judgment, an intimacy of manner, and a charm of style that gave the book the widest circulation and whetted the popular appetite for further fare.

If the exposition of economic relations which Francis Hutcheson wove into his lectures on moral philosophy did not give Adam Smith—then an admiring student—his original interest in political economy, certainly it supplied something of both form and content to the lecture course on "Justice, Police, Revenue, and Arms" which a generation later Adam Smith gave as professor of moral philosophy at Glasgow.

But the pupil went far beyond the achievement of the teacher. In part responding to the growing interest in economic affairs, in part voicing a dissenting creed, Smith gave increasing place to a discussion of the political regulations designed "to increase the riches, the power and the prosperity of a State."

The publication of the *Theory of Moral Sentiments* in 1759, and the virtual postponement of a contemplated treatise on jurisprudence, left Smith's hands free for his larger work. Probably the expectation of obtaining leisure for its pursuit, free from the press of material cares, induced him to relinquish the

[40] *Collected Works*, IX, 6.

Glasgow professorship and accept the post of traveling tutor to the young Duke of Buccleugh. Then followed two years of travel and observation, full of rich experiences and stimulating contacts. In 1766 he returned to England, to bury himself with notes and books in Kirkcaldy, not again emerging for more than brief intervals in connection with his task, until the publication of the *Wealth of Nations* in 1776.

The idea, present from the first, of a literary presentation of his university lectures had gained scope and dignity by contact with Quesnay and Turgot. The appearance of Adam Ferguson's *History of Civil Society* in 1767, with its apparent encroachment upon Smith's exposition, and the more deliberate occupation of the field by Sir James Steuart's *Principles of Political Œconomy* in the same year, contributed to cautious composition. David Hume's greeting to the published book suggested the deliberateness of its preparation: "It was a work of so much expectation, by yourself, by your friends, and by the public that I trembled for its appearance."[41]

For the inception of a science, two elements are needed: (1) a measure of consciousness and (2) a body of principles. In so far as Adam Smith wrote a scientific treatise, it was like the prose which Molière's bourgeois spoke. Trained in classical philosophy, the academic successor of Carmichael and Hutcheson, the classroom expositor of moral philosophy, it was reasonable to suppose that the economic sections of Adam Smith's work would, both in lecture outline and in final version, display the formal characteristics of a philosophy of the schools. As a matter of fact, no student of method can speak of the *Wealth of Nations* as exhibiting the deliberate scope, the systematic plan, or the logical method of a scientific treatise.

Joseph Massie, in the Dedication to his *Representation con-*

[41] Rae, *op. cit.*, p. 286.

cerning the Knowledge of Commerce, had noted in 1760, "Some Writers have considered Commerce as a Science, and endeavoured to deduce the knowledge of it from Axioms, Maxims, etc." As early at least as 1763 in his Glasgow lectures, Adam Smith had referred to jurisprudence as "that *science* which inquires into the *general principles,*" etc.[42] Some years later he had declared that the system of the Physiocrats, "with all its imperfections, is, perhaps, the nearest approximation to the truth that has yet been published upon the subject of political economy, and is upon that account well worth the consideration of every man who wishes to examine with attention the principles of that very important science."[43] And yet the *Wealth of Nations* has little of that easy, intimate use of the term "science" and the accompanying precision of arrangement which, in impressive contrast, distinguishes the immediate pre-Ricardian texts.

In part this later formalism as to definition and arrangement came from Jeremy Bentham, entering economic study through the influence of James Mill and possibly J. R. McCulloch. To a much greater degree the scientific consciousness of political economy is assignable to the influence upon English thought of the French post-Physiocratic writers.

Montesquieu had made familiar the conception of uniformity in economic relations and the possibility of an orderly arrangement of such principles. In 1763 Mirabeau had declared: "La science économique est approfondie et développée par l'examen et par le raisonnement, mais sans les calculs elle serait toujours une science indéterminée, confuse et livrée partout à l'erreur et au préjugé."[44]

[42] *Lectures* (ed. Cannan), p. 1.

[43] *Wealth of Nations* (ed. Cannan), II, 176.

[44] *Philosophie Rurale,* pp. xix–xx; quoted by Edgard Depitre in Introduction (p. xii, n. 2) to his reprint (Paris, 1911) of Dupont de Nemours, *De l'Exportation et de l'Importation des Grains* (1764).

A year later Dupont de Nemours dedicated a tract to Mme de Pompadour in recognition of "la protection décidée que vous accordez à ceux qui s'appliquent à l'étude de la Science économique ... cette Science importante et sublime."[45]

Despite the continuous influence of French politico-economic thought upon English philosophical circles, the terms "economic science" and "economic law" were, with a curious reticence, withheld from English writings. The explanation is probably to be found in the disfavor in late eighteenth-century England of all things French. Moreover, as the Physiocratic creed gained the ascendancy, the term "economic science" acquired a local signification. The circumstance that "Physiocracy"—fairly constituted by 1767—was "incontestably the first form under which economic science was presented to the world" encouraged the substitution.[46] In 1768 "la science économique" had become "la science nouvelle," and "les Économistes" the popular designation for the votaries of the system.

With the wane of the sect, the term, still localized in implication, was eschewed by economic writers. This tendency to avoidance was heightened by the popular association of the excesses of the French Revolution with the teachings of the Physiocrats. Even Dugald Stewart, in 1794, apologized for having expressed himself strongly on the merits of what he termed "the first Economists" on the score that "most of them are long since dead."[47]

Gradually, French thought released itself from local association. In 1794 Condorcet demanded: "Quelles sont les lois suivant lesquelles ces richesses se forment ou se partagent, se conservent ou se consomment, s'acroissent ou se dissipent?"[48]

[45] *Ibid.* (reprinted text), p. v.

[46] A. Dubois, Notice (p. vi) to his reprint (Paris, 1910) of Dupont de Nemours, *De L'Origine et des Progrès d'une Science Nouvelle* (1768).

[47] *Collected Works,* X, lxxix.

[48] Elie Halévy, *La Formation du Radicalisme Philosophique,* II, 221.

In 1796 Garnier maintained the prime inquiry of political economy to be "the laws or principles according to which wealth is formed in society in general, and is distributed among the different members who compose it," and he developed the same opinion nine years later in translating the *Wealth of Nations*.[49] In 1801 Canard made a crude attempt to find mathematical formulas for the laws which are the object of political economy. In 1803 J. B. Say published his *Traité d'Économie Politique* with the prefatory declaration that "political economy, like the exact sciences, is composed of a small number of fundamental principles, and of a great number of corollaries or consequences of those principles."[50]

The influence of this post-physiocratic group upon English writing was direct and immediate. The intense interest aroused by Malthus' *Essay* called attention anew to Condorcet. Canard's *Principes* was reviewed at length in the second issue of the *Edinburgh Review*. Garnier's annotated translation of the *Wealth of Nations* was cited[51] as a refreshing contrast to Playfair's defective edition. J. B. Say was acclaimed as one of the few French writers "who never sacrifices truth to display . . . . who first introduced the French nation to the true principles of political economy, and whose name will be mentioned with honour among the philosophers who have raised that important branch of knowledge to the rank of a science."[52]

As to the actual entry of the term "science" in English economic writing, George Crauford in *The Doctrine of Equivalents*, published in 1803 but ascribed to 1794, spoke of forming "the science of political economy into a comprehensive clear and familiar system." The Edinburgh reviewers referred again and

[49] *Ibid.*, p. 222.

[50] Preface, p. x.

[51] *Edinburgh Review*, January, 1806.

[52] *Westminster Review*, I, 525; quoted by Halévy, *op. cit.*, II, 348.

again to "the science" and its "principles." William Spence, champion of Physiocratic doctrines, wrote naturally enough in 1807 of "no principle in the Science of Political Economy," and Torrens in rejoinder to this tract—which brought James Mill and Thomas Chalmers also into the lists—made easy use of "the science of political economy." By 1811 Boileau could entitle his much-neglected book *An Introduction to the Study of Political Economy,* the purpose of which was "to render the science more accessible."

But if the *Wealth of Nations* showed little trace of scientific self-consciousness, it was distinguished in a very high degree by the second and more notable characteristic of an epoch-making work—a body of principles setting forth the uniformities and sequences that obtain in the subject matter assembled. As against the detached solutions of monographic writers or the unfulfilled engagements of more ambitious projectors, Adam Smith visualized the broad extent of economic purpose and result and ventured interpretations of that which he saw or pictured.

One of the most competent students of the *Wealth of Nations* has lately declared:

> Very little of Adam Smith's scheme of economics has been left standing by subsequent inquirers. No one now holds his theory of value, his account of capital is seen to be hopelessly confused, and his theory of distribution is explained as an ill-assorted union between his own theory of prices and the physiocrats' fanciful Economic Table. His classification of incomes is found to involve a misguided attempt to alter the ordinary useful and well-recognized meaning of words, and a mixing up of classification according to source with classification according to method or manner of receipt. His opinions about taxation and its incidence are extremely crude, and his history is based on insufficient information and disfigured by bias.[53]

[53] Edwin Cannan, "Adam Smith as an Economist," *Economica,* June, 1926.

However textually correct, such hypercriticism is a misleading introduction to an appraisal of "Adam Smith as an Economist." Even the acute recognition, which follows, of "three great things he did accomplish"—(*a*) the definite substitution of income for the older idea of a capital aggregation of "treasure," (*b*) the use of wealth per head in lieu of wealth in the aggregate, (*c*) approval of working and trading and investing for personal gain—leaves the impress of absorption in parts and disregard of the whole.

Another scholar of great competence, as part of a like anniversary tribute, has spoken of our hero as "the Great Founder," a phrase to which the title of my succeeding lecture ("The Founder of a School") must be "subconsciously" indebted. "In all the phenomena for which economists try to account in theory," Dr. James Bonar appraises, "he tried to show there was one element at the basis of all the rest in society as he then found it, viz. competition."[54] To have "anchored himself" to this "connecting principle," the competitive effort of individuals for gain, was a notable service. It is not a sufficient credential.

The master-quality of Adam Smith's service lay in the degree to which he envisaged the economic world of which he was a part and the confidence with which he set forth what seemed to him the principles manifest in its affairs. Much of what he presented was imperfect; more of it was loosely articulated. "A body of principles grows like a living body," Bonar reminds us, "it is not builded as a city that is compact together."[55] Adam Smith's "laws" were often unverified theories; his "theories," sometimes fanciful hypotheses. Limpid style, picturesque detail, vehement advocacy, emotional warmth, and constructive proposal mask lapses of thought and defects of logic.

[54] James Bonar, *The Tables Turned* (London, 1926), pp. 14–16.
[55] *Ibid.*, p. 51.

But withal the *Wealth of Nations* constituted a definite base line for succeeding economic thinkers. "It is in Rome that all ancient history loses itself; it is out of Rome that all modern history takes its source," declared the historian, Edward A. Freeman.[56] In this sense it is proper to speak of Adam Smith's great performance as marking "the dawn of a science."

[56] *Essays* (2d series, 3d ed.; London, 1889), p. 287.

CHAPTER II

THE FOUNDER OF A SCHOOL

JACOB H. HOLLANDER

A distinguished critic has spoken of the *Wealth of Nations* as securing for its author "as near an approach to immortality as can fall to any economic writer."[57] A formal treatise in two stately quartos, long years in the making, heralded by scholars as "equal to what has ever appeared on any subject of science whatever,"[58] the reception accorded the book was from the first impressive. David Hume had lamented within a month after its appearance that the treatise required too much thought and reflection to be popular, and the reader fresh from the pages of Gibbon's *Decline and Fall* might well have found the Scotch philosopher turgid and prolix.[59] But another and perhaps more judicial contemporary declared it doubtful even in 1793 "if there exists any book beyond the circle of the mathematical and physical sciences, which is at once so agreeable in its arrangement to the rules of a sound logic, and so accessible to the examination of ordinary readers."[60] The actual demand for the book was significant. While Sir James Steuart's quartos gathered dust on Cadell's shelves, Adam Smith's work sold well, and a fifth edition (1789) was reached in the author's lifetime.

[57] James Bonar, in Palgrave (ed.), *Dictionary of Political Economy, sub nom.*

[58] Adam Ferguson in 1773; see Rae, *op. cit.*, p. 264.

[59] *Ibid.*, pp. 285–86. Francis Horner, a faithful student of Smith's text, wrote in 1800 of "an hour immediately after dinner, while the rapid progress of digestion clouds the powers of apprehension, employed in the lighter labour of culling flowers from the style of Gibbon" (*Memoirs*, I, 129).

[60] Dugald Stewart, *Account of the Life and Writings of Adam Smith, LL.D.*, in *Collected Works*, X, 65.

For a time the French Revolution appears to have checked the popularity of Smith's book. Economic doctrines, and preeminently the doctrines of the new economic liberalism, came to be identified with French principles and the revolutionary spirit. In printing his memoir of Adam Smith read in January–March, 1793, to the Royal Society of Edinburgh, Dugald Stewart declared that at that period

> it was not unusual, even among men of some talents and information to confound, studiously, the speculative doctrines of Political Economy, with those discussions concerning the first principles of Government which happened unfortunately at that time to agitate the public mind.[61]

But the very same year, 1793, witnessed the appearance of Godwin's *Political Justice* with its bold challenge to "a public that is panic struck, and impressed with the most dreadful apprehensions of such doctrines as are here delivered."[62] We are told that the propriety of prosecuting Godwin was considered by the Privy Council; and Pitt is said to have dismissed the suggestion with the remark that "a three guinea book could never do much harm among those who had not three shillings to spare."[63] But the epigram if authentic was probably mere cover for sagacious appreciation of a change in the public mind. Four thousand copies of *Political Justice* were sold, and with its vogue liberalism became more than ever an issue in political and economic debate.

The influence of the *Wealth of Nations* on political policy and legislative action was notable. The book early became the *vade mecum* of every aspiring publicist. Buckle has industriously located thirty-seven instances between 1783 and 1800 in which the *Parliamentary History* records an appeal to Adam

[61] *Collected Works,* X, 87, n. G; quoted in Rae, *op. cit.*, p. 292.

[62] Preface, xii.

[63] H. N. Brailsford, *Shelley, Godwin and Their Circle* (New York ed.), pp. 91–92.

Smith's authority.[64] As early as 1788, the author of *New and Old Principles of Trade Compared*—a turgid *réchauffé* of the arguments of the *Wealth of Nations* as to the advantage of agriculture over commerce and of freedom of trade over mercantilist policies—asserted that Adam Smith was "an author of the first consideration, to whom the age is deeply indebted, and whose work if abridged and somewhat differently arranged would become the manual of every reflecting politician." In 1792 Pitt declared that Smith's "extensive knowledge of detail and depth of philosophical research will, I believe, furnish the best solution of every question connected with the history of commerce and with the system of political economy."[65] In 1797 Pulteney appealed to "the authority of Dr. Smith, who, it was well said, would persuade the present generation, and govern the next."[66] In 1800 Grenville could remind Pitt of their common conviction as to "the soundness of Adam Smith's principles of political economy."[67]

The influence of Adam Smith was potent in the domain of thought no less than in the field of action. The twenty-five years were far from barren of economic writings, and there was minor dissent from various quarters as to certain of Adam Smith's conclusions.[68] David Hume insisted, in curious anticipation of the Ricardian doctrine, that high prices were the cause, not the effect, of high rents. Jeremy Bentham filed a cogent brief against the impolicy of usury laws. Governor Pownall arraigned Smith's condemnation of the monopoly of the colonial trade.[69] The ag-

[64] *History of Civilization in England,* chap. iv, n. 60; *ibid.* (Amer. ed.; New York, 1890), I, 154–55.

[65] Rae, *op. cit.,* pp. 290–91.

[66] Buckle, *op. cit.,* I, 155.

[67] "Grenville," in Palgrave, *Dictionary of Political Economy.*

[68] See the present writer's "Development of the Theory of Money from Adam Smith to David Ricardo," *Quarterly Journal of Economics,* May, 1911, p. 430.

[69] Rae, *op. cit.,* p. 318.

ricultural reformers stirred uneasily at Adam Smith's renunciation of the paramount importance of agriculture. The author of the Physiocratic *The Essential Principles of the Wealth of Nations illustrated, in opposition to some false doctrines of Dr. Smith and others* urged the complete adoption of the doctrines of the Économistes. James Anderson stood out vigorously for the utility of corn-law bounties. Arthur Young admitted that he knew of "no abler work" than the *Wealth of Nations,* but added that he knew of none "fuller of poisonous errors."[70]

From the quarter where economic protest was most to have been expected—revolutionary radicalism—there was little or nothing heard. The explanation is found in the fact, as Hall has pointed out, that the early English Radicals were chiefly interested in political reform. Price, Priestley, Horne Tooke, Cartwright, and Paine directed their assaults against the political constitution of society rather than its economic organization.[71] There was, it is true, complaint against economic want, but the elements held accountable were unwise political institutions and proximate economic abuses. There was no serious challenge of ultimate economic principles. Thomas Spence in 1775 urged the nationalization of land. Whitbread in 1795 championed a return to the Elizabethan assessment of agricultural wages by justices of the peace. Paine proposed a redistribution of income through an inheritance tax on all landed property, and minor writers were at hand with reforms as specific as the construction of public granaries and the prohibition of hair powder.[72]

Despite an occasional note of criticism, the doctrinal supremacy of the *Wealth of Nations* thus remained virtually unchallenged from the date of its appearance in 1776 to the closing years of the eighteenth century. The economic thought, even

[70] Hollander, *David Ricardo: A Centenary Estimate* (Baltimore, 1910), p. 20.

[71] W. P. Hall, *British Radicalism, 1791–1797* (New York, 1912).

[72] *Ibid.,* p. 153.

more than the commercial policy and the financial practice, of Great Britain was dominated by Adam Smith.

Adam Smith lectured at the University of Glasgow as professor of moral philosophy on "Justice, Police, Revenue, and Arms" from 1752 to 1764—this exclusive of his earlier course in Edinburgh. The lectures at once attracted attention. Reid, Smith's academic successor, noted in 1764 that "there was a great spirit of inquiry abroad among the young people in Glasgow," and this result John Rae, Smith's biographer, ascribes to Smith's course:

> It had taught the young people to think. His opinions became the subjects of general discussion, the branches he lectured on became fashionable in the town, the sons of the wealthier citizens used to go to College to take his class though they had no intention of completing a university course, stucco busts of him appeared in the booksellers' windows, and the very peculiarities of his voice and pronunciation received the homage of imitation.[73]

More specifically, the lectures on politics and economics attained popularity. Mr. Rae is of the opinion that in regard to the doctrine of free trade "not the least remarkable result of his thirteen years' work in Glasgow was that before he left he had practically converted that city to his views." Certainly we know from contemporary evidence that during Smith's professorship in Glasgow many leading merchants of the city became "convinced proselytes of free trade principles." Sir James Steuart records his failure, in 1763, to "enlist them in favor of protection" because "Smith had already succeeded in persuading them completely in favor of the free importation of corn."[74]

Of any direct and immediate influence exercised by Adam Smith's lectures upon economic study and thought, I can find no trace. Mr. Rae inclines to the opinion that Foulis reprinted his economic tracts in 1750 at Smith's suggestion;[75] but there is no

[73] *Op. cit.*, p. 59.

[74] *Ibid.*, p. 61.

[75] *Ibid.*, p. 76.

positive evidence as to this, and the occasion was more probably the economic awakening of which Adam Smith's original lecture course was indeed a phase.[76]

Of the size and composition of Smith's audience we know nothing except that theological students seem to have formed a considerable part. The exposition itself was earnest and dignified, but neither eloquent nor stimulating. There is likewise no trace of any collateral accompaniment of the course in the form of required reading or class discussion. In a word, the influence of Adam Smith upon economic thought was exerted through the printed page.

The earmarks of a scientific school have been defined by Higgs as "an alliance of persons, a community of ideas, an acknowledged authority and a combination in purpose, which banded them into a society apart."[77] So understood, the physiocrats were certainly not only "the first scientific school of political economy," but, it might be added, the only school.

It is in a less rigorous but perhaps in a more substantial and a more enduring sense that I have ventured to appraise Adam Smith as "the founder of a school." The term "Smithians" is a barbarism, and "Smithianismus" has been vested with a depreciatory implication. But neither phrase suggests so intimately the quality of Adam Smith's impress upon contemporary and succeeding opinion as the formal title here used.

In a scintillating address, forming part of a course of lectures wherein British economists, much after the manner of the present series, have lately commemorated the hundred and fiftieth anniversary of the *Wealth of Nations*, Dr. James Bonar has explored the textual use and real content of the term "the classical economists." The conclusion is reached, in agreement with the careful phrasing of the thinker whom we too can term "our

[76] Cf. p. 155, *supra*. [77] *The Physiocrats* (London, 1897), p. 3.

lamented leader," Alfred Marshall, that an author was not for him "classical"

> unless either by the form or the matter of his words or deeds he has stated or indicated architectonic ideas in thought or sentiment, which are in some degree his own and which once created, can never die but are an existing yeast ceaselessly working in the cosmos.[78]

This serves as prologue to the thesis that "broadly speaking, in the England of the 19th century the word ["classical"] stood for the followers of the Classical Tradition proceeding from the *Wealth of Nations*."[79]

It is proper to appraise Adam Smith as the first and greatest of "the classical school." But the warrant lies somewhat beyond, although in general accord with, the criteria proposed. Adam Smith's classicism, if the term may be ventured, his title as "the founder of a school," lies in some degree in the formative quality of his thought. But much more it resides in the stimulus, often the original impetus given to succeeding thinkers to initiate and pursue inquiries into economic life, sometimes in supporting continuation of, more often in divergent opposition to, Smith's principles.

This influence is associated with the commentatorial activity of Dugald Stewart, the critical discipleship of Francis Horner and "the first Edinburgh reviewers," and the intellectual enlistment of Thomas Robert Malthus, Jean Baptiste Say, and David Ricardo.

Dugald Stewart succeeded his teacher, Adam Ferguson, in

[78] *The Tables Turned* (London, 1926), p. 6.

[79] *Ibid.*, p. 7. The passage is extracted from a characteristic letter (September 27, 1898) of Marshall to Bonar (*Memorials of Alfred Marshall* [ed. Pigou; London, 1925], p. 374). "With that definition," Marshall continues, "I can to my own satisfaction say pretty well whom I regard as classical economists. I think that such a large proportion of them wrote in the half century 1770–1820 that that is rightly called the classical epoch."

the chair of moral philosophy at Edinburgh in 1785. Following the traditional scope of Scotch philosophical teaching, the course of instruction included lectures on the theory of government and might naturally have been expected to broaden out so as to embrace an examination of economic institutions.

But before this expansion had taken considerable shape, the reaction from the French Revolution had put fetters upon intellectual freedom in Great Britain. Lord Cockburn records, in connection with Stewart's presentation, in January–March, 1793, to the Royal Society of Edinburgh of the *Account of the Life and Writings of Adam Smith,* referred to above, that the occasion was awaited with impatience by Stewart's enemies in the confident hope that he would be led into indiscreet utterance. Stewart himself declared, some years later, that, at the time the *Account* was read,

the doctrine of a Free Trade was itself represented as a revolutionary tendency; and some who had formerly prided themselves on their intimacy with Mr. Smith, and on their zeal for the propagation of his liberal system, began to call in question the expediency of subjecting to the disputations of philosophers, the arcana of State Policy, and the unfathomable wisdom of the feudal ages.[80]

As a matter of fact, in printing the memoir of Adam Smith, Stewart confined himself to "a much more general view" of the contents of the *Wealth of Nations* than he had originally intended,[81] and in later years he frankly explained the omission of "comments and criticisms" as made necessary by the then state of the public mind.[82] How well justified was this prudence is evidenced by the bitter protest in February, 1794, of Lord Abercromby—communicated to Stewart through Lord Craig—against essentially unoffending passages on "the use and abuse of general principles in politics" in Stewart's *Elements of the*

[80] *Collected Works,* X, 87. [81] *Ibid.,* p. 53.

[82] *Ibid.,* p. 87.

Philosophy of the Human Mind, published in 1792.[83] Stewart's reply was a dignified and convincing refusal to make the recantation demanded. But with all, there was a certain discreet bending to the storm: "As soon as I understood that the scope of some of my observations had been mistaken by a few whose characters I respect, I was anxious to guard against the possibility of such misapprehension" by the insertion of certain conservative passages in the memoir of Adam Smith, and only the fault of the printer had delayed publication. Stewart added:

> I shall ever regret that I dishonored some of my pages by mentioning with respect the name of Condorcet; but when my papers were sent to the press, he was quite unknown in any public capacity, and he enjoyed the friendship of the most respectable men in Europe.

But, most significant of all, Stewart stated:

> Ever since I was Professor of Moral Philosophy, I have concluded my course with a set of Lectures on the English Constitution, the peculiar excellencies of which I have always enlarged upon in the warmest and most enthusiastic terms. In treating of this subject, I have been so uniformly impressed with a sense of the importance of my situation, that among all the interesting questions which have, during the last nine years, divided our political parties, I have never introduced the slightest reference to any of them excepting in the single instance of the African trade, on which I formerly expressed myself with some warmth;—and even these expressions I dropped from my course, as soon as it became matter of popular discussion.[84]

Our knowledge as to the nature and substance of Stewart's economic teaching from 1785 to 1793 rests entirely upon the scanty syllabus contained in his *Outlines of Moral Philosophy,* first published in 1793.[85] Part III of this general course treated

[83] *Ibid.,* pp. lxx–lxii.

[84] *Ibid.,* pp. lxxii–lxxiv.

[85] I have not this 1793 edition and can infer its contents only from the second "enlarged" edition published in 1801, with a "postscript" explaining the alterations. Of this edition, the text in the *Collected Works* (VIII, 3–6), although a

"Of Man Considered as the Member of a Political Body." It was subdivided into chapter i, "Of the History of Political Society," and chapter ii, "Of the General Principles of Legislation and Government"; chapter ii was in turn subdivided into section i, "Of Political Economy"—comprising the four topics, "Population," "National Wealth," "Slavery," and "Education"—and section ii, "Of the Different Functions of Government."

In explanation of the minor place given to politico-economic institutions, Stewart stated in the Preface to the *Outlines:*

> The branch of Moral Philosophy which relates to the Principles of Politics being less abstract than the others, I have contented myself with a simple enumeration of the most important articles treated of in the third part of my course. It is scarcely necessary for me to mention, that, in this enumeration, I have not aimed at anything approaching to systematical arrangement; and that, in illustrating the titles it contains, I am obliged, by the term prescribed to my academical labours, to confine myself to very general sketches. As soon as my other engagements allow me sufficient leisure for such an undertaking, I shall attempt a separate Course of Lectures on this very extensive and difficult subject.

The sensitive state of public opinion indicated by the reception accorded the *Elements* in 1792 and the *Account of Adam Smith* in 1793 probably delayed the "separate course of lectures" beyond the time Stewart had contemplated. By 1800 the sky had cleared enough of revolutionary reaction, and Stewart's position in the intellectual and social world had become sufficiently secure, to justify an independent survey. Accordingly, in the winter of 1799–1800, Stewart offered a separate course of

---

later redaction, gives a serviceable basis. I have also no exact knowledge of the economic content of the *Elements* (1792) since the *Collected Works* reprint a later edition. But it is unlikely to have been anything more than the section on the "use and abuse of general principles in politics" which excited Abercromby's ire (*supra*). This section was retained unchanged with an explanatory note in the second (1802) edition and probably in the later editions of the *Elements* (see *Collected Works,* II, 219).

lectures on political economy, the lectures on economic topics being then removed from the general course, and their place taken by "a few others, calculated to illustrate the peculiar and intimate connexion between this department of Politics and the more appropriate objects of Ethics."[86] This "separate course" on political economy was repeated each year thereafter, practically until Stewart's retirement from academic office in 1809–10.

Dugald Stewart's "separate course," in so far as appears from the imperfect record preserved, consisted of a preliminary survey of the scope and development of political economy followed by a detailed consideration of population, national wealth, the poor, and, possibly, of police and of education, the whole divided into many heads and subheads. The classification was, however, less in accord with any formal theory—although the later composed Introduction makes labored attempt to demonstrate this—than to avoid any slavish following of the plan Adam Smith had used.

As a matter of fact, few of the topics, essential or incidental, of the *Wealth of Nations* escaped Stewart's attention. From year to year the original was revised and supplemented, and after Stewart's retirement from academic office there was further redaction with a view to ultimate publication. The completed manuscript was, however, burnt by Stewart's son in 1837 or earlier, so that Sir William Hamilton, in editing the *Lectures on Political Economy* for their first publication in 1855,[87] was obliged to have recourse to an earlier draft supplemented by student reports.

Whatever uncertainty there may be as to the precise content of Dugald Stewart's lectures, there is no doubt whatever as to their remarkable influence in encouraging interest in economic study and in stimulating independence in economic thinking.

[86] *Collected Works,* VIII, 3.

[87] *Ibid.,* Vols. VIII and IX.

The announcement of the course created a sensation in academic and political circles. Revolutionary reaction had waned, but the public-mind opinion still associated such instruction with "questions touching the constitution of government," and "no ordinary audience could be collected to whom the elements and phraseology of the science were not matters of surprise." In more advanced minds, the shock came from the formal entry of a "gospel of mammon" into the university curriculum. Lord Cockburn notes:

> It was not unusual to see a smile on the face of some, when they heard subjects discoursed upon seemingly beneath the dignity of the Academical Chair. The word *corn* sounded strangely in the Moral Class, and *drawbacks* seemed a profanation of Stewart's voice.[88]

The attendance was small, the average number of students during the eight sessions being forty-nine, and the withdrawal of the course for want of students being at times contemplated.[89] But the quality of the student body was extraordinary. After the death of Reid, in 1796, Stewart remained the only distinguished philosophical teacher in Great Britain.[90] The progress of the war had put restraint upon European travel, and a session in Edinburgh took the place of the "grand tour" in the education of young men for a public career. Political philosophy had been invested with a new and alluring interest by the debates of the preceding decade, and attendance upon such a course had the appeal of a daring venture. Indeed, the response came not only from undergraduates. Veitch notes that the class included "also, and even chiefly, an audience of riper years, especially members of the bar,"[91] and George Pryme, of Trinity College, Cambridge, records in 1819 that "several Members of our own University

[88] John Veitch, "Memoir of Dugald Stewart," *Collected Works,* X, li.

[89] *Ibid.,* pp. lxviii, lii.

[90] Leslie Stephen, *Dictionary of National Biography, sub nom.*

[91] *Collected Works,* X, lv.

went from the South of England to pass the winter at Edinburgh, for the purpose of attending them."[92]

Some part of the effectiveness of the course was due to Stewart's amazing eloquence. Dr. John Thomson, professor of general pathology in the University of Edinburgh, declared that the two things by which he was most impressed in the course of his life were the acting of Mrs. Siddons and the oratory of Dugald Stewart.[93] James Mill's testimony is even more striking: "I have heard Pitt and Fox deliver some of their most admired speeches; but I never heard anything nearly so eloquent as some of the lectures of Professor Stewart."[94] If, as Professor Bain suggests, this appreciation was the stirring of Mill's own philosophical aptitude, there still remain Lord Cockburn's opinion that "Dugald Stewart was one of the greatest of didactic orators,"[95] and Francis Horner's tribute:

> It is not so much from the detail of particulars that I derive improvement from this amiable philosopher's lectures, as from the general manner and spirit with which he unfolds his speculations, and delivers, in chaste and impressive language, the most liberal and benevolent sentiments, the most comprehensive and enlightened views.[96]

The correlation of economic discussion with general philosophical principles lent dignity to the treatment, and the eloquence of the lecturer added to its attractiveness. But the attendants were not encouraged, perhaps were not even permitted, to remain admiring auditors. At the conclusion of his course at the 1803–4 session, Stewart remarked that he had intended "to

[92] *A Syllabus of a Course of Lectures on the Principles of Political Economy* (2d ed.; Cambridge, 1819), pp. vii–viii.

[93] *Collected Works,* X, xxxviii.

[94] Alexander Bain, *James Mill: A Biography* (London, 1882), p. 16.

[95] *Collected Works,* X, xlv.

[96] Leonard Horner (ed.), *Memoirs and Correspondence of Francis Horner, M.P.* (London, 1843), I, 130.

have marked out a plan of reading on the different subjects which have been under our review."[97] Lacking time for this and realizing that "an enumeration of a long list of books might, not improbably, have had the effect (at least with my younger hearers) of distracting the attention, by leading to the perusal of a multiplicity of discordant and inconsistent theories," Stewart confined himself to "a few authors whose works appear to me most likely to be useful to you in the farther prosecution of these studies." Following the general arrangement of his course, Stewart recommended, under the head of "Population," Wallace's *On the Numbers of Mankind,* Hume's *Of the Populousness of Ancient Nations,* Malthus' *On the Principle of Population.* With respect to "National Wealth," the students were advised to study Adam Smith's *Wealth of Nations* as "the book with which the student may, with most advantage, *begin* his researches on this subject," and thereafter to consult Sir James Steuart's *Inquiry into the Principles of Political Œconomy,* Turgot's *Reflections on the Formation and Distribution of Riches,* Mercier de la Riviere's *Natural and Essential Order of Political Societies,* Dupont de Nemour's *Physiocratie,* and Lauderdale's *Public Wealth.* Upon the topic of "Legislation of Grain," Smith's *Three Tracts on the Corn Laws* was recommended; and upon "The Poor," Eden's *The State of the Poor* was particularized.

The actual enrolment included,[98] for the most part in the early sessions, James Mill, John Ramsay McCulloch, Thomas Chalmers, the Earl of Lauderdale, Henry Brougham, Francis Horner, Francis Jeffrey, Macvey Napier, Sydney Smith, Archibald Allison, Lord Webb Seymour, Henry Cockburn, Viscount Palmerston. These were the men who contributed most—as text-writers, as editors, as publicists, as reviewers, and as jour-

[97] *Collected Works,* X, 458.

[98] *Ibid.,* p. liv.

nalists—to the revival of economic study in England in the decade then beginning.

The effect of Dugald Stewart's instruction upon the student mind may be traced in the mental history of Francis Horner. Horner was born in 1778. He was a student at the University of Edinburgh from 1792 to 1795. During some part of this time he attended Stewart's course in philosophy, and followed with interest the lectures dealing with economic principles. In 1795, to rid his speech of "the Scotch burr," he was sent to England to pursue courses of study and reading. During this time he retained his interest in political economy. His letters to Lord Murray, then a student at Edinburgh, repeatedly express a desire to carry on economic discussion: "Let us be the Beaumont and Fletcher of metaphysics," and, more specifically: "Come, I order you in the name of Hume, and Smith and Dugald Stewart, to select a question immediately, and to begin upon it in your very first letter."[99]

Horner returned to Edinburgh in October, 1797, to prepare for admission to the bar two years thereafter. He marked out an elaborate course of reading in literature, philosophy, jurisprudence, and political economy. In particular, Condorcet and Turgot engaged his interest, a collected edition of the latter's economic writings being seriously contemplated. In November, 1798, he enrolled as a member of "Stewart's Class of Moral Philosophy," and records, on February 19, 1799, that he had "entered on a plan, with Lord Webb Seymour, of discussing with him, after Stewart's lecture, the different arguments or topics which it comprehended."

The first detailed reference to Stewart's "separate course" is contained in a letter of January 23, 1800, to Erskine:

[99] A little later he adds: "The controversy would be much the better for our friend Brougham's assistance and I shall give him a hint" (*Memoirs,* I, 91).

> Professor Stewart has lately begun a course of lectures on Political Economy; and though his plan is not quite so comprehensive as he proposes to render it next winter, yet I promise myself great instruction; and I hope he will at least have the influence to make this captivating science more popular than it has been for some time past, and that he will render us familiar with those liberal enlarged views which he forms upon sciences.

At this juncture (May, 1800) Horner realized that economic study was not merely a matter of texts, but of industrial observation. He proceeds, accordingly, rather cumbrously to acquire acquaintance with actual industrial processes, beginning with the manufacture of tobacco pipes, "which is a very neat operation," and the manufacture of iron, which is "not only the soul of every other manufacture, but the mainspring perhaps of civilized society." He also aspires to acquire a facility of interrogating "the lower orders," possessed by Locke and Franklin in an eminent degree:

> To collect information from workmen is a matter of some address, for they are in general mere machines, and not unfrequently more ignorant, literally speaking, than the tools which they employ. I may gain sufficient practice of this address in the new manufactories that are in the neighbourhood of this place, to prepare me for more ample opportunities.

Horner enrolled in the second session of Stewart's lectures in December, 1800, and supplemented classroom attendance by systematic reading of economic texts. He agreed with Lord Webb to read, or rather re-read, the *Wealth of Nations,* and "to date from this day the commencement of a regular course of political economy" (I, 157). It is possible to follow almost week by week in Horner's remarkable journal and correspondence his further development as a political economist, under the joint stimulus of Adam Smith's text and Dugald Stewart's comment. A single paragraph, of enough significance to atone for its length, must suffice:

We have been under the necessity of suspending our progress in the perusal of the *Wealth of Nations,* on account of the insurmountable difficulties, obscurity, and the embarrassment in which the reasonings of the 5th chapter are involved. It is amusing to recollect the history of one's feelings on a matter of this kind: many years ago, when I first read the *Wealth of Nations,* the whole of the first book appeared to me as perspicuous as it was interesting and new. Some time afterwards, while I lived in England, I attempted to make an abstract of Smith's principal reasonings; but I was impeded by the doctrine of the real measure of value, and the distinction between nominal and real price: the discovery that I did not understand Smith, speedily led me to doubt whether Smith understood himself, and I thought I saw that the price of labour was the same sort of thing as the price of any other commodity; but the discussion was too hard for me, and I fled to something more agreeable because more easy. The next incident that I can recollect of this narrative, is the pleasure I received from finding in a pamphlet by Lord Lauderdale, of which Professor Dalzel gave me a copy, that what had puzzled me appeared decidedly erroneous to him, and was rejected without ceremony. Mr. Stewart also devoted an elaborate lecture to this curious subject; his refutation of Smith's argument appeared to me at the time demonstrative, but the principles he proposed to substitute were not quite so satisfactory. The subject has again come before me, and I hope, with Lord Webb's aid, not to quit it without making something of it. In utter despair, however, of conducting the investigation successfully without more materials than Smith furnishes, we have betaken ourselves to some treatises in which the doctrine of money is examined in a more elementary manner.

A striking exhibit of Dugald Stewart's influence was the prominence of economic criticism in the newly founded *Edinburgh Review.* Sydney Smith has described the circumstances under which the venture was conceived:

Towards the end of my residence in Edinburgh, Brougham, Jeffrey, and myself happened to meet in the eighth or ninth story or flat in Buccleugh Place, the then elevated residence of Mr. Jeffrey. I proposed that we should set up a *Review;* this was acceded to with acclamation; I was appointed editor and remained long enough in Edinburgh to edit the first number of the *Review.*[100]

[100] Lady Holland, *A Memoir of the Reverend Sydney Smith* (London, 1885), I, 22–23.

Francis Horner's interest was promptly enlisted, and the initial number appeared in October, 1802—a larger product of Stewart's lecture-room. The project was indeed designed to effect practical reform rather than to afford philosophical exercise. From the outset it set itself to oppose in politics, in economics, and in jurisprudence that "timorous acquiescence in the actual system" which Walter Bagehot describes as a characteristic of the early nineteenth century.[101]

In the field of economic relations, its editors—idealists yet not dreamers—attempted nothing less than the formation and spread of a sound public opinion. "The principles of political economy were little understood," was Sydney Smith's opinion,[102] enforced by citation of the charges of the judges to county juries a few years before that the prevailing scarcity of grain was due to combinations of farmers. Even in more enlightened circles, Francis Horner lamented, "the superstitious worship of Adam Smith's name" stood as a bar to independent thought.

Yet in economic affairs the *Review* served as something more than "the doctrinal organ of the Whigs."[103] It became the rostrum from which expert judgment—sometimes biased, often truculent, but rarely incompetent—appraised the economic writings and happenings of the period. Over and above its achievement in affairs, there was thus an educational service and a scientific contribution. In a troubled decade when stirring events were turning men's minds to economic thinking, the *Review* was the only competent guide and expositor of economic literature intermediate between newspaper and treatise. Issue after issue was distinguished by some essay-like critique from the pen of Francis Horner, of Richard Jeffrey, of Sydney Smith, of Henry Brougham—a little later, of Malthus, James Mill, and McCulloch.

[101] "The First Edinburgh Reviewers," *Works* (Hartford, 1891), I, 13.

[102] *Ibid.*, p. 14. [103] *Ibid.*

The exactness with which the output of economic literature was followed is seen in a list of the leading economic papers appearing in the first twenty or more issues of the *Review:*

1802, Oct. Thornton, *Inquiry into the Nature and Effects of the Paper Credit of Great Britain* (1802).

1803, Jan. Canard, *Principes d'Économie Politique* (1801).

1803, Apr. *Guineas an Unnecessary and Expensive Incumbrance on Commerce* (1802).

1803, July. Lord King, *Thoughts on the Restriction of Payments in Specie at the Banks of England and Ireland* (1803).

1803, Oct. Wheatley, *Remarks on Currency and Commerce* (1803).

1804, Jan. Bishop of Landaff, *Intended Speech on the National Debt* (1803).

1804, Apr. Dumont (ed.), *Bentham's Principles of Legislation* (1802).

1804, July. Earl of Lauderdale, *Inquiry into the Nature and Origin of Public Wealth* (1804).

1804, Oct. (*a*) *Plans of National Improvement* (1803); (*b*) *Observations on the Bounty upon Exported Corn* (1804).

1805, Jan.[104]

1805, Apr. Toulongeon, *De l'Usage du Numeraire dans un grand État* (1804).

1805, July. Earl of Lauderdale, *Hints to the Manufacturers of Great Britain* (1805).

1805, Oct. Earl of Selkirk, *Emigration from Scotland* (1805).

1806, Jan. Earl of Liverpool, *Treatise on the Coins of the Realm* (1805).

1806, Apr. Oddy, *European Commerce* (1805).

1806, July. Macpherson, *Annals of Commerce* (1805).

1806, Oct. Foster, *Essay on the Principles of Commercial Exchanges* (1804).

1807, Jan. Filangieri, *Science of Legislation* (trans. Clayton; 1806).

1807, Apr. Lord Henry Petty, *Plan of Finance* (1807).

1807, July. Wheatley, *Essay on the Theory of Money and Commerce* (1807).

[104] There was default as to a long-delayed critique of Malthus' *Essay on Population:* "The person into whose hands it was put, has disappointed us, from indolence or other occupations, or a sense of the difficulty and extent of Mr. Malthus's speculations" (October, 1804, p. 191 n.).

1807, Oct. *Inquiry into the Effects of the Principles of the Poor Laws* (1807).

1808, Jan. Spence, *Britain Independent of Commerce* (1807).

1808, Apr. *The Orders in Council* (1808).

1808, July. Newenham, *Statistical and Historical Inquiry into the Population of Ireland*.

1808, Oct. Smith, *Essay on the Theory of Money and Exchange* (1807).

1809, Jan. *Pamphlets on West Indian Affairs* (1808).

1809, Apr. Spence, *Agriculture the Source of the Wealth of Britain* (1808).

In addition to the detailed review of more important economic books, briefer notices were inserted of minor publications; and a "Quarterly List of New Publications" enumerated, under the heading "Political Economy," tracts and pamphlets not otherwise noted.

The quality of the reviews was in the main distinguished. A high standard was set at the very outset by Francis Horner's notice of Thornton's *Paper Credit,* published in the first number. "The analysis of Thornton cost me a considerable degree of trouble," recorded Horner in his journal, "but this labor has served to break up the ground in one of the most necessary fields of political economy." However short of its author's estimate the critique may have fallen, it succeeded in laying before an influential public a succinct statement of the theory of paper money and an accurate description of the existing credit mechanism, and at the same time suggested that which it did not expose—the defects in Thornton's explanation of the influence of the existing paper currency upon the actual state of prices.[105]

The temper of criticism was less admirable, being at times characterized by a certain eighteenth-century vehemence. Sometimes this became Johnsonian. An unfortunate tract in defense of the bank restriction (*Guineas an Unnecessary and Expensive Incumbrance on Commerce,* 1802) was introduced with a para-

[105] Hollander, "Development of the Theory of Money from Adam Smith to David Ricardo," *op. cit.*, p. 454.

graph which accords not unfairly with Jeffrey's welcome to the *Excursion:*

> We have seldom met with a more contemptible performance. Ignorant of the very language of political œconomy, and grossly mistaken in the first principles of the science, the author has the confidence to treat of the most difficult matters of finance, and to utter his crude half-formed and incoherent opinions. . . . .[106]

In 1798 appeared a loosely printed octavo of some four hundred pages, *An Essay on the Principle of Population, as it affects the Future Improvement of Society, with Remarks on the Speculations of Mr. Godwin, M. Condorcet, and other Writers.* The publication marked the entry of Thomas Robert Malthus into the field of economic discussion. The début was, however, as indirect as it was masked. The *Essay* may be fairly described as a polemic participation in a running controversy in political science and social philosophy, rather than a deliberate contribution to economic speculation. Its antecedents were socio-philosophical texts; its inspiration was political controversy.

It has long been customary to imply this fact in the general summary that Malthus' *Essay* was evoked by Godwin's *Enquirer.* But such statement is misleading in encouraging the impression that the keynote of the *Essay,* "the principle of population," sprang full armed from an economist's brow. From the time of Montesquieu, speculation upon "the future improvement of mankind"[107] through political action had been a favorite philosophical diversion. With the development of the French Revolution and appearance of political radicalism, this debate as to "the perfectibility of man and of society"[108] grew to engage "a considerable proportion of the public attention."

Political idealism had expressed itself in Wallace's *Prospects of Mankind* (1761), in Godwin's *Political Justice* (1793),

[106] *Edinburgh Review,* April, 1803, p. 101.

[107] Preface, *Essay* (1798), p. ii.

[108] *Ibid.,* p. 7.

and in Condorcet's *Progrès de l'Esprit Humain* (1794). Each of these advocates in clearing the ground of opposing argument had of necessity paid attention to the contention, already then familiar, that the pressure of population upon subsistence would arrest the well-being of the new order. Thus Wallace asserted that no difficulty would arise from this cause "till the whole earth had been cultivated like a garden, and was incapable of any further increase of produce."[109] Condorcet, while admitting the hypothetical possibility of an increase in the numbers of men beyond their means of subsistence, maintained that such an event could take place only "at an æra, when the human race will have attained improvements, of which we at present can scarcely form a conception."[110] Godwin declared more vaguely that "myriads of centuries of still increasing population may probably pass away, and the earth be still found sufficient for the subsistence of its inhabitants";[111] while even thereafter "when the earth shall refuse itself to a more extended population" mankind through the decline of the sexual instinct "will probably cease to propagate."[112]

To Malthus, casting about for a vulnerable point in the larger issue, such treatment seemed cavalier: "All the writers on the perfectibility of man and of society, who have noticed the argument of an overcharged population, treat it always very slightly, and invariably represent the difficulties arising from it, as at a great and almost immeasureable distance."[113]

The *Essay* was thus neither novel in purpose nor original in argument. The central doctrines of Condorcet's *Progrès* and Godwin's *Political Justice*—human perfectibility and "administrative nihilism"—had already been assailed from more than one quarter. The eventual pressure of mankind upon subsis-

[109] *Ibid.*, p. 143. [110] *Ibid.*, p. 152.

[111] *Enquiry concerning Political Justice*, II (1793), 861.

[112] *Ibid.*, p. 871. [113] *Essay*, p. 142.

tence had been noted by writers of the seventeenth and eighteenth centuries, to the extent of becoming a commonplace in conjectural history. The application of this "principle of population"—even the term had been used by Arthur Young and by Godwin[114]—in opposition to schemes of social regeneration had become so familiar that the later political idealists reviewed it only as a familiar objection of the market place. Malthus entered the lists with a weapon sharpened and furbished, but not new in the sense of one theretofore unknown or even unused.

The real significance of what Malthus did was precisely what Ricardo did a decade later in the matter of the theory of money: to revive a familiar argument in a pending controversy, to clarify it by precise definition, to fortify it by positive evidence, to maintain it thereafter against controversial assault, and to establish it not so much as the barrier to the doctrine of social perfectibility, but as a factor to be reckoned with in theories of economic distribution.

In doing this, not only did Malthus the political controversialist become Malthus the economist, but the writing and thinking incident to the controversy passed from political to economic. "Originally he had used the principle of population merely as a weapon in his argument with his father about perfectibility."[115] But, from the appearance of the *Essay*, "he studied it for its own sake." In part this was due to the intense resentment which the doctrine created and the necessity for defending it from acrimonious attack; in part it was the response of Malthus' awakened interest as thinker and student.

The transition is apparent in the chronicle of Malthus' writings. Before the *Essay* in 1798, Malthus had only written *The*

[114] *Political Arithmetic* (London, 1774), p. 61; *Political Justice* (London, 1793), Book VIII, chap. vii, title.

[115] Edwin Cannan, *History of the Theories of Production and Distribution* (London, 1893), p. 133.

Crisis, "a Whig tract" never published.[116] Thereafter his activity was incessant. In 1800 appeared *An Investigation of the Cause of the Present High Price of Provisions,* still without signature. The second edition of the *Essay* was published over his full name in a stout quarto in 1803; the third in two octavo volumes in 1806, with an Appendix containing replies to critics, also published separately in quarto the same year; and the fourth without change in 1807. The *Letter to Samuel Whitbread* upon the proposed amendment to the poor-law saw light in March, 1807, and a paper on the economic condition of Ireland in the *Edinburgh Review* in July, 1808. More important than the foregoing was Malthus' relinquishment of active clerical duties to accept the professorship of history and political economy at the newly established Haileybury College in 1807. It was the first academic recognition of the science in England proper, and Malthus' incumbency lent new dignity to the study and afforded favorable occasion for its pursuit.

At the time the first edition of the *Essay* appeared, Malthus as an economist was in all essentials in agreement with Adam Smith. His acquaintance with economic literature was inconsiderable, hardly extending beyond Hume, Adam Smith, Godwin, Wallace, Price, Condorcet; and his interest in economic principles was minor, being subordinate to political science and social philosophy. In so far, however, as his economic opinions had any form, they were those of the *Wealth of Nations.* A chapter (xvi) of the *Essay* was devoted to the "probable error of Doctor Adam Smith in representing every increase of the revenue or stock of a society as an increase in the funds for the maintenance of labour." But it was introduced "with that diffidence, which I ought certainly to feel, in differing from a person so justly celebrated in the political world,"[117] and it rested on the very doubt-

[116] James Bonar, *Malthus and His Work* (1924 reprint), p. 7.

[117] *Op. cit.,* p. 302.

ful ground that only an increase of foodstuffs and not of manufactures could have "the same good effect upon the condition of the poor."[118]

Beyond this there was deferential agreement. Adam Smith was one of the four authors "from whose writings I had deduced the main argument of the essay."[119] Legislative intervention "to repress inequality of fortunes" was undesirable since "perhaps the generous system of perfect liberty, adopted by Dr. Adam Smith, and the French œconomists, would be ill exchanged for any system of restraint."[120] Adam Smith's observations on the relation of potato culture to population were cited with approval.[121] The government of exclusive companies of merchants, "as Dr. Adam Smith says very justly," was the worst of all possible governments,[122] and as to the respective effects of national parsimony and profusion, "Dr. Adam Smith's position is evidently true."[123]

A critical exposition of the *Wealth of Nations* probably formed the nucleus of Malthus' Haileybury lectures. We have no means of knowing the form and content of the commentary. The *Inquiry into the Nature and Progress of Rent,* published in 1815, contained "the substance of some notes on Rent, which, with others on different subjects relating to political economy," Malthus had "collected in the course of his professional duties at the East India College."[124] In January, 1815, Ricardo could write to Malthus: "I hope your notes on Adam Smith are in great forwardness and ready for early publication."[125] Only one set of student's notes, taken many years later, exists; and this,

[118] *Ibid.*, p. 321.

[119] *Ibid.*, Preface (2d ed., 1803).

[120] *Ibid.*, pp. 287–88 n.

[121] *Ibid.*, pp. 136–37.

[122] *Ibid.*, p. 103.

[123] *Ibid.*, p. 284.

[124] Advertisement.

[125] J. Bonar (ed.), *Letters of Ricardo to Malthus, 1810–1823* (Oxford, 1897), p. 56.

Dr. Bonar records, "adds little to our knowledge of Malthus."[126] Ricardo's forecast is perhaps the fairest estimate: "I expect that they will not only be very useful in giving correct notions to the public, but also in calling the attention of those who are well informed in the science of political economy to many points which have hitherto escaped their consideration."[127]

Jean Baptiste Say was born in Lyons on January 5, 1767, of a Protestant family which had been obliged to flee from France at the revocation of the Edict of Nantes, but which returned toward the middle of the eighteenth century.[128] Young Say received a good education, but through family reverses he was taken from school and put in a business office in Paris. Later, with his brother Horace, he went to complete his commercial studies in England, where the two lads were placed *en pension* in the village of Croyden. After a second commercial apprenticeship in London he returned to France, retaining a profound impression of his sojourn in England. He became an employee of a life insurance company, of which Clavière, later minister of finance, was manager. Clavière owned a copy of Adam Smith, of which no translation had yet been made into French. At his suggestion, Say read the book. "At once he sent for a copy to London, studied it, annotated it and thereafter kept it by him."[129]

Professor Charles Gide ranks Say with Adam Smith and Ricardo as "amongst the fathers of economic science," even though "very inferior to the first as regards historical and philo-

[126] J. Bonar, in Palgrave, *Dictionary of Political Economy, s.v.* "Malthus."

[127] *Letters of Ricardo to Malthus,* p. 56.

[128] A. Clément, in Coquelin et Guillaumin, *Dictionnaire de L'Économie Politique* (Paris, 1873), *s.v.* "J. B. Say."

[129] *Ibid.;* cf. Gide and Rist, *History of Economic Doctrines* (Eng. trans.), p. 104, citing J. B. Say's letter to his brother, Louis Say, in 1827 (*Œuvres diverses,* p. 545).

sophical knowledge and to the second in originality and depth of view."[130] There is likely to be agreement with Gide's further detail that Say introduced a terminology and a schematization which served as "a model for innumerable subsequent treatises"; that he developed doctrines which, even though now "generally discarded," have "none the less exercised an enormous influence"; and that he "contributed fundamental ideas which will always be highly valued in the science."

Notable, too, was Say's influence in spreading interest in economic study. His most important work, the *Traité d'Économie Politique,* passed through many editions and was "the first really popular treatise in political economy ever published in France." It was widely translated and circulated. An American reprint (Philadelphia, 1830) of Prinsep's London translation of the fourth edition, with an Introduction and notes by Clement C. Biddle, was perhaps the most influential manual among serious students of political economy in the United States up to the Civil War.

The early life of David Ricardo is a remarkable story of self-help.[131] Within a few years, probably before he was twenty-six, he had secured for himself economic independence. The problem of material cares disposed of, Ricardo allowed himself some relaxation from intent business activity. In part following an inclination of his boyhood, in part through the example and urging of a friend "with whom he was then very intimate," the young stockbroker devoted a part of his leisure to the popular branches of natural science—mathematics, chemistry, geology, and mineralogy. Many years later his sister told of having been invited as a child to witness some of the electrical experiments which Ricardo conducted with all the naïve pride of an amateur

[130] C. Gide, in Palgrave, *Dictionary of Political Economy, s.v.* "J. B. Say."

[131] Hollander, *David Ricardo: A Centenary Estimate* (Baltimore, 1910), pp. 35–38, from which the succeeding paragraphs have been taken.

physicist; and Fonteyraud, and after him Garnier, state, perhaps upon the same authority, that he was one of the first to introduce illuminating gas in his residence. But even more than chemistry, geology and in particular mineralogy attracted Ricardo's attention, and either at this time or a little later, he fitted up a laboratory and formed a collection of minerals. The beginnings of modern geological study in England are curiously associated with the Society of Friends, and it is possible that Ricardo may have been drawn into this coterie through his wife's connections. He does not appear to have been a member of the Askesian Society, founded in 1796, or of the British Mineralogical Society, organized in 1799. But a few years later these two organizations first merged and then reappeared as the Geological Society, a kind of semi-scientific club, formed by thirteen men dining together at the Freemason's Tavern on November 13, 1807, and meeting in a similar way once a month thereafter. Ricardo, although not one of the original thirteen, became a member of the Society in 1808, and continued more or less actively interested in its affairs until his death.

The history of science presents more than one example of an almost accidental circumstance being responsible for the original interest of a master-mind in the particular subject matter with which it was thereafter to be conspicuously identified. Certainly, casual episode was responsible for Ricardo's attraction to formal economic study. The "Annual Obituary" memoir refers to the circumstance, and McCulloch repeats the story. But the more direct and graphic version is Hobhouse's:

> March 2 [1822].—Dined with Lambton—an immense party and splendid dinner. I sat next to Ricardo, who told me that he never thought of political economy till happening one day, during an illness of his wife, to be at Bath, he saw an Adam Smith in a circulating library, and turning over a page or two ordered it to be sent to his house. He liked it so much as to acquire a taste for the study.[132]

[132] Lord Broughton, *Recollections of a Long Life,* II (1909), 179.

We can well understand that as a substantial, well-informed man of affairs, Ricardo's attention must have been arrested by the remarkable economic events that were taking place about him. Even a mind less favorably endowed or an experience less admirably equipped would have been tempted to inquire as to the cause and extent of such conspicuous phenomena as the rise in general prices, the fluctuations in foreign exchange, and the perplexing interrelations of rents and profits. It is not to be doubted that Ricardo early entertained intelligent views on these subjects; but at best they were independent and detached opinions differing only in degree of intimacy from the sentiments which so thoughtful an observer would have formed upon current social and political conditions. There was need of a determining impulse which should both definitely engage his intellect in economic speculation, and at the same time supply the positive structure to which an essentially critical mind should attach, either in affirmation or dissent, its own views. This impulse came in the form of acquaintance with Adam Smith's work. We are told that Ricardo was from the very first highly gratified by its perusal, and that the inquiries with which it is concerned continued thenceforth to engage a considerable share of his time. The story may be apocryphal, although there is no reason for assuming this; in any event, the fact is unessential. It is enough to know that in the very prime of his mental powers, when a material career had already been achieved, Ricardo's attention was definitely drawn to economic speculation by attentive reading of an economic treatise. "It is, within restricted limits," declared Fonteyraud, "the history of Archimedes' bath, of Newton's apple, of Torricelli's lamp, of Watt's kettle; the history in a word of all intellectual germs which a ray of light fructifies."

The list might indeed be extended: James Mill, who, predestined for the ministry, nevertheless enrolled in Dugald Stewart's "separate course" in 1793: "All the years I remained about Edinburgh, I used, as often as I possibly could, to steal into Mr. Stewart's class to hear a lecture, which was always a high treat." Years before he had made "the aspiring Scotchman's venture upon London," endowed with high intellectual accomplishments and great bodily charm—"The short breeches of the time showed a leg of perfect form," Professor Bain meticulously records—Mill paid ample tribute to Stewart's impress: "The taste for the studies which have formed my favorite pursuits, and which will be so till the end of my life, I owe to him."[133]

John Ramsay McCulloch, who commenced his studies at the University of Edinburgh in 1805, and of whom we are told: "Though he attended several of the classes in the University he gave his almost undivided attention to that department of science which he has done so much to illustrate and elucidate."[134]

Even Mrs. Marcet led her docile pupil along the way appointed by Adam Smith, with only a measure of uneasiness as to "some passages" when a second edition of the *Conversations* was imminent: "If she begins to listen to our controversy," wrote Ricardo to Malthus, in comment upon her application for counsel, "the printing of her book will be long delayed; she had better avoid it, and keep her course on neutral ground. I believe we should sadly puzzle Miss Caroline, and I doubt whether Mrs. B. could clear up the difficulty."[135]

Dugald Stewart, Francis Horner and the Edinburgh reviewers, Thomas Robert Malthus, Jean Baptiste Say, David Ricardo were the notable figures in the early building of "the classical political economy." Torrens, De Quincey, Senior con-

[133] Bain, *op. cit.*, pp. 16–17.

[134] *Biographical Notice of John Ramsay McCulloch, Esq.* (London, 1865), p. 3.

[135] Bonar (ed.), *Letters of Ricardo to Malthus*, p. 133.

tributed elements in the next decades; but the outline and plan of the main structure had then already been determined. Of this major group, Adam Smith was not only the first and greatest but the master. Quite apart from positive contribution of matter and doctrine, his work evoked the first interest and inspired the succeeding effort of the company whose later performance determined the scope and content of our science in the richest period of its history. In this far-reaching sense Adam Smith is to be acclaimed "the founder of a school."

CHAPTER III

ADAM SMITH AND THE CURRENTS OF HISTORY

JOHN MAURICE CLARK

I. INTRODUCTION

There has recently been a revival of interest in that type of economics which interprets things in the light of their origins, the influences which have made them what they are, and the processes by which they have reached their present state. It is from this standpoint that I am asked to speak of Adam Smith. It is frequently said that the germs of all subsequent theories are to be found in his many-sided work, and accordingly one might fairly expect to find germs of this "genetic" type of thinking also. But in view of the fact that his system is in the main an exposition of the "natural laws" and of the "natural order" of liberty, we should naturally expect that such elements of the genetic method as we might find would be of a secondary and subordinate character. And this is, in fact, what we shall find.

But this is not the end of the story. Even more interesting and significant than the search for elements of the genetic method in Adam Smith is the application of this method to his work in its entirety, seeking to interpret his non-genetic theories and principles in the light of the influences which molded them and the forces and conditions to which they were a response. Such a study, if pursued in a captious mood or without a sympathetic sense of values, may have a belittling effect, making social theories seem the playthings of historical accident and robbing their makers of the credit of originality and independence. But if the research be animated by a more open-minded and appreciative spirit, great thought will emerge from the test with renewed vitality. Elements which otherwise seem merely quaint or perverse are revealed as natural adaptations to conditions of time and place, and often acquire a degree of pragmatic validity in relation to a given situation. Such a study does not invite us to accept such doctrines literally, or to reject them *in toto* if we cannot accept them, but rather to give our own thought a relation to the conditions and needs of our time similar to that which we find in the great constructive thought of the past. To understand such thought we must take into account the conditions of the time and what went before; to select from it the elements of value for our own use we must see it in relation to what has come after and to the changed conditions which now prevail. For the first purpose we must view Adam Smith in relation to an age in which factories were tiny, the machine was still hardly more than a machine tool, the competitive system was young and struggling against eighteenth-century mercantilism and survivals of medieval restrictions which had outlived their function. For present purposes we must view Smith's individualism in the light of such facts as railroads, holding-companies, centralized banking, business barometrics and giant power. The teleology of his "unseen hand" must be appraised in terms of Darwinism; its optimism in the light of modern psychiatry. Specific doctrines will be discredited, yet something perhaps of more value, will remain.

The type of environmental interpretation of economic thought which is here attempted is far from a complete one. It deals with the relation of that thought to the larger conditions of its time rather than with the more intimately personal factors and those of particular intellectual contacts which account for so many details of doctrine. On these matters you have already heard a distinguished and original contribution.

2. AN ENVIRONMENTAL INTERPRETATION OF ECONOMICS

The balance of forces in social life is continually shifting—between the few and the many; king, nobles and common people; between authority, science, and popular opinion or free personal choice; between the need of common action and the power of individual initiative; between capital and labor, etc. Existing institutions set the mold in which forces act, and govern their relative opportunities. And, with the familiar fact of institutional lag, they are likely to be adapted to the relative position of the forces as they were when the institutions took shape, a generation or a century or more in the past. They give weight to certain forces, usually not in proportion to their present strength or capacities.

Social thought may follow this emphasis, giving weight to those forces which are dominant in the institutions of the time—then it is "conservative." Or it may emphasize those forces which may become dominant in the millennium—then it is "utopian." Or it may emphasize those forces which are now in existence but to which prevailing institutions give inadequate outlet and recognition in proportion to their present importance and force—then it is "radical" or "progressive" and becomes the keynote of forward movements. Of this general sort was the social philosophy of Adam Smith.

This emphasis may be expressed in various forms, with different degrees of dogmatism on the one side or careful qualification on the other. The practical partisan tends to one kind of statement, and the scientist or philosopher to others. But in either case, the same emphasis may be conveyed, whether in a fighting slogan which ignores all but one side of the case or in a scientific abstraction which focuses attention in certain directions and accomplishes its results by means more unobtrusive and more likely to be unsuspected. Furthermore, writers whose glimpse of truth is derived from conditions of time and place, show a tendency—shall we follow Adam Smith and call it a "natural propensity"—to universalize their particular glimpse of truth. In so doing they often give it a far stronger appeal to the men of their own time; but by the same token they make it less adaptable and less likely to survive changing conditions and issues. Even the issues of one time are seldom so unified and simple that all of them can be correctly approached via any one principle of this universalized sort. An economics made up of such principles must either be inconsistent or be wrong part of the time; but if the economics of the past had refused to employ such principles, it would have refused its most effective weapons. Whatever way it takes out of this dilemma, later students can make the necessary allowances, with the help of historical hindsight. They must strip dogmas of their universality and interpret them in relation to time and place, because only thus can they give themselves a fair chance to sift out the elements of truth which the dogmas usually contain and to re-apply it to their own problems, so far as it may be applicable.

And what happens if the theory succeeds and new institutional adjustments are made which give the new forces the recognition for which they have striven? Then the theory passes into another stage in which it becomes the gospel of things as they are: a conservative rather than a radical force. Its continuing growth is likely to be self-perpetuating; new developments building on the theory itself and carrying it through to its logical conclusions. As to the disturbing forces of the new era, theory is likely to adapt itself to these with as little change as possible rather than make them the keynote of the system. And ultimately the process may have to be repeated.

In all this it is worth while emphasizing that the new theory, while it may be in accord with the manifest destiny of the time, does not therefore necessarily weigh things exactly according to their present force and importance. It must emphasize the things the age does not yet see, not those on which its institutions are consciously founded. Thus when Alfred Marshall speaks of self-reliant, deliberate, foresightful judgment as a fundamental characteristic of modern industrial life, he presumably has in mind the characteristics which are fundamental to an understanding of our more recent and conscious social adjustments; and he justifies this interpretation by seeking chiefly the characteristics which distinguish this age in contrast to previous ages.[1] What makes a thing fundamental for theory may be the fact that it is recent enough to raise problems of conscious readjustment.

This method of interpretation of economic doctrines leads, among other things, to the following maxim: To understand any forceful writer and to make the necessary allowances, find out what it was against which he was reacting. You may then expect to find the value of his message in the direction in which he is swaying the thought of his time, not in the exact distance to which he may carry it. As Smith himself said: "If the rod be bent too much one way, in order to make it straight you must bend it too much the other." He made this remark of the Physiocrats' emphasis on agriculture, but it applies quite as well to the emphasis on liberty which Smith and the Physiocrats had in common.

Furthermore, the errors and excesses of the prevailing system may be diagnosed by observation; but the corresponding errors and excesses of a system which is advocated and is not now in full force, must be largely matters of conjecture. Thus theories are likely to have greater scientific validity as reactions away from previous error than as embodiments of ultimate truth: they serve better to indicate a direction of motion than a final goal.

[1] See *Principles of Economics* (5th ed.), pp. 5–10.

In the light of this approach, what was Adam Smith? He was the interpreter of the forces of economic liberty against certain types of restraints prevalent in the mid-eighteenth century, and of the interest of the country as a whole, viewed from a standpoint in which the common man had a large part, as against the exploitive interests of the particular classes then in power. And he had the rare fortune to stand at a changing-point of historical eras when the world stood ready to accept and use his ideas as part of a great economic transformation. Liberty was about to be supremely justified in the riches brought by the industrial revolution, especially to England, which took the lead in this movement. And the masses were about to gain political power, so far as voting equality could give it; a great increase in economic power; and the embodiment of their interests in the accepted ideal of economic policy: the good of the greatest number.

This theory of liberty has persisted into a new era when new issues are arising in bewildering variety; not so much taking the place of the older issues as added to them. So far as the older issues persist, the truths embodied in Smith's message persist also, but they cannot be expressed with the old degree of generality and emphasis. Fortunately, Smith has set the example, not of dogmatic and universal absolutes, but of a sane and balanced treatment of conflicting interests, consciously adjusted to the conditions and needs of his own time.

Let us now look in more detail, first at his environment, and then at his doctrines.

3. ADAM SMITH'S ENVIRONMENT

The close of the eighteenth century, which witnessed the publication of the *Wealth of Nations,* saw also the American Revolution, the French Revolution, and the Industrial Revolution. These marked the end of the first era of modern Nationalism and the beginning of the second, which appears already to have worked out its destiny in bringing us well into a third.

The epoch which was coming to its close in 1776 was that of dynastic-aristocratic Nationalism: the dark ages of modern times. It had passed through the heroic days of idealized buccaneering typified in Francis Drake, and had subsided into the more commercialized, calculating, and materialistic attitude which characterized the first half of the eighteenth century. One of the dominant forces was war, and the mutual rivalries of the various nations, viewed from the standpoint of dynastic aggrandizement, and with war never far in the background. Such nations naturally did not think in terms of mutual advancement in their dealings with one another; rather, a nation felt that it gained from the losses of its rivals, apart from its own absolute advancement in wealth or welfare. A large population, national self-sufficiency, and industries subserving the army and navy—all were ends in themselves; while a high level of wealth for the masses was not a goal of national policy but—strange as it may seem—rather the opposite, as expressed by numerous candid spokesmen of the dominant undemocratic materialism. Aggregate rather than per capita wealth was the economic goal.

Socially, education was still the privilege of the few, and the common people were rather frankly regarded as instruments of production, food for powder, and means of sustaining the elegance of the gentry. The state of humanitarian feeling may be exemplified by the death penalty for theft, replaced in practice by transportation, but remaining on the statute books. Liberty could have little meaning for the great majority. The chief practical exponents of increased freedom were the mercantile classes; and the liberty for which they spoke was not general liberty but particular liberties in which they had an interest. The increasing liberty of the masses, largely expressed in the substitution of the wage system for the feudal status, was hardly an articulate movement, or a part of the dominant philosophy of the time. Liberty of thought, however, already existed to a large extent in England, though in France the Mercantilist Abbé Galiani defined eloquence as the art of saying everything without going to the Bastile.

Politically, Englishmen had won rights and representation of which they were justly proud, but the system was far from democratic in theory or ideal in operation. The government was largely in the hands of the landed aristocracy, though seats in Parliament were marketable commodities which members of other classes were able to purchase. The methods of filling positions of public trust were marked by a certain genial inappropriateness which was saved from worse results chiefly by the fact that the landed gentry in their blundering and amateurish way still showed a well-meaning conscientiousness about fulfilling the responsibilities which their station placed upon them. (In France, the lack of this saving quality paved the way for the Revolution.) Commissions in the army were bought and sold; prisons were farmed out; and of government as a tool adapted to the enlightened discernment of social needs and the efficient prosecution of them, there was little trace. For such tasks the government of the time was not fitted; even less so than the government of today.

On the economic side, the early system of Nationalism was marked by a great increase in the scope of free contract and free exchange as compared to the medieval economy of local units, largely self-sufficing and governed to a great extent by status. In this local economy, rural tenants paid their customary dues in kind, and town craftsmen received their customary "just price" and controlled entry into their "mysteries." This idea of a "just price" was not applicable to distant trade, or indeed to any but dealings within a small and closely knit community;

and it weakened with the increase of distant trade and disappeared with the transition from the guild craftsman to the capitalist employer. Free exchange in determining the prices of goods was paralleled by the wage system and contractual rents payable in money. The king built up his paid standing army in place of the feudal levies, and his strength began to be measured by his treasure rather than by lands, vassals, and retainers. The vast supply of precious metals from the New World reinforced the emphasis on specie, which was natural in this situation, and drew the nations into a conscious struggle for their share.

In this situation arose the well-known system of Mercantilism, which we think of as a system of restrictive control, but which was, from an historical standpoint, based on a transfer to the nation of controls previously exercised locally, in which process most of them were considerably relaxed. Within the boundaries of the nation, the principle and practice of free trade and exchange made great headway, as already indicated, despite the retarding effect of many survivals of earlier restrictions, including apprentice laws, the law of parish settlements in England, and local customs duties in France.

Early Nationalism strove to keep money in the country by the direct and crude method of prohibitions on the export of specie. These not only proved unworkable but they unduly restricted trade and were opposed by the growing interests of the mercantile classes. These interests found in the theory of the balance of trade a defense for their desire for a greater degree of freedom, harmonizing it with the accepted notion of the importance of conserving the specie supply and showing how the traders could be permitted certain kinds of profitable trade while the country's interest in its money supply would be promoted more effectually than before.

This theory represented a rudimentary form of scientific economics, examining the effects of transactions and policies in order to show how desired results could be better obtained by indirect than by direct means, taking advantage of the natural laws of exchange and utilizing them. Thus the balance-of-trade theory was not solely the result of a desire for increased specie, but rather a combination of this with the merchants' direct interest in greater freedom of trade. But it served the interests of freedom only to a limited extent, and it was not to be expected that this material interest would remain permanently content with the precise degree of freedom which this theory justified.[2] It was a compromise, representing a temporary and unstable equilibrium between the various interests concerned. It did not represent the interests of consumers, for whom Adam Smith spoke, nor did it regard trade fundamentally as an instrument for the acquisition of more goods for all to enjoy.

In the meantime, the same forces which built the national economy were developing the basis for a more democratic view and a more inclusive treatment of interests. The disruption of feudal status ushered in a struggle for a new adjustment of the powers of different classes, from which the people at large could not be permanently excluded. As they gained political representation, their economic interests could not longer be ignored, though at first they were spoken for largely by members of other classes, animated by the humanitarian sentiments which began to be respectable as the democratic movement proceeded. From this time on, Mercantilist economics, or any economics expressing solely or primarily the interests of the mercantile classes, could not hold an uncontested supremacy.

The new economy was also laying the basis for the development of scientific economics as we know it: a more or less quantitative study of the natural results of a system based on free

[2] The main features of this interpretation are similar to that of Alfred Marshall. See his *Principles of Economics* (5th ed.), Appendix B, "The Growth of Economic Science," esp. p. 755.

exchange. In medieval times, free exchange was most evident in distant trade, and distant trade was adventurous and speculative to an extent which almost precluded the observation of quantitative regularities. Interest on loans for sea commerce, besides being concealed to avoid the laws against usury, contained such a large element of premium for risk that the interest-component was indistinguishable. Manufacturing capital consisted of the simple tools of the craftsman; and domestic loans were largely for non-productive purposes. It is not safe to assume that the laws of supply and demand were wholly atrophied in domestic trade, but the restraints on mobility prevented them, under ordinary conditions, from getting far out of line with the customary standards which the medieval system enforced as just.

But with the broadening of the economic unit to national size, and the development of domestic free exchange and competition, profits and interest became more distinguishable and more nearly standardized; and wages also reached something like a system of levels under the visible operation of the laws of supply and demand. The loan for productive purposes began to take the place of the loan for consumption, as the typical form of transaction; and interest became a more regular thing, with an observable relation to business earnings. In short, more and more regularities were appearing in the unregulated behavior of economic phenomena, governed by the principle of self-interest and checked by competition and the forces of demand and supply. Thus the subject matter of economics took on a shape susceptible of analysis into laws of a scientific character, as they are generally understood.

Meanwhile the concept of laws in social life had been set up as a goal by the Encyclopedists; and the Physiocrats identified the natural order with the order of liberty; and both with the most efficient development of society. With this weapon they attacked not only the restrictions of Mercantilism but also the hideously unjust, corrupt, and inefficient tax system—or rather tax chaos—then prevailing in France. The system laid crippling burdens on trade and enterprise, and especially on the labor of the peasants; and exempted the church and the landowning aristocracy. Thus Physiocracy was an attack on the greatest vested interests of the time, though it was sugar-coated by the argument that these interests already bore the ultimate burdens of taxation and that if they should bear them directly they would actually have more left than before, on account of the increased productivity which would result from removing the burdens on work and enterprise. Whatever may have been the intellectual roots of this idea, it seems clear that without such a sugar-coating no doctrinal attack on the exemptions of the privileged classes could have failed to bring its advocates to the Bastile.

The Physiocrats were still monarchists, believing in the enlightened sovereign who should follow the laws of the natural order as the conductor of an orchestra follows the laws of musical harmony. This again was the only safe form of liberalism in France at that time. Thus the very features of Physiocracy which we cannot accept, were, consciously or unconsciously, adaptations to environment, marking this as the only liberal doctrine which could be openly advocated at that time and place. Even so, the beginnings of a practical application of Physiocratic principles, by Turgot, was more than the privileged interests would tolerate; and his reforms were promptly extinguished. France was not ready for freedom through reason, but had to wait for a political revolution, after which the peculiar conditions no longer existed which had given appropriateness to the peculiar features of Physiocratic doctrine, and the principle of liberty naturally found its expression in a different form.

The vogue of the Physiocratic doctrine bears witness to the

readiness of the world to listen to ideas of liberty despite obscurities and extravagances which taxed human credulity. Elsewhere, other general advocates of liberty were being heard, and the way was paved for Adam Smith's synthesis of liberty and economic science. This, then, was the situation, and these were the issues at which his thinking was directed. And his mind grasped them largely, constructively, and on the side of human progress. He was great in the sense of being the child of his time, but the child of its unsatisfied urges rather than of its established complacencies.

While the issues of the time furnished the material and governed the trend of his thinking, the thought of the time gave him tools with which he worked and preconceptions with which he approached his task. One of these was the idea of an order of nature, to be found by searching nature itself for the universal or the original. He was in the current of a notable revival of liberal thought in the Scotch universities; and from Hutcheson he had the opportunity to absorb, among other things, the idea of the good of the greatest number. His personal bent led him to amass a great array of facts, so that he has been called the best-informed man since Aristotle. In either case, it is only fair to judge the accuracy of the information in the light of available sources and prevailing standards in the matter of verification. Aristotle's equipment of "facts" included many an astounding fable.

Smith also had a considerable historical perspective, seeking for the roots things have in the past. He was a realist; hence he never forgot such facts as the existence of classes; but his standards of welfare looked beyond the mere *fait accompli* of present power and took in the welfare of the undistinguished masses, giving them in an unspectacular way more fundamental importance than the ambitions of the rich. And this, needless to say, marks a great advance on the Mercantilist attitude.

4. ADAM SMITH'S DOCTRINES

Not all of Adam Smith's specific doctrines, of course, are direct attempts to puncture Mercantilist fallacies or to set up antitheses to them. But most of them have some relation, direct or indirect, to this great controversy. And one fancies, in reading the *Wealth of Nations,* that where the relation is most direct the style acquires an added zest which is very revealing. Smith reveled in exposing the false standards of economic policy which served to mask the interests of particular producing classes and in setting up instead the basic standard of producing more goods for people at large to consume.

Money, instead of being a great desideratum, was with him a tool, of which it was as wasteful to use more than was needed as it would be to use two wagons to haul one load. This dethroning of money as an end of all things probably carried with it a certain underestimate of its importance as a tool: an error which we are now attempting to rectify. Exports were not good in themselves, nor were imports in themselves forms of economic calamity; rather imports were goods to be consumed, and exports were the means of securing imports and paying for them. To secure general acceptance of this view was no small contribution. By defining Mercantilism in terms of its monetary notions, Smith put its most vulnerable aspect foremost and not only strengthened his case against it but enabled himself, without evident inconsistency, to adopt some of the sounder standards of national policy on which the mercantile system in a larger sense was built.

His own ideas, then, of the ends of economic policy were a mixture, in which anti-Mercantilist elements held the central place, while other special purposes were allowed as justifying particular departures from the general rule of laissez faire. In setting up consumable goods as the prime desideratum, he also adopted the criterion of per capita rather than aggregate wealth, but this standard finds little reflection in his later discussions of those methods of production which set a maximum amount of productive labor in motion. He also urges that it is only just that those who feed, clothe, and lodge the whole society (it is labor which does this) should themselves be tolerably well fed, clothed, and lodged. And he nowhere expresses similar solicitation for the consumption of the rich! He does not claim that all men are equal, though he does consider the difference between a philosopher and a street porter mostly a matter of environment.

A characteristic example of his point of view is found in his treatment of the struggle with the American colonies. He minimized the burdens laid on the colonists, but condemned the restrictions as violations of "natural rights." And he gave decisive weight to the inevitable pressure of the minority of "natural leaders" in the colonies toward a chance to make the most of their talents and position. This affords an almost ironic contrast to the language of a certain great Declaration which these same "natural leaders" were then on the point of signing. Though Smith shared the belief that men were *born* (approximately) equal, his practical mind solved problems in terms of the inequalities they acquired after birth. In these terms he not only argued for giving the colonies (or their "natural leaders") representation in Parliament, but calmly contemplated the time when they would outweigh the British Isles and when the capital might be moved across the Atlantic!

On the other hand, he not only reacts against Mercantilism and attacks its premises and standards; he also borrows some of its less controversial features. He recognizes national ends as vital. "Defense is more important than opulence," and economic measures looking to this end are justifiable. They must, however, appear in their true colors and not pose as means of economic gain when they are really economic burdens undergone for the sake of a more important end. He is a Nationalist, though his Nationalism is not primarily invidious, being colored by his philosophy of mutual gain in international exchange. But when he justifies the Navigation Acts, invidious Nationalism certainly enters in, and the rivalry between England and Holland is continually before his eyes. While he does at times suggest viewing the world as one economic society, he thinks prevailingly of the societies we actually have. He is a Nationalist because he is a realist.

But perhaps the strongest feature of his work—unless it be his mass of descriptive evidence—is the strengthening of its claims to scientific standing by the theory of value and distribution which forms, in one sense, the backbone of his book. This theory seems not to be related to specific points in the Mercantilist controversy, though it has an indirect relation. Smith's labor measure of value helps to bring into relief changes in the value of specie, and this in turn helps to weaken the claims of money to the homage formerly paid it. And the theory of the tendency of values to natural levels is part of a system of natural equilibrium whose naturalness carries some weight of approval. The tendency toward equalization of the real attractiveness of different occupations is part of this system and helps it to appear good as well as natural. The mere fact that Smith's individualism is part of the argument which centers around the science of value lends it a certain force.

But logically there are conspicuously weak points in the chain of connection between these two ideas, and the individualism is logically far more independent of the value theory than is usually supposed. And Smith's theory of value was not sufficiently coherent or complete to afford a permanently adequate basis for the science of economics. From our present standpoint his individualism would be weakened rather than strengthened by being made to rest on this as its sole foundation.

The annual revenue of the society consists of the "exchangeable value" of the commodities produced; and a large revenue of this sort is desirable, though admittedly it does not measure the utilities received. This end is to be promoted by putting in motion as much productive labor as possible and allotting this labor between the different branches of production in accord with the strength of the respective demands. But demand, as a criterion of what is socially desirable, remains unsupported, hanging in the air. Thus under critical examination, Smith's rule of laissez faire finds but weak support in his theory of value.

It is more directly supported by a number of more practical observations. Smith noted that scarcities of foodstuffs seldom degenerated into famine if supplies were free to distribute themselves in response to demand; or rather, he noted that where famines occurred, there was always some obstacle to the free movement of supplies from less afflicted regions. As to standards of workmanship, he stated that the customer is the best source of trade discipline—better, that is, than the rules of guilds or of national officers. Would he have maintained this faith in the modern era of synthetic substitutes and jerry-building? He argued that freedom of international trade brought the consumers more goods: a proposition not fundamentally dependent on any one theory of value.

Another aspect of the extra-logical character of his individualism is seen in his theory of human nature. He did not believe in the competence of man's reason to guide and control his destiny. In the "Theory of Moral Sentiments" we learn that nature implants impulses in man's breast which are wiser than his reason, since nature intends always the good of the species and endows man with social sentiments. And this despite the fact that the "Theory of Moral Sentiments" is as full of vices as of virtues. The pursuit of happiness through wealth is delusive, but justified by its results through this same wisdom of nature. Yet its results include the stultifying effects of the subdivision of labor on the mass of routine laborers, of which Smith in one passage draws a truly appalling picture. Why select the good effects as those which nature intends? If one replies that the benevolent order of nature was an idea which Smith absorbed from his contemporaries, this merely forces us back to the question why this idea was growing in force at this time. Was it not perhaps fundamentally because this aspect of economic liberty was precisely the one which at this time most needed to be interpreted to a world whose established order was built on its negation? If so, an interesting conclusion follows. We of today have no such justification for giving this idea the same place in our economics that Smith gave it in his.

The "invisible hand" did not prevent Smith from making many departures from laissez faire. He followed it only so far as the facts appeared to him to warrant. And the warrant of facts was found chiefly in the errors of Mercantilism, of the apprentice laws, of the law of parish settlements, and other outworn restrictions on the general liberty to choose one's trade and to produce what the market might demand. The superiority of natural liberty is really a relative superiority: relative to the forms of control then in vogue and to the existing capabilities of private enterprise. And Smith continually falls back on such comparisons to support it.

5. WAS SMITH A GENETIC ECONOMIST?

To what extent did Smith himself appreciate the relation between economic doctrine and the forces of history which lie back of it? And to what extent was he a "genetic economist"? As to the first question, it seems clear that if he had regarded his doctrines as no more than the reflection of a particular and passing historical situation, they would have been robbed of their greatest effect. And as to the question of Smith's claims to rank as a genetic economist, the answer may hinge on the choice of a definition. And a fair definition for the purpose in hand is not easy, since to the modern mind the term "genetic" has a content which it could not possibly have had to anyone who lived and died in the eighteenth century. It implies explaining things in terms of the conditions out of which they arose. And a genetic economist would naturally be one in whom this element is so fundamental as to give him a sense of the relativity of all institutions to the circumstances of their origin. To this the modern mind adds the idea of endless evolution, not directed by rational purpose toward any previsioned end nor explainable by a tendency toward any ultimate "natural" system. Purposes are among the impelling forces, but are not supreme; and none of them explains the ultimate outcome. Indeed there is no outcome that can be called ultimate. It is clear at the start that no economics can be fully "genetic" in which the purposes of nature and the "natural order" of liberty play so basic a part as they do in the system of Adam Smith.

Smith's treatment of origins falls partly in the class of "hypothetical history," serving mostly to explain how the forces of "natural liberty" might have operated under primitive conditions. His "propensity to truck and barter" must probably be placed in this class, on account of its slight basis in actual historical evidence. Here also belongs his rationalized picture of exchange leading to the division of labor in a hunting society and to a labor basis of value under primitive conditions. Here also belongs his idea that rent arises when all the land is owned and his discussion of the origins of money. It is noticeable that he takes legal tender as an institution for granted, the only question being what materials had this quality in different stages of development.

But Smith deals far more with actual than with hypothetical history. He traces the policy of Europe from the fall of Rome, showing how it has consistently favored town as against country industry. He holds that this has been the result of the prejudices of different classes, but has given rise to different systems of political economy. This is a truly genetic point of view, but he stops short of applying it to his own system. Even Mercantilism he interprets, as we have seen, too much in terms of a single dogma about money and too little in terms of its whole institutional setting and purport.

He discusses at length the development of water trade, how ancient civilizations centered around the Mediterranean, and how commerce led to a taste for the finer manufactures. But all this appears to be in support of his general doctrine that the division of labor is limited by the extent of the market. He also traces the different progress of opulence in the different nations; but he finds therein a natural order of development, the reflection of his static "natural order," often thwarted and distorted by human institutions. Indeed, this is the light in which institutions are typically mentioned. He thinks of productivity as relative to the development of institutions, for he speaks of countries as having developed the full degree of productiveness which their institutions permit; but here again the stage of development of institutions is regarded in the light of a greater or less approximation to the system of natural liberty. More promising is his discussion of the manner in which commerce leads the rich to buy goods rather than keep retainers, leading to a surrender of their power and permanence of position; but even here one seems to see the change as a setting free of the forces of natural liberty from the trammels of customary status.

To sum up: Smith used genetic evidence, and it lent his system much of its strength. It gave him a sense of the relativity of institutions—some institutions—those which thwarted the laws of natural liberty, but not those which followed these laws. And it gave him a sense of the relativity of systems of political economy—some systems, but not his own. It gave him a sense of probable future change, but only toward a predetermined goal. The germs of a genetic treatment are there, but they are tributary and subordinate to the system of natural liberty.

6. THE SPIRIT OF SMITH IN THE LIGHT OF LATER CONDITIONS

The immediate success of Adam Smith's views in England, especially in the practical work of freeing her from the restraints he attacked, undoubtedly had much to do with the fact that class interests had shifted and no longer required these restraints. But this topic belongs to a later lecture in this series. Let us pass, then, to the question: What can we learn from Smith today? Viewing the heritage he has left us in the light of its origins, how much can we keep? The most fundamental thing to preserve is the thing which gave his thought its power and vitality; namely, its grasp on the interests of his time to which the institutions of the time gave inadequate opportunity and expression. And since these interests and institutions have changed greatly in a century and a half, our answer must change correspondingly; otherwise we shall not be imitating Smith in the most significant sense.

The theory which traces its lineage most directly to Adam Smith has now reached that second stage of development in which it expresses the forces on which the prevailing order is consciously built. It takes care of certain interests, as the theory of the balance of trade did; but it is not sufficiently comprehensive for modern conditions. In the first place, Mercantilism is still with us, complicated by the abnormal state of international indebtedness. This affords ample opportunity for pouring new facts into the mold of Smith's analysis and for renewing his outspoken exposures of false standards, inconsistency, and unworkability. But these matters are less paramount; other issues have grown to an even more insistent importance, especially those of industrial relations and the control of large-scale industry.

There have been immense developments of control in the interests of labor, which Smith said were always just. But we must remember that the reason he gave was that these regulations must run the gauntlet of a government which represented the employing interests, and that this reason no longer holds good to anything like the same extent. Universal suffrage has given an opposite bias, against which the employing interests wage a struggle, with varying fortunes.

Our intellectual tools and preconceptions have also developed. In Smith's time the world was just awakening to a scrutiny of institutions and retained a bias toward justifying them by finding that they were in accord with original nature. Since then we have passed through the age of Bentham, who would test them by their results, but who viewed them too much as bits of machinery to be tinkered with at the will of the tinkerer. We are now realizing that while they are not eternally natural in any one form, they are the results of natural forces, both of change and of stability. And while we still submit them to Bentham's test, we cannot hope to mend their shortcomings by a light-hearted shifting of gears or substitution of rolls. We must study them as living things and influence their growth by indirect as well as by direct means, expecting many failures and disappointments.

The modern economist, like Smith, is forced to use the yardstick of price for what it may be worth; but he is developing statistical data and techniques which enable him to study the physical quantities that lie behind the money measure and to supplement it in other ways. Like Smith, we may recognize standards of welfare and of public policy independent of price: and at present we are returning to an attitude more like his in that we do not trust the all-sufficiency of reason, but lay increasing emphasis on the impulses. One school builds its chief criterion of welfare out of the "impulses implanted by nature." But, needless to say, the eighteenth-century concept of nature has been revolutionized by Darwinism. Darwinism justifies the idea that nature intends the good of the species only so far as the environment remains substantially the same as that in which the present human characters were developed. Our fitness to the new environment which we ourselves have made remains an open question and a serious one.

One thing we must, of course, reject is Smith's idea that corporations cannot operate industry efficiently. But if we wish to develop the best capabilities of these organizations, we have not yet done with the sources of weakness he pointed out. We can no longer be content to take corporations for granted as artificial economic men and build on them a pseudo-individualism which Smith himself would have instantly rejected. On this point perhaps the best model for a would-be follower of today is found in his discussion of an established church. He approves of small-scale competitive enterprise in religion on the basis of its effects on the actual individuals engaged—both clergy and parishioners.

The modern economist who would follow the lead of Smith must be alert to new alignments of classes, to their conflicting interests and to the habits of mind and limitations of intelligence which they exhibit. He will not be a doctrinaire democrat or a socialist. He will neither despise government nor idealize it as the all-sufficient social agency. He must strike for himself some balance between the new departmentalized representative government and the new integrated industry; between the liberties of individuals, increased industrial output, and the pressure of various brands of "natural leaders" toward scope for their talents.

Above all, he must search for interests which have outgrown the customary avenues of expression. And in the light of this search he may modify Smith's attitude toward trade associations and other co-operative agencies; indeed, Smith's purely negative attitude is now clearly untenable. We must recognize the dangers of group power and selfishness, but we must also see the part such agencies are playing and are destined to play in preventing evils and injuries which unregulated free exchange does not prevent and in protecting interests which it leaves unprotected.

Indeed, the modern follower of the spirit of Smith might be justified in concentrating his emphasis on such controlling, moralizing, and associative agencies, not because the principle of free exchange has lost its validity, but because these moralizing agencies are the things which are new and undeveloped, relative to the place they seem destined to fill. On the other hand, so long as mercantilism persists and revolutionary communism remains an active possibility, the basic serviceability of free exchange cannot safely be left wholly out of sight. The range of alternatives to which our economics must be relevant has increased. Between the "thesis" of free exchange and the "antithesis" of communism we are challenged to build up a working synthesis which may have a relation to the needs of our time similar in kind, if not in genius, to that achieved by Adam Smith. One may even conjecture what the keynote of the synthesis will be: the building of moralized economic communities, expressing and protecting by appropriate agencies all the essential interests concerned.

But whatever one's conclusion may be on that point, it seems clear that we also stand at a changing-point of historical eras. The raw materials for a new synthesis lie temptingly about us; and the place it can fill, if successful, can hardly be overestimated. We face a need no less insistent and an opportunity no less commanding than that which was so greatly met by a certain absent-minded Scotch professor in the year 1776.

CHAPTER IV

SMITH'S THEORY OF VALUE AND DISTRIBUTION

PAUL H. DOUGLAS

The contributions of Adam Smith to the theory of value and of distribution were not great, and in commemorating the publication of the *Wealth of Nations* it might seem to be the path of wisdom to pass these topics by in discreet silence and to reserve discussion instead for those subjects, such as the division of labor, where his realistic talents enabled him to appear at a better advantage. Yet the errors of an able thinker are, if properly interpreted, only slightly less illuminating than his substantive contributions, and deserve analysis in the history of economic thought. There is, however, another reason why Smith's doctrines on value and distribution merit examination. This is because Smith's formulation of the problems of exchange value and of the distribution of the national product among the factors of production was such as almost inevitably gave rise to the doctrines of the post-Ricardian socialists and to the labor theory of value and the exploitation theory of Karl Marx.

I. THE REJECTION OF UTILITY AS A DETERMINANT OF VALUE AND THE ACCEPTANCE OF THE LABOR THEORY

In a society with a highly developed division of labor, exchange necessarily becomes ubiquitous, and the ratio at which the goods or services one produces exchange for the goods and services one desires becomes an ingredient element in individual, and indeed in national, prosperity. It is not enough to produce a large physical quantity of goods. If one is to be comfortable it is also necessary, as the farmers in the United States have found, that the exchange ratios of these goods in terms of other products should be sufficiently high to yield a comfortable real income in goods, and hence ultimately in pleasures to the producers. To the theory of production is therefore necessarily joined the theory of value.

What, then, did determine the ratio at which commodities exchanged? Smith had considered the possibility of utility but dismissed it because of the paradox which Locke, Hutcheson,[1] Law,[2] and Harris had pointed out before him between the relative value of water and diamonds. "Nothing is more useful," wrote Smith,[3] "than water, but it will purchase scarce anything; scarce anything can be had in exchange for it. A diamond, on the contrary, has scarce any value in use; but a very great quantity of other goods may frequently be had in exchange for it." From this he concludes that "value in use," or utility is of an entirely independent nature from "value in exchange" and has no part in the determination of the latter. "The things which have the greatest value in use have frequently little or no value in exchange; and, on the contrary, those which have the greatest value in exchange have frequently little or no value in use."[4] Here the break between the two concepts is complete. Not only is utility not a determinant of exchange value, but—and here Smith goes much farther than Ricardo and later exponents of the labor theory of value—it is not even a necessary prerequisite.

The main reason why Smith and those who followed him abandoned utility as a determinant of value was, of course, because they were comparing the total utilities yielded by varying types of objects rather than their marginal utilities.

[1] Hutcheson, *A System of Moral Philosophy*, II, 53-54.

[2] Law, *Money and Trade Considered* (1705), chap. i.

[3] Smith, *Wealth of Nations* (Cannan edition), I, 30.

[4] Smith, *op. cit.*, p. 30.

The existence of free goods is striking proof of the fact that the utility afforded by a class of commodities need bear no relation to its exchange value. It was not until it was pointed out that we should compare the exchange ratios of individual units rather than of whole classes of commodities that the water-diamond paradox could be solved. When this was done, it was not difficult to see that *a* diamond had a greater value than a gallon of water because in comparison with the intensity of the desires for diamonds and for water, the former was less plentiful than the latter.

Smith's failure to consider the relative scarcity of commodities in connection with their respective utilities is all the more striking in view of the very clear approaches to this point of view which had been made by Locke and Harris. Thus, Locke had written:

> What more useful or necessary things are there to the being or well-being of men than air and water? And yet these generally have no price at all, because their quantity is immensely greater than their vent in most places of the earth. But as soon as ever water comes anywhere to be reduced into any proportion to its consumption, it begins presently to have a price and is sometimes sold dearer than wine. Hence it is that the best and most useful things are commonly the cheapest, because, though their consumption be great, yet the bounty of providence has made their production large and suitable to it.[5]

and Harris, applying himself to the very commodities which Smith later considered, had explicitly written that

> . . . . Water is of great use and yet ordinarily of little or no value because in most places, water flows spontaneously in such great plenty as not to be withheld within the limits of private property; but all may have enough without other expense than that of bringing or conducting it. . . . . On the other hand, diamonds being very scarce, have upon that account a great value, though they are but of little use.[6]

[5] Locke, *Considerations of the Lowering of Interest and Raising the Value of Money,* p. 41.

[6] Harris, *Essay upon Money and Coins,* p. 5.

By failing to follow up the hints which these writers had developed,[7] Smith helped to divert the writers of the English Classical school into a cul-de-sac from which they did not emerge, in so far as their value theory was concerned, for nearly a century, while he also helped, as we shall see, to give rise to the economic doctrines of nineteenth-century socialism.

When, by observation, by the mathematical assumptions of Dupuit, the demand concepts of Cournot,[7a] and by the experiments of Weber, the principle of diminishing utility was grasped, the further fact emerged that the economic importance of an object was determined by the relative utility yielded by the last of a series of such articles. From these simple phenomena, Gossen,[7b] Jevons,[7c] and Wicksteed[8] built up their elaborate analyses of individual behavior to demonstrate how men would dispose of their time and money in such a way that utilities of the last units of each set of commodities would be equal, while the Austrian school deduced the laws of short-run price.

Smith's moralistic sense was probably a further reason why he failed to follow up the analysis of utility as a possible cause of value. In his thrifty Scotch manner with its opposition to ostentation as almost sinful he concluded that diamonds had "scarce any value in use." But, of course, as the moralists from Ruskin on have pointed out, economic values are not necessarily moral values. It is not necessary that commodities should be "good" for people in order that they may have value. It is only

[7] For a discussion of the various value theories prior to 1776, see Sewall, *The Theory of Value before Adam Smith,* especially pp. 66–124.

[7a] Cournot, *Recherches sur les principes mathématiques de la Théorie des richesses* (1838). English translation by Bacon, *Mathematical Principles of the Theory of Wealth* (1897).

[7b] Gossen, *Entwickelung der Gesetze des Menschlichen Verkehrs* (1854). Gossen to be sure developed this theory independently.

[7c] Jevons, *The Theory of Political Economy,* chap. iii.

[8] Wicksteed, *The Common Sense of Political Economy.*

necessary that they be desired and that they exist in less than sufficient quantity to satisfy the demand. A large proportion of what is produced today is indeed "illth" rather than "wealth" in the original sense of the latter word, and yet these articles sell in the market for a money price. We are, indeed, likely to fall into the confusion of Smith if we do not recognize that ethical value and economic value are by no means identical and that the absence of the former by no means signifies the absence of the latter.

Having discarded utility, save in so far as it helped to determine temporary market price, Smith turned to labor as both the measure and the source of value. This in turn necessitated the conception of a unit of labor. What was the common denominator to which all labor could be reduced? Time by itself, Smith pointed out, was not sufficient, since[9] "the different degrees of hardship endured or ingenuity exercised must likewise be taken into account." "There may be more labour," he remarked,[10] "in an hour's application to a trade which it cost ten years labour to learn, than in a month's industry at an ordinary and obvious employment."

2. THE REDUCTION OF TIME, HARDSHIP, AND INGENUITY TO A COMMON MEASURE: THE DISCUSSION OF DIFFERENCES IN WAGES

But to equate time, hardship, and ingenuity to a common unit was, as Smith admitted, "not easy." How, then, was it accomplished? "By the higgling and bargaining of the market," Smith replied,[11] "according to that rough sort of equality which, though not exact, is sufficient for carrying on the basis of common life." There is here the same tendency toward circular reasoning which marks the thinking of both Ricardo and of

[9] *Wealth of Nations*, p. 33.

[10] *Wealth of Nations*, p. 33.

[11] Smith, *Wealth of Nations*, I, 33.

Marx upon this point. For if it is labor which is to serve as the measure and source of value, then we must explain the latter by the quantity of the former. Yet here we find Smith appealing to market values to determine the quantity of labor.[12]

But Smith may perhaps be saved from circuity of reasoning by his celebrated chapter on differences in wages. Differences in monetary remuneration as between occupations are caused, he holds, by differences in (1) the agreeableness of the employments, (2) the relative difficulty in learning them, (3) the degree of regularity of employment, (4) the relative trust imposed on those employed, and (5) the relative possibility of success.

Analyzed more closely, it will be seen that those differences in wages which are caused by differences in the regularity of employment are primarily daily and not yearly differences. Smith pointed out that the wages of the masons were higher than those of journeymen in manufacturing, who had equal skill, in order to compensate the former for the smaller number of days in which they had an opportunity to labor. Over the year—or at best, if we are to use modern parlance, over the course of a business cycle—these differences would be equalized and an equality of earnings for otherwise similar work be established.

In a similar fashion, the necessity for paying skilled labor more than unskilled in order to compensate for the years of apprenticeship when money earnings were lower than those secured by common laborers would not by itself, over the course of a working lifetime, give greater earnings to the skilled than to the less expert. All that Smith tells us is that in later life the

[12] Ricardo: "The estimation in which different qualities of labor are held comes soon to be adjusted in the market with sufficient precision for all practical purposes." *Principles of Political Economy* (Everyman edition), p. 11. Cf. Marx: "The different proportions in which different sorts of labour are reduced to unskilled labour as their standard are established by a social process which goes on behind the backs of the producers." *Capital* (Kerr edition), I, 52.

former must have higher earnings to balance the lower earnings which they obtained during the earlier years. Equality of money earnings would in the long run be the inevitable result were we not to resort to the relatively modern doctrines of time preference. We may say that the skilled worker is not compensated by receiving later in life the same number of dollars which he had earlier foregone. The higher earlier earnings of the unskilled might in most youthful minds outweigh the greater subsequent earnings of the skilled, and in order to induce some of the boys to forego them, it would probably be necessary to promise them more dollars in the future than they were abandoning in the present. Thus there is probably something in the nature of interest in the wages of the skilled. While this latter point is certainly not Smith's, it is thoroughly consistent with his theory. For here the greater wages received over the course of a life by the skilled as compared with the unskilled workers would only be enough to compensate them for the greater psychic loss which they experienced in giving up their cake in the years of their youth. For each unit of discomfort experienced, the remuneration of labor would be the same.

This is the basic principle throughout Smith's discussion. It is strikingly evidenced in his first reason for such differences, namely, that wages varied[13] "with the ease or hardship, the cleanliness or dirtiness, the honourableness or dishonourableness of the employment." Blacksmiths, adduced Smith, received more than weavers because their work was dirtier, while miners received still more because their work was even more disagreeable. These added money sums had to be paid to the workers in order to compensate them for the intrinsic unpleasantness of their occupations, but supposedly were just enough to provide for this. For equal amounts of sacrifice, however, the remuneration would be equal. Similarly, those whose positions

[13] *Wealth of Nations,* I, 102.

are attended with public honor will be willing to work for less than will others who do not receive such social esteem.

The reasoning that wages must be higher in those occupations where trust is reposed is more ambiguous. Goldsmiths are said to be paid more than other workmen of equal ingenuity because "of the precious metals with which they are intrusted."[14] Here, apparently, the reasoning is that those who are subjected to great temptations need added rewards to prevent them from yielding. A higher wage and a higher level of living would lessen this pressure of temptation. Since such workers would then live on a more expensive scale, they would not need to steal in order to surpass their fellows. Higher wages in such cases were in the nature of necessary insurance policies against theft and betrayal. Since men do not believe that virtue is its own reward, it is necessary to furnish more tangible incentives.

But Smith evidently had more in mind than merely the foregoing:

> We trust our health to the physician . . . . our fortune, and sometimes our life and reputation, to the lawyer and attorney. Such confidence could not safely be reposed in people of a very mean or low condition. Their reward must be such therefore as may give them that rank in the society which so important a trust requires.[15]

There are two possible explanations of these sentences. The first is that the responsibility involved in such positions was so irksome that it was necessary to pay extra sums to attract persons who, without such a compensation, would avoid the responsibility involved. Such an explanation is of course thoroughly consistent with the doctrine that wages are equal for equal amounts of disability experienced.

The other possible explanation is, however, more difficult to reconcile with the general theory. Smith implies that people would not patronize professional men who did not live upon a

[14] *Wealth of Nations*, p. 107. [15] *Ibid.*, p. 107.

standard considerably above that of the rest of the community. This may well be true in such a society as our own, where men tend to be valued according to what they spend and waste rather than according to what they are. Under such conditions, lavish personal expenditure may be a necessary competitive advertising expense which is required if one is to secure prestige and consequently public patronage. To maintain this scale of living, higher charges will have to be made. But this is not in harmony with the general tenor of Smith's thought. For in such a case the higher remuneration is being paid not so much to compensate men for added exertions, as to provide the favored professions with those comforts which the snobbish mind of the public persists in regarding as the infallible stamp of worth.

The fifth assigned reason for differences in wages is even less in harmony with the general theory that the differences are but compensatory. In some occupations, such as the mechanical trades, the entrants would have the surety of making at least a modest living; while in others, such as the law, there would be great and glittering prizes for the few, but very small stipends for most of the remainder. Smith's position here has been frequently interpreted to mean that merely the modal, or most frequent, wage would be lower in those occupations where only a few would rise to the top, but that the very high remuneration of these few would be sufficient to bring the arithmetic average of earnings in these occupations to an equality with that in those occupations where the deviation from the average was but slight. But this was not Smith's meaning. He declares:

> The counsellor at law who at forty begins to make something at his profession, ought to receive the retribution, not only of his own so tedious and expensive education, but of that of more than twenty others who are never likely to make anything by it. How extravagant so ever the fees of counsellors at law may sometimes appear, their real retribution is never equal to this.[16]

[16] *Wealth of Nations,* p. 108.

Smith believed, therefore, that in those occupations which had great prizes, the average rate of remuneration was lower than in other pursuits. But if this were so, it may be inquired why men would continue to enter such occupations? Would there not be a tendency for them to turn elsewhere and consequently force the level of payment in the given occupation to rise? Smith saw, however, that this was offset by the almost inveterate tendency of men to overestimate their abilities and their chances for success. Despite the large percentage of failures in these occupations, men would continue to pour into them because each one would believe that he at least would, because of his ability and good fortune, be the one to rise to the top.

Were men perfectly rational and calculating, then, the existence of a few great rewards would not depress the general average below that of other occupations. It does so only because men are not so expert in judging their own qualities and chances as they are in appraising other market situations. Even the Scotchman, whom Bagehot said Smith postulated as inside every man, had a blind spot as regards his own probable advancement.

With the exception of the fifth and, in part, of the fourth reason, however, the differences in wages are not real differences. They either equate out in money terms over the course of a lifetime or are just sufficient in the long run to balance any differences in the relative amounts of sacrifice involved. The force depended upon to effect this nice equilibrium is of course that of competition. If in one occupation the rewards per unit of sacrifice or disutility are greater than in others, then a larger number of men will enter these occupations and a smaller number will enter others until an equilibrium is restored. There is, of course, implied in such reasoning, the assumption that competition is indeed free, and that men are equal in abilities. Smith admitted that competition was not wholly free, but the restrictions which he conceived were legal rather than social and economic in their nature. It remained for Mill and Cairnes to point out the significance of non-competing groups and to demonstrate that equality of remuneration for equal units of sacrifice applied only within, and not between, these non-competing groups.

The assumption that there were no innate differences between men which could enable one man with the same amount of effort to secure a higher wage was natural enough in an age in which Locke's dictum[17] that the mind at birth was a *tabula rasa* upon which experience could write as it would, and in the same year in which Jefferson, on our side of the Atlantic, declared that it was self-evident that "all men are created free and equal." "The difference between the most dissimilar characters, between a philosopher and a common street porter," wrote Smith,[18] "seems to arise not so much from nature as from habit, custom and education." In a society thus peopled by men of approximately equal talents, freedom of competition was all that was needed to bring wages to an equality. To the modern mind, accustomed by the work of Darwin, Galton, Pearson, and the host of educational psychologists to appreciate the importance of innate differences, this view seems almost incredibly naïve; but it was thoroughly in harmony with the associationist psychology of the day as taught by Smith's bosom friend and fellow-Scotchman, David Hume.

This somewhat lengthy discussion of differences in wages may seem to be a digression from the main theme of the labor theory of value. But it is not in reality. Smith believed he had established the fact that equal units of labor in the sense of disutility were at any one time compensated for by equal amounts of money wages. The market, according to Smith, thus does reduce the various elements composing labor to a common measure.

[17] Locke, *Essay on Human Understanding.*

[18] Smith, *Wealth of Nations,* I, 17.

It should be noted in passing that this doctrine that at any moment of time equal money units represent equal amounts of labor paves the way for a value theory based on the money cost of production, which can also be found lurking in Smith's discussion. Profits and rent need only to be added to wages and then one can say, as Smith did, that

> . . . . when the price of any commodity is neither more nor less than what is sufficient to pay the rent of the land, the wages of the labour and the profits of the stock employed in raising, preparing, and bringing it to market, according to their natural rates, the commodity is then sold for its natural price.[19]

3. THE LABOR-COST AND LABOR-COMMAND THEORIES OF VALUE[20]

We have hitherto spoken of Smith's labor theory of value as though it were unitary; there are however, in fact, the outlines of two very different theories which are embodied in it, namely, the labor-jelly or labor-cost theory, and the labor-command theory. These two explanations of value are very different in nature, yet they rub elbows with each other on almost the same pages. Smith seems, indeed, to give almost equal emphasis to each and to fail to distinguish between them. The labor-jelly theory declares that the value of an object is determined by the quantity of labor units required to produce it, while the labor-command theory declares that the value of an object is determined by the amount of labor which can be purchased with it.

The labor-jelly theory is expressed in the following quotations:

> The real price of everything, what everything really costs to the man who wants to acquire it, is the toil and trouble of acquiring it.[21]

[19] *Wealth of Nations*, p. 57.

[20] For a competent treatment of this subject, see Whitaker, *History and Criticism of the Labor Theory of Value*, pp. 16–40; see also Wieser, *Natural Value*, pp. xxvii–xxix. See also the suggestive discussion by C. M. Walsh, *The Fundamental Problem of Monetary Science*, pp. 46–53; *The Four Kinds of Value*, pp. 4–10.

[21] Smith, *Wealth of Nations*, p. 32.

At all times and places that is dear which it is difficult to come at, or which it costs much labor to acquire; and that cheap which is to be had easily or with very little labour.[22]

That money or those goods . . . . contain the value of a certain quantity of labour which we exchange for what is supposed, at the time to contain the value of an equal quantity.[23]

In that early and rude state of society which precedes both the accumulation of stock and the appropriation of land, the proportion between the quantities of labour necessary for acquiring different objects seems to be the only circumstance which can afford any rule for exchanging them for one another. . . . . It is natural that what is usually the produce of two days' or two hours' labour should be worth double of what is usually the produce of one day's or one hour's labour.[24]

On the other hand, the labor-command theory is clearly stated in a number of passages, of which the following are perhaps the most notable:

The value of any commodity therefore, to the person who possesses it, and who means not to use it or consume it himself, but to exchange it for other commodities, is equal to the quantity of labour which it enables him to purchase or command.[25]

Its value [wealth] to those who possess it and want to exchange it for some new productions, is precisely equal to the quantity of labour which it can enable them to purchase or command.[26]

Wealth [Mr. Hobbes says] is power. . . . . His fortune is greater or less, precisely in proportion to the extent of this power; or the quantity either of other men's labour or, what is the same thing, of the produce of other men's labour, which it enables him to purchase or command. The exchangeable value of everything must always be precisely equal to the extent of this power which it conveys to its owner.[27]

It is sometimes said, as by Wieser, that the labor-cost theory was only intended for an explanation of value in a primitive society, and that Smith designed the labor-command theory as an explanation of how values were set in more advanced societies.

[22] *Ibid.*, p. 35.

[23] *Ibid.*, p. 32.

[24] *Ibid.*, p. 49.

[25] *Ibid.*, p. 32.

[26] *Ibid.*, p. 33.

[27] *Ibid.*, p. 33.

This is only partially true. The labor-cost theory was applied to this primitive stage, but it was also applied at times to more modern communities as well.

What, then, is the difference between these two conceptions? If those who labored to turn out a product received all of that product or all which it brought in exchange, as Smith assumes was the case in primitive times, then the two would be identical. There would be neither a deduction for rent nor for interest; and hence if commodities exchanged according to the amount of labor required to produce them, they would command equal quantities of labor in the form of goods or personal services. Thus, if five hours or "units" of labor were expended on the average to produce a pair of shoes, then this pair of shoes would exchange for a price which would be sufficient to hire other labor for five "units" also. The value of the pair of shoes would then be the same in terms both of labor cost and labor command.

But if rent and profits were deducted from the prices at which all of the articles sold, there would then be a discrepancy between the two measures of value. For if commodities exchanged according to the amount of labor embodied in them, then this would be less than the amount of labor which they could command. Thus, if the share of labor amounted only to two-thirds of the total product, then the workers who expended the five units of labor required for the shoes would receive in return commodities in which only three and one-third labor units were contained. The given pair of shoes would indeed sell in the market for a price which would enable it to purchase seven and one-half units of labor.[28] This would be its value from the standpoint of labor command; but from the standard of labor cost, it would be but five units. There is thus a very real difference between the labor cost of commodities and the command of these commodities over labor. This very real distinction was not

[28] I.e., $3.33 : 5.0 = 5 : 7.50$.

perceived by Smith, but was understood by Ricardo, who struggled in some of the most difficult and obscure pages of all economic literature[29] to make the contradiction evident.

It was Karl Marx,[30] however—who, as a value theorist, was indeed the last great figure in the classical school—who most clearly pointed out the economic contradictions involved. He tried to restore the labor theory of value by making the value of laboring power (i. e., human effort expended in production) that of the commodities required to support and maintain the laborers and those who were to replace them. In other words, the number of labor "units" expended in producing the food, clothing, and shelter consumed by the workers constituted the value at which their services exchanged for other commodities. Since, however, the laborers expended more units of labor than were embodied in the commodities which they consumed, the balance appropriated by the recipients of rent, interest, and profits was termed by Marx "surplus value." The most distinctive feature of Marxian economics comes directly therefore from Smith's confusion between labor-cost and labor-command.

But it may be objected that while it is true that there is a lack of coincidence between the labor cost and the labor command theories as long as we either compare commodities (1) with labor offered for sale, or (2) with each other in terms of absolute units of value, there is nevertheless virtual identity between the two as long as we deal only with the exchange ratios of material commodities for each other. Thus, even though our

[29] I.e., the latter part of Section I of the first chapter of his *Principles of Political Economy*. It should also be noted that according to the labor command theory, the amount of commodities offered for a day's labor will always have the same value since they command a constant amount of labor. The wages of the workmen would accordingly not alter in value, although they might increase or decrease as regards their composite physical quantity or the satisfaction afforded.

[30] See Marx, *Capital* (Kerr edition), Vol. I, especially chaps. i, vi, and vii; also *Value, Price, and Profit*.

pair of shoes contained five units of labor and could command seven and one-half such units, nevertheless it would exchange on equal terms for another commodity in which there were five units of labor and which could also command seven and one-half units. The values of these commodities would therefore be equal upon either the labor-cost or labor-command basis.

But while the consistency of Smith's teachings may perhaps be still maintained for the mutual exchange of commodities, the still further inner inconsistencies which were involved in the labor-cost theory were abundantly displayed in the attempts by Ricardo, McCulloch, and Marx to rehabilitate it. In the first place, it soon became apparent that a bushel of wheat produced on good land had an equal exchange value with that raised on poor land, despite the fact that much less labor had been expended upon the former than upon the latter. Ricardo tried to meet this difficulty by comparing only the respective amounts of labor contained in the marginal units of different commodities and of regarding these as setting the exchange ratios between them. Although a city man, he nevertheless could see only the importance of the margin in the case of agriculture and mineral products. Although writing in a period when England had just won the Napoleonic Wars because of her newly developed factory system, he persisted in thinking of industry as being conducted under those conditions of constant cost which were so characteristic of handicraft.

But there was an even greater difficulty which grew with the passage of time: the payment of interest, or of profits, as the classicists used the phrase, was a reality. The wages of the workmen were advanced to them by the capitalists for the period intervening between the production of goods and their sale, and for this the capitalists collected interest at a given rate per cent per year. But the period required to produce different commodities varies greatly. Pop corn takes relatively little time to produce, even when the corn is taken into account as well as the popping. But a yard of cloth, if the labor expended upon the machinery as well as upon the textiles themselves be considered, requires labor spread out over a considerable period of time. The amounts of labor expended upon the pop corn and upon the cotton cloth may be equal; but since the wages expended in producing the latter have been advanced over a longer period of time, there has been a greater accumulation of interest upon the cloth than upon the pop corn. Either the rate of wages paid per unit of labor must therefore be less upon the cloth than upon the corn, which in view of Smith's assumptions of free competition is impossible, or the cloth must exchange for pop corn with more units of labor embodied in it. If this is so, however, then commodities plainly do not exchange according to the relative amounts of labor jelly of which they are composed. Ricardo clearly pointed out this difficulty in the fourth and fifth sections of his celebrated first chapter, but, in order to simplify the problem, for the rest of his discussion chose to disregard these troubling factors and to make the heroic assumption that all commodities were produced with capitals of equal duration and with equal rapidity of turnover. And yet the fact that this disturbing issue continued to bother Ricardo is evidenced from his correspondence with McCulloch:

> I sometimes think that if I were to write the chapter on value again which is in my book, I should acknowledge that the relative value of commodities was regulated by two causes instead of by one, namely, by the relative quantity of labour necessary to produce the commodities in question, and by the rate of profit for the time that the capital remained dormant and until the commodities were brought to market.[31]

It was indeed upon this very point that the Marxian theory of value finally collapsed. For if only labor creates exchange value, then it is only the capital which is advanced in the form of

[31] *Letters of Ricardo to McCulloch* (edited by J. H. Hollander), p. 71.

wages which creates a surplus and gives rise to profit. The labor crystals of value supposedly contained in machinery which is used up and in the raw materials fabricated will then merely pass over into the finished product without diminution or increase. But this in turn means that those industries where the proportion of raw materials and machinery is low in comparison with the wages paid must have correspondingly higher profits than those where the situation is reversed. This would mean (1) that equal capitals make different rates of profits according to their "organic composition" and (2) that the less advanced industries make larger profits than those where the process of mechanization has progressed farther. The plain variance of these conclusions from the commonly known facts of economic life led Marx in his third volume to make his famous attempt to reconcile the labor-cost theory with the tendency of profits toward an equality. As is well known, he tried to effect this by declaring that goods sold (1) at the value of the "constant" capital used up in producing them plus (2) the amount advanced in wages or variable capital plus (3) that proportion of the total amount of surplus value secured in society which the sum of the constant and variable capital employed in the given industry formed of the total supply. In this way, although profits were supposed to accrue only from the expenditure of variable capital, they were distributed out over constant as well as over variable capital. Differences in the organic composition of capital thus created no variations in the rates of profit received. A unit of constant capital received as much profit as a unit of variable. But this amounted to the virtual abandonment of the labor-cost theory of value, since accumulations of interest came to affect exchange value as well as the quantity of labor expended. Commodities in actual life did not exchange therefore in proportion to the days of labor embodied within them, but according to the wages advanced to the workers plus an average rate of profit for the time periods during which the wages were advanced.

Marx has been berated by two generations of orthodox economists for his value theory.[32] The most charitable of the critics have called him a fool and the most severe have called him a knave for what they deem to be the transparent contradictions of his theory. Curiously enough, these very critics generally commend Ricardo and Adam Smith very highly. Yet the sober facts are that Marx saw more clearly than any English economist the differences between the labor-cost and labor-command theories and tried more earnestly than anyone else to solve the contradictions which the adoption of a labor-cost theory inevitably entailed. He failed, of course; but with him Ricardo and Smith failed as well. There are, it seems to me, few more unfair instances in economic thought than the almost complete unanimity with which the English-speaking economists of the chair have heaped condemnation upon the overworked and poverty-stricken Marx, who worked under such great difficulties, and, save for the comments of Jevons and a few others, have heaped praises upon Smith and Ricardo. The failure was the failure not of one man but of a philosophy of value, and the roots of the ultimate contradiction made manifest to the world in the third volume of *Das Kapital* lie imbedded in the first volume of the *Wealth of Nations.*

4. THE DEDUCTIONS FROM THE WHOLE PRODUCE OF LABOR AND THE IMPETUS TO BRITISH SOCIALISM

Smith declared that in the primitive stages of industry, before land is owned privately or capital accumulated, "the whole

[32] As instances of this type of attack, see Böhm-Bawerk, *Karl Marx and the Close of His System;* Joseph, *The Labor Theory of Value in Karl Marx;* Skelton, *Socialism: A Critical Analysis.*

produce of labour belongs to the labourer."[33] This is a phrase of great importance in the history of socialist thought,[34] and it is most significant to find it in Adam Smith, by whom it was indeed repeated no less than five times.[35]

But this economic Eden does not last long, for

> As soon as stock has accumulated in the hands of particular persons some of them will naturally employ it in setting to work industrious people whom they will supply with materials and subsistence in order to make a profit by the sale of their work, or by what their labour adds to the value of the materials. In exchanging the complete manufacture . . . . something must be given for the profits of the undertaker of the work who hazards his stock in this adventure. The value which the workmen add to the materials, therefore, resolves itself in this case into two parts, of which the one pays their wages, the other the profits of their employer upon the whole stock of materials and wages which he advanced.[36]

In other words, the worker adds all value but he does not receive all of it. As Smith says again, "In this state of things the whole produce of labour does not always belong to the labourer.

[33] *Wealth of Nations,* I, 49.

[34] A clear statement of the doctrine is given by Locke in the days when handicraft prevailed, to justify private property: "Every man has a property in his own person; this nobody has any right to but himself. The labour of his body and the work of his hands, we may say, are properly his. Whatsoever then he removes out of the state that nature hath provided and left in, he hath mixed his labour with and joined to it something that is his own and therebye makes it his property. It being by him removed from the common state nature hath placed it in, it hath by this labour something annexed to it, that excludes the common right of other men. For this labour being the unquestionable property of the labourer, no man but he can have a right to what that is once joined to, at least where there is enough, and as good, left in common for others." *Essay on Civil Government,* chap. v; *On Property,* ss. 27.

[35] See p. 49, already referred to, and also pp. 51, 66, 67, 68. Another similar passage is that of p. 80: "It is but equity, besides, that they who feed, cloath and lodge the whole body of the people, should have such *a share of the produce of their own labour* as to be themselves tolerably well fed, cloathed and lodged" (italics mine).

[36] *Wealth of Nations,* p. 50.

He must in most cases share it with the owner of the stock which employs him." These deductions by the owner of capital are not merely a compensation for the

> labour of inspection and direction. They are, however, altogether different, are regulated by quite different principles, and bear no proportion to the quantity, the hardship, or the ingenuity of this supposed labour of inspection and direction. They are regulated altogether by the value of the stock employed, and are greater or smaller in proportion to the extent of this stock.[37]

While Smith did not therefore distinguish the investing capitalist from the entrepreneur a differentiation which was left for the Frenchman, Say, to make a little over a quarter of a century later—he did distinguish between profits and the wages of management. So also did he distinguish between interest and the compensation for risk as is shown by the passage "the lowest ordinary rate of interest must be something more than what is sufficient to compensate the occasional losses to which lending, even with tolerable prudence, is exposed."[38]

In a similar fashion, Smith seems generally to regard rent as a deduction from values created by labor and one which did not represent any affirmative contribution by land. In a striking passage he writes: "As soon as the land of any country has all become private property, the landlords like to reap where they never sowed and demand a rent even for its natural produce."[39] And in another place he states that "as soon as the land becomes private property, the landlord demands a share of almost all the produce which the laborer can either raise or collect from it."[40]

A natural conclusion from such contentions as these would naturally seem to be that if labor produces all value and if rent and interest are but deductions representing no concrete serv-

[37] *Ibid.*, p. 51.

[38] *Ibid.*, pp. 97–98.

[39] *Ibid.*, p. 51.

[40] *Ibid.*, p. 67.

ice, it should follow ethically that labor ought to receive all and that wages should be the only share in distribution. But this interpretation seems never to have entered Smith's practical mind. Landlords and men of industrial and commercial property were dominant in the society in which he wrote and he accepted them as part of the order of nature. With his hard-headed Scotch way of accepting the *status quo,* he never thought of inquiring whether it would be possible to create an economic society in which profits and interests would disappear so that thus, as in his suppositious primitive society, the workers should enjoy the full produce of their labor. The doors of Eden had been irrevocably closed to man and there was no possibility of his ever re-entering them.

The declaration that the laborers should receive their full produce was left for the little group of socialist writers, including William Thompson, Thomas Hodgskin, John Gray, and John Francis Bray, who fell between the period of Ricardo and that of Marx and who have been somewhat inappropriately labeled, by Professor Foxwell[41] and Miss Lowenthal,[42] the Ricardian Socialists. They may, however, better be termed the Smithian Socialists, since they derive their inspiration from Smith rather than from Ricardo. This can be demonstrated in a number of ways. In the first place it should be remembered that whereas Adam Smith had taught that labor *caused* value, Ricardo merely held that commodities exchanged in proportion to the relative amounts of labor embodied in them. If there were even ratios of capital to labor in the various lines of industry, which Ricardo assumed for the purpose of his construc-

[41] Foxwell, Introduction to Menger, *The Right to the Full Produce of Labour,* p. lxxxiii: "It was Ricardo, not Owen, who gave the really effective inspiration to English Socialism."

[42] In her able monograph, *The Ricardian Socialists.* Miss Lowenthal has pointed out, however, the slight influence of Ricardo upon this group.

tive theory, then it would still be possible for capital to make a contribution to the value of commodities and yet, because of this even distribution of capital, for commodities to exchange according to the proportion of labor expended upon them. Labor is thus, in the Ricardian analysis, the measure of value rather than the cause of value.

In the second place, Thomas Hodgskin is apparently the only one of the group who had studied Ricardo at first hand, although Bray makes a few references to him. The others, and possibly Bray as well, knew Ricardo only through the medium of James Mill's and McCulloch's texts. All of the writers, on the other hand, had apparently read Adam Smith, and the phrase "the whole produce of labour" which had been given such wide circulation by Smith, or equivalent expressions are repeated very frequently by them.

Thus Thomas Hodgskin wrote[43] that since the economists have declared that "the labour of a man's body and the work of his hands are to be considered as exclusively his own," they should "henceforth maintain that the whole produce of labour ought to belong to the labourer." This sentiment was frequently repeated with certain differences in phrasing in his *Popular Political Economy*.[44]

William Thompson expressed the same principle when he wrote[45] that "all the products of labour should be secured to the producers of them," and perhaps more frequently than any other of the group used, to justify his position, such phrases as the "whole produce of labour," "entire produce," and charac-

[43] Hodgskin, *Labour Defended* (Cole edition), p. 83.

[44] Thus, in *Popular Political Economy*, pp. 29, 30, 237, 237, 237, 245, 249, 255. I am indebted to one of my students, Mr. Henry J. Bitterman, for ascertaining these and the subsequently cited page references.

[45] William Thompson, *The Distribution of Wealth* (1850 edition), p. 139.

terized the payment of rent and interest by the terms "forced abstraction" and "deduction" or "deprival."[46]

John Gray, by his own statement, owed his initial interest in economics to Adam Smith. After coming up to London as a young man, he writes[47] that he "procured a copy of Dr. Smith's *Wealth of Nations*" and after reading the first volume of it, I set to work to reduce my theory to a written form." This theory that production should be the cause of demand rather than the effect of it led Gray to a theory of business depressions which was virtually identical with that at present advanced by Foster and Catchings. Depressions were caused by the fact that production increased faster than the supply of gold, which led to a consequent fall in the general price level. As he wrote:

> All stocks on hand would therefore require to be sold at a loss. And this is an evil which does not and cannot cure itself, for as commodities must always be produced in apparent super-abundance *before* any fall can take place in their money price, they must uniformly be sold at a loss wherever they are produced in such quantities as to lower themselves in money price; the *higher* price of production preceding the *lower* price of sales.[48]

This to Gray was the force by which[49] "production is constantly checked and retarded by the fear that is ever present in the manufacturer's mind of producing too much. It is the quantity that can be sold at a profit and not the quantity that can be made

[46] See the following page references in his *Distribution of Wealth* for the given phrases: (*a*) "Whole produce of labour," pp. 51, 52, 181, 132, 379, 449, 450, 455; (*b*) "Entire produce of labour," pp. 28, 31, 32, 33, 34, 35, 79, 85, 125, 136, 248, 253, 255, 436, 439; (*c*) "Forced abstraction," pp. 4, 33, 46, 50, 51, 52, 53, 54, 91, 126, 172, 252, 308, 321, 439, 442, 445; (*d*) "Deduction" or "deprival," pp. 32, 35, 41, 50; 66, 96, 221, 393; (*e*) "Part of the produce of labour," pp. 28, 30, 92, 133, 135, 169, 446; (*f*) Clear statements of the right to the whole produce of labor can be found on pp. 4, 5, 61, 85, 137, 139.

[47] John Gray, Appendix to *The Social System* (1831), p. 340.

[48] *The Social System,* p. 271 (the italics throughout are Gray's).

[49] *Ibid.,* p. 59.

that is the present limit of production." Gray proposed several measures to meet these difficulties, notably the socialization of production and distribution, and the issuance of paper money to keep pace with the increase in production. He laid especial emphasis upon this second remedy in his later writings,[50] and was thus perhaps the first of those who have sought to stabilize the price level by controlling the issue of money.

But while the control of business depressions was Gray's chief aim, he nevertheless did emphasize the doctrine that labor created all value and should receive it. Thus he called the attention of his readers to what he declared[51] to be the "undisputed doctrine of Political Economy, originally seen and demonstrated by Dr. Adam Smith that labour is the one and only source of wealth." Similar references[52] indicate that Smith's doctrines influenced him greatly on this point. His desire to make the ethical application of the labor theory led him indeed into a proposal which was in reality inconsistent with his program of stabilizing the price level. His belief that a day's labor had the same value-creating powers at one time as another caused him to propose that there should be a fixed daily *money* wage for labor.[53] But as production increased, this would mean lower costs and hence lower prices per unit, which was the very event Gray was trying to avert. In order to stabilize the price level it would be necessary for day wages to rise proportionately with output. Constant piece rates rather than constant day rates were therefore needed to prevent a price fall. To the ex-

[50] See especially *Lectures on the Nature and Use of Money* (1848), pp. 334. One of the most interesting of the parallelisms between Gray and Foster and Catchings is that upon the publication of this book he offered a prize of 100 guineas to anyone who, in the opinion of impartial judges, could successfully disprove his theory! A more comprehensive study of Gray's theories is being made by Mr. Henry J. Bitterman, and will, I hope, shortly be published.

[51] Gray, *Lectures on the Nature and Use of Money*, p. 36.

[52] Notably *ibid.*, p. 6.

[53] *Ibid.*, p. 74.

tent therefore that Gray took the labor theory of value into his system, the source of his inspiration is plainly Adam Smith rather than Ricardo.[54]

John Francis Bray, the Socialist printer, quotes Adam Smith as well as Ricardo, James Mill, and McCulloch. The following passage shows the judgment which he passed upon the doctrine that labor created value but that capital received part of it.[55]

> The wealth which the capitalist appears to give in exchange for the workman's labour was generated neither by the labour nor the riches of the capitalist, but it was originally obtained by the labour of the workman; and it is still daily taken from him, by a fraudulent system of unequal exchanges. The whole transaction therefore, between the producer and the capitalist, is a palpable deception, a mere farce: it is, in fact, in thousands of instances no other than a barefaced though legalised robbery by means of which the capitalists and proprietors contrive to fasten themselves upon the productive classes, and suck from them their whole subsistence.

In several other passages Bray asserts the right of labor to the entire fruits of industry,[56] although he abstains from using the precise phrase the "whole produce of labour." Taken as a whole, however, there seems to be but little doubt that he was influenced by Adam Smith more than by Ricardo, although this influence may have been in part strained through the writings of Thompson and Gray as well as derived directly from the source.

It is then from the Whiggish pages of the *Wealth of Nations* that the doctrines of the English Socialists, as well as the theoretical exposition of Karl Marx, spring. The history of social thought furnishes many instances where theories elaborated by

[54] In his "Lecture on Human Happiness" (1825), now chiefly available in Freund's German translation, *vom Menschlichen Glück,* there are several clear references to the "right to the whole produce." See especially pp. 65 and 74.

[55] Bray, *Labour's Wrongs and Labour's Remedies,* pp. 49–50.

[56] See, for instance, the following pages in *Labour's Wrongs:* pp. 57, 60, 87, 100, 101, 153, 181.

one writer have been taken over by others to justify social doctrines antagonistic to those to which the promulgator of the theory gave adherence. But had the gift of prevision been granted to those men, few would have been more startled than Adam Smith in seeing himself as the theoretical founder of the doctrines of nineteenth-century socialism.

5. WHAT DETERMINES THE AMOUNTS AND SHARES RECEIVED BY THE OWNERS OF CAPITAL AND LAND AND BY THE LABORERS

Profits and rent are, then, deductions from the annual product for which no corresponding contributions have been made. But what, then, makes it possible for their recipients to levy tribute upon industry, and what determines the amount and proportion of their toll?

The capitalist is able to collect profits because it is he who primarily maintains the workers during the period when they are manufacturing commodities prior to their sale. Here are the main origins of the wages-fund doctrine, as is evidenced by the following passages:[57] "It seldom happens that the person who tills the ground has wherewithal to maintain himself till he reaps the harvest. His maintenance is generally advanced to him from the stock of a master, the farmer[58] who employs him." But this is as true of manufacturing as of agriculture, since "In all arts and manufactures the greater part of the workmen stand in need of a master to advance them the materials of their works and their wages and maintenance till it be completed. He shares in the produce of their labour, or in the value which it adds to the materials upon which it is bestowed, and in this share consists his profit."[59] The capitalist is then a grub-staker who, by

[57] *Wealth of Nations,* I, 67.

[58] The word "farmer" is of course used here in the English usage to denote one who is the tenant of a large landowner and who hires laborers in turn to help him on the leased land.

[59] *Wealth of Nations,* p. 67.

his possession of working capital, is able to induce the workers because of their present necessities to surrender to him a portion of their final product. It should be noticed, however, that Smith regards the period for which the advances are made as only that which exists at any one stage of production between the purchase of the raw materials and the sale for money of the fabricated article. This, however, as Taussig has pointed out, is by no means a sufficient analysis, since the incidence of the advances has merely been transferred to another capitalist when the goods at one stage of production are sold to the next. It is the capitalistic class as a whole, rather than individual capitalists, which makes the advances.

If we ask how it was that the capitalists managed to secure control over capital and why they charge what they do for its use, Smith gives us small comfort. He indulges in no such suppositious anthropology on the origin of private property and inequality as characterized the musings of the Austrian school on how canoes, fishhooks, and nets came originally to be saved, and a subsequent leisured class to be established. It was enough for Smith that property did belong to the few. Once holding such power, it was only natural that they should make a charge for its use, for why would a master employ workmen[60] "unless he expected from the sale of their work something more than what was sufficient to replace his stock to him, and he could have no interest to employ a great stock rather than a small one, unless his profits were to bear some proportion to the extent of his stock."

But how much "more" does the capitalist expect, and what are the minima, which he will demand as the price of advancing his stock? An attempt to answer these questions would lead us into the very heart of the interest problem; but Adam Smith does not make it.

[60] *Ibid.*, p. 50; for a similar reference, see p. 67.

Smith instead attempts to explain the rate of profits and of interest as varying inversely with the accumulation of capital. When capital is scanty, the owners of it are able to secure a high return; but an increase in its amount "tends to lower its profit."[61] "When the stocks of many rich merchants," Smith writes, "are turned into the same trade, their mutual competition naturally tends to lower its profit; and when there is a like increase of stock in all the different trades carried on in the same society, the same competition must produce the same effect in them all." It might seem that the term "the amount of stock" is quite vague, but by this Smith means the amount relative to the supply of labor. This is clearly evidenced by his explanation that profits are lower in the cities where the amount of "stock" is large in comparison with the number of workers than they are in the country where the ratio of stock of labor is less.

> In a thriving town the people who have great stocks to employ, frequently cannot get the number of workmen they want, and therefore bid against one another in order to get as many as they can, which raises the wages of labour and lowers the profits of stock. In the remote parts of the country there is frequently not stock sufficient to employ all the people, who therefore bid against one another in order to get employment which lowers the wages of labour and raises the profits of stock.[62]

Profits and wages thus varied in opposite directions, profits rising as wages fell, and falling as the latter rose. Only in new countries or when new trades or territories were being opened up was it possible to combine high wages and high profits. Here it should be noted that Smith is of course speaking of wages in terms of the amount per worker and of profits in terms of percentage. Unlike Ricardo, he devotes little attention to the relative share of each in the total product.

The minimum below which wages could not permanently fall (save in a decaying society) was the basic amount needed

[61] *Ibid.*, p. 89. [62] *Ibid.*, p. 91.

to support a worker, for[63] "a man must always live by his work and his wages must at least be sufficient to maintain him." Since it is necessary to rear children in order to maintain the population intact without diminution and increase, this minimum tends indeed to be more than this. Cantillon had estimated that the earnings of the wife would serve to maintain her, but that the husband must be given enough to support four children if two were ultimately to be reared. With characteristic caution, however, Smith declines to pass judgment upon the accuracy of Cantillon's estimates,[64] and merely points out that provision must be made for some children unless the population is to decline. This minimum is "the lowest which is consistent with common humanity," although it may well be doubted whether it is the benevolence of the employer which prevents the rate from falling below this point.

But this is only the minimum. Wages may rise above this point if the demand for labor is sufficiently great. This demand for labor consists of the capital set aside by the employing class with which to hire labor, and which in a later section[65] Smith identifies with circulating capital. If the quantity of circulating capital increases, then wages must rise.[66] The greater the rel-

[63] *Ibid.*, p. 69.

[64] Dr. Louis I. Dublin and A. J. Lotka have recently estimated that *fertile* American families need on the *average* to have 3.1 children if the population is to be held constant. This does not mean, however, that the head of the family will have this number of children dependent upon him *throughout* his working years, for such would be far from the truth. For an analysis of the tangled facts of family composition, see my article, "Is the Family of Five Typical?" *Journal American Statistical Association* (September, 1924), and chap. iii of *Wages and the Family* (1925), and Miss Eleanor Rathbone's *The Disinherited Family*.

[65] *Wealth of Nations*, pp. 265–66: "All useful machines and instruments of trade are originally derived from a circulating capital which furnishes the materials of which they are made and the maintenance of the workmen who make them."

[66] That is, if the supply of labor remained constant or did not increase commensurately.

ative rise in the amount of capital, the greater must be the advance in wages. This is why in an advancing state of society wages tend to move upward. Where the supply of capital is, on the contrary, decreasing, the wage level will fall.

But—and here is a very clear adumbration of Malthusianism—as the amount of capital swells and wages rise, the population increases, for[67]

> . . . . Every species of animals naturally multiplies in proportion to the means of its subsistence. . . . . The liberal reward of labour, by enabling them to provide better for their children, and consequently to bring up a greater number, naturally tends to widen and extend those limits It deserves to be remarked, too, that it necessarily does this as nearly as possible in the proportion which the demand for labour requires. If this demand is continually increasing, the reward of labour must necessarily encourage in such a manner the marriage and multiplication of labourers as may enable them to supply that continually increasing demand by a continually increasing population.

If, on the other hand, wages "in the inferior ranks of society" fall below the minimum, then[68] "the scantiness of subsistence can set limits to the further multiplication of the human species, and it can do so in no other way than by destroying a great part of the children which their fruitful marriages produce."

The rate of multiplication of the population thus attunes itself to the rate of increase of stock, for[69]

> . . . . If the reward should at any time be less than what was requisite for this purpose, the deficiency of hands would soon raise it; and if it should at any time be more, their excessive multiplication would soon lower it to this necessary rate. The market would be so much under-stocked with labour in the one case and so much over-stocked in the other, as would soon force back its price to that proper rate which the circumstances of the society required.

While there is some verbal ambiguity as to the meaning of the term "proper rate," it is nevertheless quite clear that Smith

[67] *Wealth of Nations,* pp. 81–82.

[68] *Ibid.,* p. 81.

[69] *Ibid.,* p. 82.

meant by this the ratio between the amount of capital and the number of laborers.

This raises the further question as to whether there was a tendency for this ratio to be approximated and hence establish a wage which would tend to approach uniformity through time. That such was Smith's idea is apparent from a number of passages. It is true that he recognizes a rise in real wages in Great Britain during the eighteenth century which was directly evidenced in the increase in money wages and the fall in the price of necessities. But he does not seem to have regarded this as a permanent tendency. Thus, he states that in a country where the absolute amount of capital is large but where it has not been increasing for some time, which he assumes to be true of China, the population will have already expanded up to the limit permitted by this supply of capital and the rate of wages will in consequence be approximately that low quantum which he had set as the minimum.[70] This tendency of wages toward the minimum is forecast by implication in the passage,[71] "It is this demand [for men] which regulates and determines the state of propagation in all the different countries of the world, in North America, in Europe, and in China; which renders it rapidly progressive in the first, slow and gradual in the second, and altogether stationary in the last." Though there is here no direct statement, the purport of this sentence seems to be that North

[70] "Though the wealth of a country should be very great, yet if it has been long stationary, we must not expect to find the wages of labour very high in it. The funds destined for the payment of wages . . . . may be of the greatest extent; but if they have continued for several centuries of the same, or very nearly of the same extent, the number of labourers employed every year could easily supply, and even more than supply, the number wanted the following year. . . . . If in such a country the wages of labour had ever been more than sufficient to maintain the labourer and to enable him to bring up a family, the competition of the labourers and the interest of the masters would soon reduce them to this lowest rate which is consistent with common humanity" (*ibid.*, p. 73).

[71] *Wealth of Nations,* p. 82.

America will tend to move into the slow rate of growth of Europe, and the latter into the stationary condition of China.

This tacit forecast of the stationary state which was more fully elaborated three-quarters of a century later by John Stuart Mill is much more directly stated in another passage:

> In a country which has acquired that full complement of riches which the nature of its soil and climate, and its situation with respect to other countries allowed it to acquire, which could, therefore, advance no further, and which was not going backwards, both the wage of labour and the profits of stock would probably be very low. In a country fully peopled in proportion to what either its territory could maintain or its stock employ, the competition for employment would necessarily be so great as to reduce the wages of labour to what was barely sufficient to keep up the number of labourers, and, the country being already fully peopled, that number could never be augmented. In a country fully stocked in proportion to all the business it had to transact, as great a quantity of stock would be employed in every particular branch as the nature and extent of the trade would admit. The competition therefore would everywhere be as great and consequently the ordinary profit as low as possible.[72]

Population would therefore ultimately be at a standstill and the rate of profits at that minimum where there would be no inducement for any further savings, since, if such savings were made, the fund available for the payment of labor would rise and wages consequently increase. What this minimum rate was, Smith, like Ricardo and J. S. Mill, did not definitely state beyond the fact that it must be more than a compensation for risk and losses and for management. By his statement,[73] however, that in such a state it would be "impossible for any but the very wealthiest people to live upon the interest of their money," it is plain that he thought of it as quite low. He thought that Holland was "approaching near to this state,"[74] and there the rate of interest was 2 per cent.[75] The minimum was then apparently somewhere between 1 and 2 per cent.

[72] *Ibid.*, p. 96; for a similar passage, see p. 98.

[73] *Ibid.*, p. 98. [74] *Ibid.*, p. 98. [75] *Ibid.*, p. 93.

Virtually all of the features which characterize the later classical writers were then present in the *Wealth of Nations;* the labor theory of value, Malthusianism, the tendency of profits to a minimum, and the stationary state are all contained in the writings of Adam Smith. The *Wealth of Nations* was indeed a rich quarry in which the later classicists could find the ideas and hints which they molded into more systematic form.

Before passing from the subject of wages, it is well to note (1) Smith's recognition of the disparities in bargaining power between employers and workers, and (2) his sturdy opposition to the mercantilistic doctrine that lower wages were needed in order to force the laborers to work more and thus make England prosperous.

There have been few more pungent summaries of the relative bargaining strength of labor and capital than Smith's quiet comment[76] that while "in the long run the workman may be as necessary to his master as his master is to him; the necessity is not so immediate." Smith also saw that it was easier for the employers to limit competition between each other for workmen than it was for the workers to restrict their competition for positions:

> The masters, being fewer in number, can combine much more easily; and the law, besides, authorizes, or at least does not prohibit their combinations, while it prohibits those of the workmen. . . . . We rarely hear, it has been said, of the combinations of masters; though frequently of those of workmen. But whoever imagines, upon this account, that masters rarely combine, is as ignorant of the world as of the subject. Masters are always and everywhere in a sort of tacit, but constant and uniform combination, not to raise the wages of labour above their actual rate.[77]

Smith thus was in a sense a bargain theorist who held that the employer's superiority enabled him to reduce wages below the point at which they would otherwise have rested, although they

[76] *Ibid.*, p. 68. [77] *Ibid.*, p. 68.

could not fall below that minimum which was needed to maintain the workers.

The English mercantilists had wished to depress the real earnings of the workers in order to force them to work more days in a week, and opposed increasing their remuneration on the ground that it would merely induce them to work for a correspondingly shorter time. This assumed of course that the desires of the workers were relatively fixed and that a higher wage would merely enable them to satisfy those wants, and that the workers would then rest. The way to increase the wealth of the state was therefore thought to lie in decreasing the daily wages of the manual workers.[78] Even Smith's contemporary, Arthur Young, held substantially similar views. Smith, however, could not justify such a public policy which made of the laborers mere instruments for the enrichment of others and which regarded them not as members but as slaves of the state. To his mind, an "improvement in the circumstances of the lower ranks" was of distinct advantage to society, since[79]

> . . . . Servants, labourers and workmen of different kinds make up the far greater part of every political society. But what improves the circumstances of the greater part can never be regarded as an inconveniency to the whole. No society can surely be flourishing and happy, of which the far greater part of the members are poor and miserable.

It was here that he added the certainly modest plea that "it was but equity beside that they who feed, cloath, and lodge the whole body of the people, should have such a share of the produce of their own labour as to be themselves tolerably well fed, cloathed, and lodged."

Smith also took decided issue with the doctrine that high

[78] For a summary of these doctrines, see E. S. Furniss, *The Position of the Laborer in a System of Nationalism,* and an article by T. E. Gregory in Vol. I of *Economica.*

[79] *Wealth of Nations,* p 80.

wages led to less effort, and asserted on the contrary that they increased "the industry of the common people," for[80] "a plentiful subsistence increases the bodily strength of the labourer and the comfortable hope of bettering his condition . . . . animates him to exert that strength to the utmost." In support of this contention he cited the superiority of English workmen to the Scotch artificers, although the wages of the former were appreciably higher. He admitted that high wages might lead some to be idle part of the week, but stoutly asserted that this was "by no means the case with the greater part."

In matters of practical policy, therefore, Smith did not sympathize with the efforts of the employing class to reduce wages through superior economic and political power, and he resolutely opposed the reactionary theory of the mercantilists that the great masses of mankind can be driven to work only under the whip-lash of want. The mercantilistic theory has virtually ceased to be applied to white labor, but it has been taken over by the imperialistic countries as a justification of their treatment of tropical labor. What was thought to be true of "trueborn Englishmen" in the seventeenth and eighteenth centuries is now asserted to be true of the black and yellow races.

Turning now to the rent of land, the question naturally presents itself as to how the landlord is able to collect rent and what fixes its amount. In the passages which have been previously quoted the implication is that the landlord secures it because he "demands" it. But we may make the same retort to such an explanation that Hotspur made to Glendower's boast that he "could call the spirits from the vasty deep," namely, "You can call them, but will they come?"

It is not enough to demand rent; it is also necessary to secure it. Analyzed more closely, Smith is, however, seen to have offered no less than three different explanations of rent other

[80] *Ibid.*, p. 83.

than the main one which has been previously quoted. These are, namely, explanations on the ground of (1) monopoly, (2) differential advantages, and (3) the bounty of nature. Thus Smith speaks of rent beginning when *all* of the land of a country "has become private property." And he continues,

> The wood of the forest, the grass of the field and all the natural fruits of the earth, which when land was in common cost the labourer only the trouble of gathering them, come, even to him, to have an additional price fixed upon them. He must then pay for the license to gather them and must give up to the landlord a portion of what his labour either collects or produces.[81]

In another place Smith states[82] directly that "the rent of land therefore . . . . is naturally a monopoly price."

In other places Smith approaches the position ultimately worked out by Anderson, West, and Ricardo and makes rent a differential resulting from superior advantages. "The rent of land," he writes,[83] "not only varies with its fertility, whatever be its produce, but with its situation, whatever be its fertility."

A final explanation taken over from Quesnay and the Physiocrats, which Smith offered for rent, was that it was a surplus due to the bounty of nature. In an extraordinary passage[84] he stated that

> The labourers and labouring cattle, therefore, employed in agriculture, not only occasion, like the workmen in manufactures, the reproduction of a value equal to their own consumption, or to the capital which employs them together with its owners' profits; but of a much greater value. Over and above the capital of the farmer and all its profits, they regularly occasion the reproduction of the rent of the landlord. This rent may be considered as the produce of those powers of nature, the use of which the landlord lends to the farmer. . . . . It is the work of nature which remains after deducting or compensating everything which can be regarded as the work of man. It is seldom less than a fourth and frequently more than a third of

[81] *Ibid.*, p. 51.

[82] *Ibid.*, p. 146.

[83] *Ibid.*, p. 148.

[84] *Ibid.*, p. 343.

the whole produce. No equal quantity of productive labour employed in manufactures can ever occasion so great a reproduction. In them nature does nothing; man does all; and the reproduction must always be in proportion to the strength of the agents that occasion it.

But "in agriculture nature labours along with man, and though her labour costs no expense, its produce has its value, as well as that of the most expensive workmen." Here it is the plenty of nature rather than its niggardliness which enables rent to be paid. It was precisely this position which Malthus, as the defender of the English landlord, urged over forty years later in his discussion with Ricardo[85] when he declared that rent was a payment for added riches rather than a diversion of an existent stock. This position of Smith seems in part inconsistent with his dictum that rent is a subtraction from the whole produce of labor. Yet it might be possible for someone to urge, although Smith did not do so, that although the land might be productive, the landlord was not, and that the bounty of nature should flow to the workers.

As Cannan has pointed out and as we have already stated, Smith interested himself primarily in the question of profits per cent, wages per head, and rent per acre. He did not grapple seriously with the question of the relative share which capital, labor, and land received of the total national product. In one place he asserts[86] that the progress of improvement causes the landlord's share of "the whole produce" to rise, but in another he declares[87] that "in the progress of improvement, rent, though it increases in proportion to the extent, diminishes in proportion to the produce of the land." He concludes that the interests "of those who live by profit" are opposed to the progress of society, since this will mean a fall in the interest rate.[88] This, however, clearly omits to consider the total amount of capital saved,

[85] See *Letters of Ricardo to Malthus*, edited by James Bonar, and Malthus, *Principles of Political Economy*.

[86] *Wealth of Nations*, I, 247. [87] *Ibid.*, p. 317. [88] *Ibid.*, p. 249.

which might of course be so much greater that even with the reduction in the rate, the total amount of interest and even its share in the total product might be greater than before.

Rent is thought of by Smith in the main as a residual element and not as a cost. It is true that the first edition declared that the price of a commodity must be sufficient to "purchase, command, or exchange for an additional quantity of labour, in order to enable the person who brings it to market to pay this rent," but this was clearly inconsistent with his doctrine that the taxation of rent as such could not be shifted, since "it would fall altogether upon the owner of the ground-rent who acts always as a monopolist and exacts the greatest rent which can be got for the use of his ground."[89] Under the probable influence of Hume the former passage was reworded to make it consistent with his doctrine of incidence.

Profits are said in the first volume to be a necessary cost, but in the second it appears that this only applies to compensation for risk and management, and not to interest;

> . . . . As a tax upon the rent of land cannot raise rents, because the net produce which remains after replacing the stock of the farmer, together with his reasonable profit can not be greater after the tax than before, so for the same reason, a tax upon the interest of money could not raise the rate of interest, the quantity of stock or money in the country, like the quantity of land, being supposed to remain the same after the tax as before.[90]

This would, of course, be true were the supply of capital to be fixed or to be absolutely inelastic. It is because this is approximately true in the case of land that taxes on economic rent cannot be shifted. Whether capital, however, has such a supply curve may well be doubted, although many, notably the Webbs, have so contended. If not, and if a tax by lowering the rate of interest were to decrease the amounts saved, then other forces would be set into effect which would not make interest such a pure residual.

[89] *Wealth of Nations,* II, 328.
[90] *Ibid.,* II, 332.

CHAPTER V

ADAM SMITH AND LAISSEZ FAIRE[1]

JACOB VINER

I. THE HARMONIOUS ORDER OF NATURE

An endeavor to make a just appraisal of Adam Smith's original contributions to economic doctrine would even today be a task of extraordinary difficulty. On the one hand, what was serviceable in his doctrines has become so thoroughly incorporated in our modern thinking that we discover it upon the slightest provocation in whatever we may read that was written before his day, and we are especially prone to make a virtue of obscurity in his predecessors by taking it for granted that it conceals premature insight rather than unduly prolonged lack of it. On the other hand, there is always great danger lest what we credit to a writer as priority of doctrine may not in reality be merely an indecent exposure of our own ignorance concerning his predecessors. There is much weight of authority and of evidence, however, that Smith's major claim to originality, in English economic thought at least, was his detailed and elaborate application to the wilderness of economic phenomena of the unifying concept of a co-ordinated and mutually interdependent system of cause and effect relationships which philosophers and theologians had already applied to the world in general. Smith's doctrine that economic phenomena were manifestations of an underlying order in nature, governed by natural forces, gave to

[1] References to Adam Smith's writings are to the following editions: *History of Ancient Physics,* and *Theory of Moral Sentiments,* in "Essays Philosophical and Literary by Adam Smith" (Ward, Lock & Co., London, n.d.); *Wealth of Nations,* Cannan edition; *Lectures,* Cannan, editor.

English economics for the first time a definite trend toward logically consistent synthesis of economic relationships, toward "system-building." Smith's further doctrine that this underlying natural order required, for its most beneficent operation, a system of natural liberty, and that in the main public regulation and private monopoly were corruptions of that natural order, at once gave to economics a bond of union with the prevailing philosophy and theology, and to economists and statesmen a program of practical reform.

Smith was *the* great eclectic. He drew upon all previous knowledge in developing his doctrine of a harmonious order in nature manifesting itself through the instincts of the individual man. The oldest source in which he expressly finds an approach to his own views is in the science of the classical philosophers: "In the first ages of the world . . . . the idea of a universal mind, of a God of all, who originally formed the whole, and who governs the whole by general laws, directed to the conservation and prosperity of the whole, without regard to that of any private individual, was a notion to which [the Ancients] were utterly strangers . . . . [but] as ignorance begot superstition, science gave birth to the first theism that arose among those nations, who were not enlightened by divine Revelation."[2]

The Roman *jus naturale,* through Grotius and Pufendorf, strongly influenced Smith's thinking. The Renaissance emphasis on the individual, the naturalistic philosophy of Shaftesbury, Locke, Hume, Hutcheson, the optimistic theism of the Scotch philosophers, the empiricism of Montesquieu, were more immediate and more powerful influences. Science, philosophy, theology, psychology, history, contemporary observation of facts—all of them were made to produce, under Smith's capable management, an abundance of evidence of the existence of an order

[2] *History of Ancient Physics,* pp. 391, 392.

in nature in which beneficent intentions toward mankind could be discerned. If Smith at times showed more catholicity than scientific discrimination in what he accepted as supporting evidence, if some of this evidence appeared upon close scrutiny to be conjectural, contradictory, irrelevant, or inconclusive, the richness of argument, the power of his exposition, the attractiveness of his conclusions served to overwhelm the captious critic and to postpone closer scrutiny to a later day.

Smith's major claim to fame, as I have said, seems to rest on his elaborate and detailed application to the economic world of the concept of a unified natural order, operating according to natural law, and if left to its own course producing results beneficial to mankind. On every detail, taken by itself, Smith appears to have had predecessors in plenty. On few details was Smith as penetrating as the best of his predecessors. There had been earlier pleas for freedom of internal trade, freedom of foreign trade, free trade in land, free choice of occupations, free choice of place of residence. Some philosophers, notably Shaftesbury and Smith's own teacher, Hutcheson, had already extended to economic phenomena, though sketchily, the concept of an underlying natural order manifesting itself through the operation of physical forces and individual psychology. But Smith made an original forward step when he seriously applied himself to the task of analyzing the whole range of economic process with the purpose of discovering the nature of the order which underlay its surface chaos. Claims have been made for the Physiocrats, but the evidence indicates that Smith had already formulated his central doctrine before he came into contact with them or their writings. As early as 1755 Smith had publicly asserted his claim to priority, as against some unnamed rival, in applying to the economic order the system of natural liberty. In doing so, he cited a lecture, delivered in 1749, which even in the fragment which has survived contains the essence of his fully developed doctrine, as expounded in the *Wealth of Nations.* It even uses an English equivalent of the very phrase "laissez faire," which the Physiocrats were soon to make the war cry of the system of natural liberty.

> Projectors disturb nature in the course of her operations on human affairs, and it requires no more than to *leave her alone* and give her fair play in the pursuit of her ends that she may establish her own designs. . . . . Little else is required to carry a state to the highest degree of affluence from the lowest barbarism but peace, easy taxes, and a tolerable administration of justice; all the rest being brought about by the natural course of things. All governments which thwart this natural course, which force things into another channel, or which endeavor to arrest the progress of society at a particular point, are unnatural, and, to support themselves, are obliged to be oppressive and tyrannical.[3]

In his *Theory of Moral Sentiments,* Smith develops his system of ethics on the basis of a doctrine of a harmonious order in nature guided by God, and in an incidental manner applies his general doctrine with strict consistency to the economic order. In his later work, the *Wealth of Nations,* Smith devotes himself to a specialized inquiry into the nature of the economic order. It is a commonplace among the authorities on Adam Smith that it is impossible fully to understand the *Wealth of Nations* without recourse to the *Theory of Moral Sentiments.* The vast bulk of economists, however, who have read the *Wealth of Nations* without reading the *Theory of Moral Sentiments,* have not regarded Smith's masterpiece as an obscure book, as one especially hard to understand. On the other hand, the very authorities who are most emphatic in asserting the need of reference to the *Theory of Moral Sentiments* to understand the *Wealth of Nations,* once they embark upon their self-imposed task of interpreting the latter in the light of the former, become immersed in difficult problems of interpretation for which

[3] Rae, *Life of Adam Smith,* p. 62. Italics mine.

scarcely any two writers offer the same solution. The system of individual liberty is much in evidence among the interpreters of Smith, but that natural harmony which should also result is strikingly lacking. The Germans, who, it seems, in their methodical manner commonly read both the *Theory of Moral Sentiments* and the *Wealth of Nations,* have coined a pretty term, *Das Adam Smith Problem,* to denote the failure to understand either which results from the attempt to use the one in the interpretation of the other. I will endeavor to show that the difficulties of the authorities result mainly from their determination to find a basis for complete concordance of the two books, and that there are divergences between them which are impossible of reconciliation even by such heroic means as one writer has adopted of appeal to the existence in Smith's thought of a Kantian dualism. I will further endeavor to show that the *Wealth of Nations* was a better book because of its partial breach with the *Theory of Moral Sentiments,* and that it could not have remained, as it has, a living book were it not that in its methods of analysis, its basic assumptions, and its conclusions it abandoned the absolutism, the rigidity, the romanticism which characterize the earlier book.

II. THE "THEORY OF MORAL SENTIMENTS"

In the *Theory of Moral Sentiments,* Smith develops the doctrine of a beneficent order in nature, manifesting itself through the operation of the forces of external nature and the innate propensities implanted in man by nature. The moral sentiments, self-interest, regulated by natural justice and tempered by benevolence, operate in conjunction with the physical forces of nature to achieve the beneficent purposes of Nature. Underlying the matter-of-fact phenomena of human and physical nature is benign Nature, a guiding providence, which is concerned that natural processes shall operate to produce the "happiness and perfection of the species." Smith is unfortunately far from explicit as to just how Nature makes certain that nature shall not betray the former's intentions, though he does say that Nature dictates to man the laws which he shall follow.[4] It seems, however, that the essence of Smith's doctrine is that Providence has so fashioned the constitution of external nature as to make its processes favorable to man, and has implanted *ab initio* in human nature such sentiments as would bring about, through their ordinary working, the happiness and welfare of mankind. The many titles by which this beneficent Nature is designated must have taxed severely the terminological resources of the Scotch optimistic theism. Among them are: "the great Director of Nature,"[5] "the final cause,"[6] "the Author of Nature,"[7] "the great judge of hearts,"[8] "an invisible hand,"[9] "Providence,"[10] "the divine Being,"[11] and, in rare instances, "God."[12] Smith definitely commits himself to the theism of his time. The harmony and beneficence to be perceived in the matter-of-fact processes of nature are the results of the design and intervention of a benevolent God.

> The idea of that divine Being, whose benevolence and wisdom have, from all eternity, contrived and conducted the immense machine of the universe, so as at all times to produce the greatest quantity of happiness, is certainly of all the objects of human contemplation by far the most sublime. . . . . The administration of the great system of the universe, ... the care of the universal happiness of all rational and sensible beings, is the business of God and not of man. To man is allotted a much humbler department, but one much more suitable to the weakness of his powers, and

[4] *Theory of Moral Sentiments*, p. 75.

[5] *Ibid.*, p. 71 n.

[6] *Ibid.*, p. 80.

[7] *Ibid.*, p. 96.

[8] *Ibid.*

[9] *Ibid.*, p. 163.

[10] *Ibid.*, p. 163.

[11] *Ibid.*, p. 210.

[12] *Ibid.*, pp. 80, 97.

to the narrowness of his comprehension; the care of his own happiness, of that of his family, his friends, his country.[13]

Thus self-preservation, and the propagation of the species, are the great ends which Nature seems to have proposed in the formation of all animals. . . . . But though we are . . . . endowed with a very strong desire of those ends, it has not been intrusted to the slow and uncertain determinations of our reason to find out the proper means of bringing them about. Nature has directed us to the greater part of these by original and immediate instincts. Hunger, thirst, the passion which unites the two sexes, the love of pleasure, and the dread of pain, prompt us to apply those means for their own sakes, and without any consideration of their tendency to those beneficent ends which the great Director of nature intended to produce by them.[14]

Society can get along tolerably well even though beneficence is absent and self-interest and justice alone operate. "Society may subsist among different men, as among different merchants, from a sense of its utility, without any mutual love or affection; and though no man in it should owe any obligation, or be bound in gratitude to any other, it may still be upheld by a mercenary exchange of good offices according to an agreed valuation." Beneficence "is the ornament which embellishes, not the foundation which supports, the building. . . . . Justice, on the contrary, is the main pillar that upholds the whole edifice." "Society may subsist, though not in the most comfortable state, without beneficence; but the prevalence of injustice must utterly destroy it."[15]

There are no serious flaws in the harmonious operation of natural forces, even in the economic order, where self-interest, which is ordinarily a virtue, but if not regulated by justice may degenerate into vice, is the most powerful of the impulses to action:

If we consider the general rules by which external prosperity and adversity are commonly distributed in this life, we shall find, that notwithstanding the disorder in which all things appear to be in this world, yet even

[13] *Ibid.*, p. 210. [14] *Ibid.*, p. 71 n. [15] *Ibid.*, p. 79.

here every virtue naturally meets with its proper reward, with the recompense which is most fit to encourage and promote it; and this too so surely, that it requires a very extraordinary concurrence of circumstances entirely to disappoint it.

What is the reward most proper for encouraging industry, prudence, and circumspection? Success in every sort of business. And is it possible that in the whole of life these virtues should fail of attaining it? Wealth and external honours are their proper recompense, and the recompense which they can seldom fail of acquiring.[16]

The poorer classes have little if any ground for complaint as to their lot in life, and no reason to seek to improve it except by methods which contribute to the general welfare of society. "In the middling and inferior stations of life, the road to virtue and that to fortune . . . . are, happily, in most cases, very nearly the same. . . . . The good old proverb, therefore, that honesty is the best policy, holds, in such situations, almost always perfectly true."[17] Beneficent Nature so operates the machinery behind the scenes that even inequality in the distribution of happiness is more apparent than real:

[The rich] are led by an invisible hand to make nearly the same distribution of the necessaries of life which would have been made had the earth been divided into equal portions among all its inhabitants, and thus without intending it, without knowing it, advance the interest of the society, and afford means to the multiplication of the species. When Providence divided the earth among a few lordly masters, it neither forgot nor abandoned those who seemed to have been left out in the partition. These last, too, enjoy their share of all that it produces. In what constitutes the real happiness of human life, they are in no respect inferior to those who would seem so much above them. In ease of the body and peace of the mind, all the different ranks of life are nearly upon a level, and the beggar, who suns himself by the side of the highway, possesses that security which kings are fighting for.[18]

[16] *Ibid.*, p. 146.

[17] *Ibid.*, 58.

[18] *Ibid.*, p. 163.

Smith concedes that the processes of nature operate at times with what, by man's standards, are results so unjust that they arouse our indignation:

> Fraud, falsehood, brutality, and violence, ... excite in every human breast such scorn and abhorrence, that our indignation rouses to see them possess those advantages which they may in some sense be said to have merited, by the diligence and industry with which they are sometimes attended. The industrious knave cultivates the soil, the indolent man leaves it uncultivated. Who ought to reap the harvest? Who starve, and who live in plenty? The natural course of things decides it in favour of the knave; the natural sentiments of mankind in favour of the man of virtue.[19]

This is a familiar dilemma of the optimistic theology, but Smith is precluded from adopting the familiar solution that "the ways of the Lord are inscrutable" by the fact that he is at the moment engaged in the task of formulating with great precision and assurance just what the ways of the Lord are. A contemporary economist of Adam Smith, Josiah Tucker, who was also by the necessity of his profession a theologian, when faced with an apparent conflict between the processes of nature and the "fundamental Principle of Universal Benevolence" found an ingenious solution in the conclusion a priori that there must be something wrong in the appearance of things: "I conclude *a priori,* that there must be some flaw or other in the preceding Arguments, plausible as they seem, and great as they are upon the foot of human Authority. For though the Appearance of Things makes for this Conclusion . . . . the Fact, itself, cannot be so."[20] Smith also succeeded in keeping his theory alive when the force of conflicting fact seemed to threaten to destroy it, but his method was more gentle to the facts. Man has been given by nature one standard by which to judge it, but nature has retained another and different standard for itself. "Both are

[19] *Ibid.,* pp. 147, 148.

[20] *Four Tracts* (Gloucester, 1774), p. 12.

calculated to promote the same great end, the order of the world, and the perfection and happiness of human nature."[21] Only an inordinately exacting critic would suggest that this solution is not wholly satisfactory, since Smith can have logically reached it only by applying to nature its own standard, which it was not appropriate for man to use. But if this solution does not satisfy, Smith has another one. If we despair of finding any force upon earth which can check the triumph of injustice, we "naturally appeal to heaven, and hope that the great Author of our nature will himself execute hereafter what all the principles which he has given us for the direction of our conduct prompt us to attempt even here; that he will complete the plan which he himself has thus taught us to begin; and will, in a life to come, render to every one according to the works which he has performed in this world."[22] If, judged by men's standards, the order of nature does not result in perfect justice on earth, we apparently have two alternative explanations: either that man's standards are an inadequate basis for appraisal, or that there is opportunity in a future state for redress of the injustices of the present one.

What we have, therefore, in the *Theory of Moral Sentiments* is an unqualified doctrine of a harmonious order of nature, under divine guidance, which promotes the welfare of man through the operation of his individual propensities. Of these, self-interest is the most important one, in so far as economic life is concerned, though it is subject to the regulations of natural justice, to which it must conform. "In the race for wealth, for honours, and preferments, he may run as hard as he can, and strain every nerve and every muscle, in order to outstrip all his competitors. But if he should jostle, or throw down any of them, the

[21] *Theory of Moral Sentiments*, p. 148.

[22] *Ibid.*, p. 149.

indulgence of the spectator is entirely at an end. It is a violation of fair play, which they cannot admit of."[23] In economic matters, benevolence plays but a minor rôle. There is no express formulation of a principle of laissez faire, and no explicit condemnation of governmental interference with individual initiative; but it is quite clearly implied that self-interest, if regulated by justice, which may be natural justice, but is likely to be more effective if it is administered by a magistrate, is sufficient to attain the ends of Nature in the economic world. There is convincing evidence from other sources that Smith was already an exponent of the system of natural liberty.

III. THE SYSTEM OF NATURAL LIBERTY IN THE "WEALTH OF NATIONS"

Traces of the general doctrine expounded in the *Theory of Moral Sentiments,* that there is a beneficent order in nature which, if left to take its own course, will bring to mankind maximum happiness and prosperity, are undoubtedly to be discovered in the *Wealth of Nations.* Traces of every conceivable sort of doctrine are to be found in that most catholic book, and an economist must have peculiar theories indeed who cannot quote from the *Wealth of Nations* to support his special purposes. But it can be convincingly demonstrated, I believe, that on the points at which they come into contact there is a substantial measure of irreconcilable divergence between the *Theory of Moral Sentiments* and the *Wealth of Nations,* with respect to the character of the natural order.

In the first place, the emphasis in the *Theory of Moral Sentiments* upon a benevolent deity as the author and guide of nature is almost, though not quite, completely absent in the *Wealth of Nations.* There are only a few minor passages in the later work which can be adduced as supporting evidence of the

[23] *Ibid.,* p. 76.

survival in Smith's thought of the concept of a divinity who has so shaped economic process that it operates necessarily to promote human welfare: an incidental allusion to "the wisdom of nature";[24] a remark that with respect to smuggling the laws of the country had "made that a crime which nature never meant to be so";[25] and a more famous passage, the main reliance of those who would completely reconcile the doctrines expounded in the two works, in which Smith repeats the phrase "the invisible hand" which he had used in the *Theory of Moral Sentiments*.[26] The only explicit reference to God is one which could have given but scant comfort to the natural theology of his time: "Superstition first attempted to satisfy this curiosity [about natural phenomena] by referring all those wonderful appearances to the immediate agency of the gods. Philosophy afterward endeavored to account for them from more familiar causes, or from such as mankind were better acquainted with, than the agency of the gods."[27] To the extent that Smith in the *Wealth of Nations* does expound a doctrine of a harmonious order in nature, he accounts for it, as a rule, and perhaps even invariably, by reference to "more familiar causes [and] to such as mankind were better acquainted with, than the agency of the gods." The significance for our purposes of this virtual disappearance from the *Wealth of Nations* of the doctrine of an order of nature designed and guided by a benevolent God is that it leaves Smith free to find defects in the order of nature without casting reflections on the workmanship of its Author.

To some extent Smith makes use of this freedom. In both works he finds an inherent harmony in the order of nature, whereby man, in following his own interests, at the same time and without necessarily intending it serves also the general interests of mankind. In the *Theory of Moral Sentiments*, this

[24] *Wealth of Nations*, II, 174.

[25] *Ibid.*, II, 381. [26] *Ibid.*, I, 421. [27] *Ibid.*, II, 256.

harmony, as I have shown, is represented as universal and perfect. In the *Wealth of Nations,* this harmony is represented as not extending to all elements of the economic order, and often as partial and imperfect where it does extend. Where harmony does prevail, it is as a rule a sort of average or statistical harmony, revealing itself only in the general mass of phenomena and leaving scope for the possibility that natural processes whose general effect is beneficial may work disadvantageously in individual cases or at particular moments of time. As a rule, though not invariably, Smith qualifies his assertions of harmony by such phrases as "in most cases," "the majority," "in general," "frequently." For example, the exercise of common prudence is a prerequisite if the system of natural liberty is to operate harmoniously, and "though the principles of common prudence do not always govern the conduct of every individual, they always influence that of *the majority* of every class or order."[28] "It is advantageous to the great body of workmen . . . . that all these trades should be free, though this freedom may be abused in all of them, and is more likely to be so, perhaps, in some than in others."[29] Drawbacks "tend not to destroy, but to preserve, what it is *in most cases* advantageous to preserve, the natural division and distribution of labour in the society."[30]

There are a number of well-known passages in the *Wealth of Nations* in which Smith asserts the existence of a more-or-less complete harmony between the general interests of society and the particular interests of individuals.

> It is not from the benevolence of the butcher, the brewer, or the baker, that we expect our dinner, but from their regard to their own interest. We address ourselves, not to their humanity but to their self-love, and never talk to them of our own necessities but of their advantages. . . . .[31] Every individual is continually exerting himself to find out the most advantageous

[28] *Ibid.*, I, 278. Italics mine.

[29] *Ibid.*, I, 456.

[30] *Ibid.*, II, 1. Italics mine.

[31] *Ibid.*, I, 16.

employment for whatever capital he can command. It is his own advantage, indeed, and not that of the society, which he has in view. But the study of his own advantage naturally, or rather necessarily leads him to prefer that employment which is most advantageous to the society. . . . . [32] As every individual, therefore, endeavors as much as he can both to employ his capital in the support of domestic industry, and so to direct that industry that its produce may be of the greatest value; every individual necessarily labours to render the annual revenue of the society as great as he can. He generally, indeed, neither intends to promote the public interest, nor knows how much he is promoting it. By preferring the support of domestic to that of foreign industry he intends only his own security; and by directing that industry in such a manner as its produce may be of the greatest value, he intends only his own gain, and he is in this, as in many other cases, led by an invisible hand to promote an end which was no part of his intention. . . . . [33] The natural effort of every individual to better his own condition, when suffered to exert itself with freedom and security, is so powerful a principle, that it is alone, and without any assistance, not only capable of carrying on the society to wealth and prosperity, but of surmounting a hundred impertinent obstructions with which the folly of human laws too often incumbers its operations; though the effect of these obstructions is always more or less either to encroach upon its freedom, or to diminish its security.[34]

But whereas in the *Theory of Moral Sentiments* such general statements as these comprise the main substance of the doctrine of a harmonious order in the economic world, in the *Wealth of Nations* they play a much more modest rôle. Though Smith in the *Wealth of Nations* frequently makes general statements intended apparently to apply to the entire universe, he has always before him for consideration some concrete problem, or some finite section of the universe. In no instance does Smith rely heavily upon his assertions as to the existence of harmony in the natural order at large to establish his immediate point that such harmony exists within the specific range of economic phenomena which he is at the moment examining. Such dem-

[32] *Ibid.*, I, 419. [33] *Ibid.*, I, 421. [34] *Ibid.*, II, 43.

onstration he accomplishes primarily by means of reference to the nature of these specific phenomena, by appeal to some self-evident principles of human psychology, by citation of historical object lessons, or by inference from contemporary experience. The general statements, though they may, as has been asserted, reveal the secret basis of Smith's conclusions, are given the appearance of mere obiter dicta, thrown in as supernumerary reinforcements to an argument already sufficiently fortified by more specific and immediate data. Smith's argument for the existence of a natural harmony in the economic order, to be preserved by following the system of natural liberty, is, in form at least, built up by detailed inference from specific data and by examination of specific problems, and is not deduced from wide-sweeping generalizations concerning the universe in general. What were the secret mental processes of Adam Smith whereby he really reached his conclusions it seems at this late date somewhat difficult to talk about with any degree of assurance.

Nowhere in the *Wealth of Nations* does Smith place any reliance for the proper working of the economic order upon the operation of benevolence, the emphasis upon which was the novel feature in the account of human nature presented in the *Theory of Moral Sentiments*. In the *Wealth of Nations,* benevolence is not merely as a rule left out of the picture of the economic order; when mentioned, it is with the implication that it is a weak reed upon which to depend. "By pursuing his own interest he frequently promotes that of the society more effectually than when he really intends to promote it. I have never known much good done by those who affected to trade for the public good. It is an affectation, indeed, not very common among merchants, and very few words need be employed in dissuading them from it."[35] The only other instance in which Smith concedes the possible operation of benevolence in the economic world he also does not take too seriously:

[35] *Ibid.,* I, 421.

Whatever part of the produce . . . . is over and above this share, he [i.e., the landlord] naturally endeavors to reserve to himself as the rent of his land, which is evidently the highest the tenant can afford to pay in the actual circumstances of the land. Sometimes, indeed, the liberality, more frequently the ignorance, of the landlord, makes him accept of somewhat less than this portion. . . . . This portion, however, may still be considered as the natural rent of land, or the rent for which it is naturally meant that land should for the most part be let.[36]

The consequences of the intervention of liberality apparently are not "natural," are not in accordance with the intent of nature! Smith shows little faith in the prevalence of benevolence in the economic sphere. "Man has almost constant occasion for the help of his brethren, and it is in vain for him to expect it from their benevolence only. . . . . It is not from the benevolence of the butcher, the brewer, or the baker, that we expect our dinner, but from their regard to their own interest."[37] "The late resolution of the Quakers in Pennsylvania to set at liberty all their negro slaves, may satisfy us that their number cannot be very great. Had they made any considerable part of their property, such a resolution could never have been agreed to."[38] Even the college professor cannot be expected to expend much energy in teaching effectively, cannot even be depended upon to teach at all, if it is not made to his interest to do so.[39] In the case of the clergy, the situation seems even more desperate. If they are endowed, they become indolent, and their zeal and industry become impaired. If, on the other hand, they are dependent upon voluntary contributions for their support, they become too zealous. He quotes from his skeptical friend Hume:

. . . . This interested diligence of the clergy is what every wise legislator will study to prevent; because, in every religion except the true, it is highly pernicious. . . . . Each ghostly practitioner, in order to render himself more precious and sacred in the eyes of his retainers, will inspire them with the most violent abhorrence of all other sects, and continually

[36] *Ibid.*, I, 145.

[37] *Ibid.*, I, 16.

[38] *Ibid.*, I, 365.

[39] *Ibid.*, II, 250 ff.

endeavor, by some novelty, to excite the languid devotion of his audience. No regard will be paid to truth, morals, or decency in the doctrines inculcated. Every tenet will be adopted that best suits the disorderly affections of the human frame. Customers will be drawn to each conventicle by new industry and address in practising on the passions and credulity of the populace.[40]

Smith laid little stress even in the *Theory of Moral Sentiments* upon the importance of benevolence in the economic order. But writers who have labored under a sense of obligation to find a basis for reconciliation of the *Wealth of Nations* with the *Theory of Moral Sentiments* have nevertheless discovered a problem in the insignificant rôle assigned to benevolence in the *Wealth of Nations*. Buckle's solution of the problem was that in the *Wealth of Nations* Smith was deliberately abstracting from all principles of human nature except self-interest, whereas in the *Theory of Moral Sentiments* he aimed at a complete picture of human nature. Not a trace of evidence is discoverable, however, that Smith in the *Wealth of Nations* was aware that he was abstracting selected elements from the totality of human nature. It awaited a later and keener mind, Ricardo, to exploit the possibilities of the technique of deliberate abstraction in the field of economics. A more ingenious attempt at reconciliation rests, in part, on the identification of self-interest as used in the *Wealth of Nations* with rational pecuniary interest, with a desire for more wealth, and by demonstrating that Smith takes into account other motives than the rational desire for more wealth, claims to demonstrate that Smith did not exclude all principles but self-interest from the economic sphere. But self-interest meant to Smith not only the desire for wealth, but self-love in all its possible manifestations. "It is the interest of every man to live as much at his ease as he can."[41] "Avarice and ambition in the rich, in the poor the hatred of labour and the love of present ease and enjoyment," envy, malice and resentment,[42]

[40] *Ibid.*, II, 273 ff. [41] *Ibid.*, II, 250. [42] *Ibid.*, II, 203.

all of these are manifestations of self-interest; the agreeableness, the ease or hardship, the cleanliness or dirtiness, the honorableness or dishonorableness, of the different employments are all factors affecting the attractiveness to labor of different occupations, as well as the wages paid: "Honour makes a great part of the reward of all honourable professions."[43] Smith distinguishes also between what a man is interested in and what is to his interest. Man is sometimes ignorant of the latter. "But though the interest of the labourer is strictly connected with that of the society, he is incapable either of comprehending that interest, or of understanding its connexion with his own."[44] It is what a man regards as his interest, even though mistakenly, that controls his actions. But every possible impulse and motive to action is included under self-interest except a deliberate intention to promote the welfare of others than one's self.

From his examination of the operation of self-interest in specific phases of the economic order and of the consequences of government interference with the free operation of self-interest, Smith arrives at an extensive program for the extension of the system of natural liberty through the abolition of existing systems of governmental regulation, though he nowhere brings the several items in that program together. Four main reforms are advocated. Free choice of occupations is to be established through the abolition of the apprenticeship regulations and settlement laws; free trade in land, through the repeal of laws establishing entails, primogenitures, and other restrictions on the free transfer of land by gift, devise, or sale; internal free trade, where such does not already prevail, by the abolition of local customs taxes; and most important of all, free trade in foreign commerce, through the abolition of the duties, bounties, and prohibitions of the mercantilistic régime and the trading monopolies of the chartered companies. These various restrictions

[43] *Ibid.*, I, 102.

[44] *Ibid.*, I, 249.

and regulations are objectionable either because they operate to keep commerce, labor, or capital from following the channels in which they would otherwise go, or because they attract to a particular species of industry a greater share of the factors than would ordinarily be employed in it. In all of these cases there is close harmony, under the system of natural liberty, between the interests of individuals and the public interest, and interference by government, instead of promoting, hinders, though it does not necessarily prevent, the attainment of prosperity.

In England all of this program has been achieved, and in so far as such things can be traced to their source, the influence of the *Wealth of Nations* was an important factor in bringing about the reforms. That they were genuine reforms most economists will admit, though even in England there is no longer the unanimity there once was on these matters. It is a somewhat ironical coincidence that the least important plank in Smith's program, the reform of the English law of property, should be in process of achievement only as the permanence of the greatest of his victories, the establishment of free trade in foreign commerce, faces its first serious threat in sixty years.

IV. FLAWS IN THE NATURAL ORDER

The foregoing is familiar matter. What is not so familiar, however, is the extent to which Smith acknowledged exceptions to the doctrine of a natural harmony in the economic order even when left to take its natural course. Smith, himself, never brought these together; but if this is done, they make a surprisingly comprehensive list and they demonstrate beyond dispute the existence of a wide divergence between the perfectly harmonious, completely beneficent natural order of the *Theory of Moral Sentiments* and the partial and limited harmony in the economic order of the *Wealth of Nations*. Masters and workmen have a conflict of interest with respect to wages, and the weakness in bargaining power of the latter ordinarily gives the advantage in any dispute to the former.[45] Masters, traders, and apprentices, on the one hand, and the public on the other, have divergent interests with respect to apprenticeship rules.[46] The interest of merchants and manufacturers is in high profits, which are disadvantageous to the public.[47] Merchants and manufacturers have interests opposed to those of the farmers and landlords,[48] and of the general public.[49] "People of the same trade seldom meet together, even for merriment and diversion, but the conversation ends in a conspiracy against the public, or in some contrivance to raise prices. It is impossible indeed to prevent such meetings, by any law which either could be executed, or would be consistent with liberty and justice."[50] The corn-dealer, on the whole, performs a useful service, but because of his "excess of avarice he does not perform it perfectly."[51] The merchant exporter sometimes finds it to his interest, when dearth prevails both at home and abroad, "very much to aggravate the calamities of the dearth" at home by exporting corn.[52] Men commonly overestimate their chances of success in risky ventures, with the consequence that too great a share of the nation's stock of capital goes into such ventures.[53] It being the custom to pay attorneys and clerks according to the number of pages they had occasion to write, their self-interest led them "to multiply words beyond all necessity, to the corruption of the law language of, I believe, every court of justice in Europe."[54] Private initiative cannot be trusted to take proper care of the roads.[55] Division of labor operates to impair the intelligence, enterprise, martial courage, and moral character of

[45] *Ibid.*, I, 68–69.
[46] *Ibid.*, I, 125.
[47] *Ibid.*, I, 100; II, 112 ff.
[48] *Ibid.*, I, 129.
[49] *Ibid.*, I, 250, 428.
[50] *Ibid.*, I, 130.
[51] *Ibid.*, II, 26.
[52] *Ibid.*, II, 40.
[53] *Ibid.*, II, 64–65.
[54] *Ibid.*, II, 213.
[55] *Ibid.*, II, 217.

the laborers,[56] though division of labor is itself "the necessary, though very slow and gradual, consequence of a certain propensity in human nature . . . . the propensity to truck, barter, and exchange one thing for another."[57] In old countries, "rent and profit eat up wages, and the two superior orders of people oppress the inferior one."[58] This is only a partial list of the defects in the natural order, even when left to take its own course, which Smith points out, though it would suffice to provide ammunition for several socialist orations. This is a far cry from the account given in the *Theory of Moral Sentiments* of a perfectly harmonious order of nature, operating under divine guidance, to promote its "great end, the order of the world, and the perfection and happiness of human nature."

In the *Theory of Moral Sentiments* Smith started out with a few general propositions about the nature of the universe which any educated Scotchman of his day would have vouched for as self-evident truths; and following them wherever they led him, he picked up en route a few more self-evident truths about the nature of human nature, and finally reached conclusions of the sort we have examined. Failing to compare his conclusions with the facts, he saw no necessity for qualifying them, and no reason for re-examining his premises. Unfortunately, these premises were in special need of careful scrutiny, for they were all drawn from a peculiar class of axioms which urgently require, but are incapable of, proof. In his earlier work Smith was a purely speculative philosopher, reasoning from notions masquerading as self-evident verities. In the *Wealth of Nations* Smith made use of a rich harvest of facts gathered by personal observation at home and abroad, by conversation and correspondence with many keen and intelligent observers of the current scene, by wide reading in a miscellany of sources from law books to travelers' tales. With this factual material Smith

[56] *Ibid.*, II, 267. [57] *Ibid.*, I, 15. [58] *Ibid.*, II, 67.

kept close contact, and he never departed from it for long. He still, it is true, retained his flair for resounding generalizations of heroic range. There is a long-standing feud between sweeping generalization and run-of-the-mill factual data, and when Smith brought them together he did not always succeed in inducing altogether harmonious relations. But Smith's strength lay in other directions than exactly logical thinking, and he displayed a fine tolerance for a generous measure of inconsistency. It is to his credit that when there was sharp conflict between his generalization and his data, he usually abandoned his generalization.

There would be little ground for insistence upon reconciliation between the *Theory of Moral Sentiments* and the *Wealth of Nations* if it were simply a case of comparing one book written in 1757 with another written in 1776. It may not be as common as it should be for a man in his full maturity to advance beyond the level of his first book; but it surely is not a rare phenomenon requiring to be explained out of existence. In every respect which is of concern to the economist as such, with the possible exception of his treatment of benevolence, the apparent discrepancies between the *Theory of Moral Sentiments* and the *Wealth of Nations* mark distinct advances of the latter over the former in realism and in application of the saving grace of common sense. But in the last year of his life Smith made extensive revisions and additions to the *Theory of Moral Sentiments,* without diminishing in any particular the points of conflict between the two books. This would make it seem that in Smith's mind, at least, there was to the last no consciousness of any difference in the doctrines expounded in the two books. Though we grant this, however, are we obliged to accept his judgment and to strain interpretations in order to find consistency prevailing where inconsistency appeareth to reign supreme? I think not. There persisted within the *Wealth of Nations,* througn five successive editions, many, and to later eyes obvious, inconsistencies. When Smith revised his *Theory of Moral Sentiments* he was elderly and unwell. It is not altogether unreasonable to suppose that he had lost the capacity to make drastic changes in his philosophy, but had retained his capacity to overlook the absence of complete co-ordination and unity in that philosophy.

V. THE FUNCTIONS OF GOVERNMENT

Adam Smith, as has been shown, recognized that the economic order, when left to its natural course, was marked by serious conflicts between private interests and the interests of the general public. This would seem to suggest that there was an important sphere in which government interference with private interests might promote the general welfare. In his one deliberate and comprehensive generalization dealing with the proper functions of the state, Smith made it clear, however, that he would narrowly restrict the activities of government. "According to the system of natural liberty, the sovereign has only three duties to attend to; . . . . first, the duty of protecting the society from the violence and invasion of other independent societies; secondly, ... the duty of establishing an exact administration of justice; and, thirdly, the duty of erecting and maintaining certain public institutions and certain public works."[59] Even here, however, he grants to government a somewhat more extensive range of proper activities than in many scattered dicta throughout the remainder of the book, where he was primarily condemning some specific governmental activity and was not really giving serious consideration to the wider problem of the proper range of governmental activity. Smith had himself undermined what is ordinarily regarded as his principal argument for laissez faire, by demonstrating that the natural order, when left to take its own course, in many respects

[59] *Ibid.*, II, 185.

works against, instead of for, the general welfare. How can his adherence, notwithstanding, to a policy of narrow limitation of the functions of government be explained?

The *Wealth of Nations,* though it was from one point of view only a segment of a larger and systematic treatise on social philosophy, was at the same time a tract for the times, a specific attack on certain types of government activity which Smith was convinced, on both a priori and empirical grounds, operated against national prosperity, namely, bounties, duties, and prohibitions in foreign trade; apprenticeship and settlement laws; legal monopolies; laws of succession hindering free trade in land. Smith's primary objective was to secure the termination of *these* activities of government. His wider generalizations were invoked to support the attack on *these* political institutions. Everything else was to a large degree secondary. Smith made many exceptions to his general argument for laissez faire. But his interest as a reformer and a propagandist was not in these exceptions. He nowhere gathered together in orderly fashion the exceptions which he would have made to his general restriction of government activity to protection, justice, and the maintenance of a few types of public works and public institutions. When considering in general terms the proper functions of government, he forgot all about these exceptions. If he had been brought face to face with a complete list of the modifications to the principle of laissez faire to which he at one place or another had granted his approval, I have no doubt that he would have been astounded at his own moderation. I once heard a president of a state bankers' association at the afternoon session of its annual convention make the theme of his presidential address the unmitigated iniquity of government interference with business and the necessity of more business men in government in order that they should see to it that there was less government in business. In the evening of the same day he introduced to the audience the state commissioner of banking as one to whom the bankers were deeply indebted, because by promoting the enactment of sound regulations governing the entrance into the banking field and the practice of banking he had secured the suppression of irresponsible and fraudulent banking, to the benefit of the solid and respectable bankers there assembled and of the general public. He was as sincere in the evening as he had been that afternoon. Not only was Smith fully capable of this type of inconsistency, but there is in the *Wealth of Nations* an almost exact parallel of this modern instance.[60]

There is no possible room for doubt, however, that Smith in general believed that there was, to say the least, a strong presumption against government activity beyond its fundamental duties of protection against its foreign foes and maintenance of justice. In his *Lectures,* Smith had said: "Till there be property, there can be no government, the very end of which is to secure wealth [i. e., to make wealth secure] and to defend the rich from the poor,"[61] following closely Locke's dictum that "Government has no other end but the preservation of property." In the *Wealth of Nations* he was more guarded: "Civil government, so far as it is instituted for the security of property, is in reality instituted for the defence of the rich against the poor, or of those who have some property against those who have none at all."[62] What were the considerations which brought Smith to his laissez faire conclusions? His philosophical speculations about a harmonious order in nature undoubtedly made it easier for him to reach a laissez faire policy, though I believe that the significance of the natural order in Smith's economic doctrines has been grossly exaggerated. But was not government itself a part of the order of nature, and its activities as "natural" as those of the individuals whom it governed? Smith is obscure on this point, and an adequate answer to this ques-

[60] Cf. *ibid.*, II, 307. [61] *Lectures,* p. 15. [62] *Wealth of Nations,* II, 207.

tion, if possible at all, would require a detailed examination of Smith's position in the evolution of political theory, especially with respect to the origin of government and the character of the state of nature in the absence of government. It is clear, however, that to Smith the activities of government in the maintenance of justice are an essential part of the order of nature in its full development, and that such activities are not interferences with the system of natural liberty.

In the *Theory of Moral Sentiments* there is a vague passage which seems to suggest that government itself is an agency of the order of nature, and to imply that all of its activities may, therefore, be as "natural" as those of individuals.[63] In the *Wealth of Nations,* Smith is a little more precise. He draws a definite line between those activities of government which are, and those which are not, in accord with the natural order, on the basis of empirical data. Government activity is natural and therefore good where it promotes the general welfare, and is an interference with nature and therefore bad when it injures the general interests of society. Whether in particular circumstances it works well or ill is to be determined only by examination of the character of those circumstances, though in most cases such examination may be expected a priori to reveal that it works badly.

This general presumption against government intervention in the affairs of mankind was itself largely the product of direct inference from experience. Against those particular activities of government which he subjected to special attack, viz., mercantilistic regulations, settlement and apprenticeship laws, legal monopolies, Smith thought he had specific objections, drawn from the results of their operation, sufficient to condemn them. Aside from protection and justice, these were the important activities of the governments of his day. In condemning them he

[63] *Theory of Moral Sentiments,* pp. 163–64.

was not far from condemning all the main types of government activity, aside from justice and protection, which were prominently in the public view. To justify these activities, it was necessary, Smith believed, to credit government with better knowledge of what was to a man's interest than the ordinary man himself was endowed with. This Smith could not concede. The standards of honesty and competence of the governments of his day with which Smith was acquainted were unbelievably low, moreover, not only in comparison with what they are today in England, Germany, and the Scandinavian countries, but apparently even in comparison with earlier periods in English political history. Smith had encountered few instances in which government was rendering intelligent and efficient service to the public welfare outside of the fields of protection and justice. The English government of his day was in the hands of an aristocratic clique, the place-jobbing, corrupt, cynical, and class-biased flower of the British gentry, who clung to the traditional mercantilism not so much because of a strong faith that it met the problems of a growing trade struggling to burst its fetters, but because they did not know anything else to do. Even when Smith was prepared to admit that the system of natural liberty would not serve the public welfare with optimum effectiveness, he did not feel driven necessarily to the conclusion that government intervention was preferable to laissez faire. The evils of unrestrained selfishness might be better than the evils of incompetent and corrupt government.

In this connection, Smith has, indeed, a lesson to teach the "new economics" of the present day, which is peddling antique nostrums under new trademarks, and which has substituted for the answer to all economic problems of the classically trained parrot, "demand and supply," the equally magical phrase, "social control." If the standards of public administration are low, progress from a life regulated by the law of demand and supply to a life under the realm of social control may be progress from the discomforts of the frying-pan to the agonies of the fire.

> It is the highest impertinence and presumption, therefore, in kings and ministers, to pretend to watch over the economy of private people, and to restrain their expense, either by sumptuary laws, or by prohibiting the importation of foreign luxuries. They are themselves always, and without any exception, the greatest spendthrifts in the society. Let them look well after their own expence, and they may safely trust private people with theirs. If their own extravagance does not ruin the state, that of their subjects never will.[64] . . . . The violence and injustice of the rulers of mankind is an ancient evil, for which, I am afraid, the nature of human affairs can scarce admit of a remedy.[65]

Where, by exception, good government made its appearance, Smith was ready to grant it a wider range of activities.

> The orderly, vigilant, and parsimonious administration of such aristocracies as those of Venice and Amsterdam, is extremely proper, it appears from experience, for the management of a mercantile project of this kind. But whether such a government as that of England; which, whatever may be its virtues, has never been famous for good economy; which, in time of peace, has generally conducted itself with the slothful and negligent profusion that is perhaps natural to monarchies; and in time of war has constantly acted with all the thoughtless extravagance that democracies are apt to fall into; could be safely trusted with the management of such a project, must at least be a good deal more doubtful.[66]

Smith believed, moreover, that there were evils involved in the economic order which it was beyond the competence of even good government to remedy. To repeat a useful quotation: "People of the same trade seldom meet together, even for merriment and diversion, but the conversation ends in a conspiracy against the public, or in some contrivance to raise prices. It is impossible indeed to prevent such meetings, by any law which could be executed, or would be consistent with liberty and justice."[67] We have tried, in this country, to abolish Gary dinners

[64] *Wealth of Nations,* I, 328.
[65] *Ibid.,* I, 457.
[66] *Ibid.,* II, 303.
[67] *Ibid.,* I, 130.

by law. Whether we have succeeded seems still to be open to argument.

So much for the negative aspects of Smith's theory of the functions of the state. Let us examine now what concessions he made to the possibilities of the promotion of human welfare through governmental action. Smith conceded that it was the duty of the government to provide protection against external foes, and on the ground of their necessity for defense, he approved of commercial regulations which on purely economic grounds he would condemn. "The act of navigation is not favourable to foreign commerce, or to the growth of that opulence which can arise from it. . . . . As defence, however, is of much more importance than opulence, the act of navigation is, perhaps, the wisest of all the commercial regulations of England."[68] In the same spirit, Smith mildly supported bounties on manufactures necessary for defense, which would not otherwise be produced at home.[69]

Smith assigned to government also "the duty of establishing an exact administration of justice." Unfortunately, Smith never succeeded in carrying out his original plan of writing a treatise on jurisprudence, and the scattered materials in the *Wealth of Nations* and the meager outline in the *Lectures* are insufficient to give us a trustworthy judgment as to what he would include under "justice." His own definition in the *Wealth of Nations*, "the duty of protecting, as far as possible, every member of the society from the injustice or oppression of every other member of it,"[70] if broadly interpreted, would assign to government the task of a major reconstruction of the economic order, since Smith, as has been shown, recited many phases of it in which injustice and oppression prevailed. It seems clear, however, that Smith, like later and more doctrinaire exponents of laissez faire, took for granted the inevitability of private property and class

[68] *Ibid.*, I, 429. [69] *Ibid.*, II, 23. [70] *Ibid.*, II, 185.

conflict, and understood by justice the whole legal and customary code of his time dealing with individual rights, privileges, and obligations under that system of economic organization. It is also likely that Smith failed to see how far acceptance of even the prevailing code of justice carried him from a simple order of nature in which natural justice automatically emerges from the harmony of individual interests, independently of governmental machinery and sanctions. Punishment and enforcement of redress after the act in case of dishonesty, violence, fraud, clearly would be included under the "administration of justice." Smith would, perhaps, include as a proper phase of this function such preventive measures as would tend to give security against the perpetration of dishonesty, extortion, and violence. In any case, he does not oppose such regulations, though his *Lectures* indicate that he would include them under "police" rather than "justice."[71] "The institution of long apprenticeships can give no security that insufficient workmanship shall not frequently be exposed to public sale. When this is done it is generally the effect of fraud, and not of inability; and the longest apprenticeship can give no security against fraud. Quite different regulations are necessary to prevent this abuse. The sterling mark upon plate, and the stamps upon linen and woollen cloth, give the purchaser much greater security than any statute of apprenticeship."[72] Unqualified adherence to the principle of *caveat emptor* was apparently not a necessary implication of Smith's laissez faire doctrines. Enforcement of contracts is specified as an important function of government,[73] and a law obliging masters to pay wages in money rather than in kind is justifiable as a protection to the workers against fraud. "It imposes no real hardship upon the masters. It only obliges them to pay that value in money, which they pretended to pay but did not always really pay, in

[71] *Lectures,* 154 ff. [72] *Wealth of Nations,* I, 123. [73] *Ibid.,* I, 97.

goods."[74] "Where there is an exclusive corporation, it may perhaps be proper to regulate the price of the first necessary of life."[75] Protection of slaves against violence by their masters is approved of both as in accord with common humanity and as promoting the productivity of slave labor.[76] Smith recognized the existence of a higher social justice, which may override the "natural liberty" of the individual, but he would invoke it sparingly. Regulations of paper money banking "may, no doubt, be considered as in some respect a violation of natural liberty. But those exertions of the natural liberty of a few individuals, which might endanger the security of the whole society, are, and ought to be, restrained by the laws of all governments; of the most free, as well as of the most despotical. The obligation of building party walls, in order to prevent the communication of fire, is a violation of natural liberty, exactly of the same kind with the regulations of the banking trade which are here proposed."[77] But "To hinder . . . . the farmer from sending his goods at all times to the best market, is evidently to sacrifice the ordinary laws of justice to an idea of public utility, to a sort of reasons of state; an act of legislative authority which ought to be exercised only, which can be pardoned only in cases of the most urgent necessity."[78] We have here, perhaps, the germ of that later maxim of convenient vagueness, that every individual should be protected in his natural rights, but only to the extent to which they do not interfere with the natural rights of others. There is no evidence that Smith would include as a proper phase of the administration of justice any drastic revision of the content of these rights.

There remains to be considered the third government function: "erecting and maintaining certain public works and certain public institutions, which it can never be for the interest of

[74] *Ibid.*, I, 143.

[75] *Ibid.*, I, 144.

[76] *Ibid.*, II, 88.

[77] *Ibid.*, I, 307.

[78] *Ibid.*, II, 41–42.

any individual, or small number of individuals, to erect and maintain; because the profit could never repay the expence to any individual or small number of individuals, though it may frequently do much more than repay it to a great society."[79] Smith here clearly assigns to the government a duty of promoting the general welfare other than in connection with protection and justice, if the means to do so are within the power of the government, but not within the power of individuals. What the relationship of this function is to the natural order Smith does not discuss in the *Wealth of Nations*. The attention given to it by Smith has been attributed to the influence of the Physiocrats. In the *Theory of Moral Sentiments* there is one passage which appears to praise such institutions, but may have been intended in a satirical sense:

> The same principle, the same love of system, the same regard to the beauty of order, of art and contrivance, frequently serves to recommend those institutions which tend to promote the public welfare. . . . . It is not commonly from a fellow-feeling with carriers and waggoners that a public-spirited man encourages the mending of high roads. When the legislature establishes premiums and other encouragements to advance the linen or woollen manufactures, its conduct seldom proceeds from pure sympathy with the wearer of cheap or fine cloth, and much less from that with the manufacturer or merchant. The perfection of police, the extension of trade and manufactures, are noble and magnificent objects. . . . . They make part of the great system of government, and the wheels of the political machine seem to move with more harmony and ease by means of them. . . . . All constitutions of government, however, are [ought to be?] valued only in proportion as they tend to promote the happiness of those who live under them.[80]

In the *Lectures*, the only relevant passage is a passing reference under the general heading of "Police" to what may be regarded as a detailed phase of this function of government, the promotion of cleanliness, presumably of the streets.[81]

[79] *Ibid.*, II, 185.

[80] *Theory of Moral Sentiments*, pp. 163–64.

[81] *Lectures*, p. 154.

In the *Wealth of Nations* the discussion lacks somewhat in breadth, perhaps because it is merely incidental to Smith's discussion of the financial aspects of government. The public works and public institutions in this class, says Smith, "are chiefly those for facilitating the commerce of the society, and those for promoting the instruction of the people."[82] He nowhere purports to give a complete list of the public works proper to government, but he mentions highways, bridges, canals, and harbors. In discussing the propriety of particular projects, however, he completely ignores the criterion he had laid down at the beginning of his discussion, namely, the impossibility of their being conducted profitably as private enterprises. The only reason he gives for his approval of government maintenance of the highways is that private management would not have a sufficient incentive to maintain them properly, and therefore could not be trusted to do so.[83] He apparently approves of government operation of canals, though he grants that they can be left safely in private hands,[84] and that they can be profitably managed by joint-stock companies.[85]

The modern issue of the propriety of government participation in commerce and industry is dealt with by Adam Smith almost solely from the viewpoint: Can the government make a net revenue out of it? He takes coinage for granted as a government function without considering any possible alternative. He apparently approves of government operation of the post-office, but if so, the only ground given is the ability of the government to manage it with successful financial results.[86] He in general disapproves of government ventures into business, but solely on the ground that the government is a poor trader and a poor manager. The public domain, except what may be needed

[82] *Wealth of Nations,* II, 214.

[83] *Ibid.*, II, 217.

[84] *Ibid.*, II, 217.

[85] *Ibid.*, II, 247.

[86] *Ibid.*, II, 303.

for parks, should be disposed of, because the sovereign is a poor farmer and forester. Smith apparently could not read German, and makes no references to German literature. Knowledge of the success of some of the German principalities in managing the public domain, and in other phases of public administration, would perhaps have lessened Smith's opposition to government ventures into industry. The modern advocate of laissez faire who objects to government participation in business on the ground that it is an encroachment upon a field reserved by nature for private enterprise cannot find support for this argument in the *Wealth of Nations*.

Of government "institutions," other than public works, intended to facilitate commerce, Smith opposes legal monopolies in general, though he concedes the validity of a temporary monopoly when a trading company undertakes, at its own risk and expense, to establish a new trade with some remote and barbarous nation, and he indicates that he approves for the same reason of the institutions of patent and copyright.[87]

Smith supports the participation of the government in the general education of the people, because it will help prepare them for industry, will make them better citizens and better soldiers, and happier and healthier men in mind and body. Public education is made necessary to check as far as may be the evil effects on the standards, mentality, and character of the working classes of the division of labor and the inequality in the distribution of wealth.[88] Here once more Smith draws a picture of the economic order under the system of natural liberty which is quite different from that beatific state which he dreamed about in the *Theory of Moral Sentiments*.

It is quite probable that Smith overlooked some current activities of government to which he would have given his approval if they had been called to his attention. The absence, for

[87] *Ibid.*, II, 245. [88] *Ibid.*, II, 267 ff.

instance, in the *Wealth of Nations* of any discussion of poor relief as a public function has often been commented upon, and is generally regarded as having been due to oversight. But we have not yet revealed the full extent to which Smith showed himself prepared to depart from a rigid policy of laissez faire. The one personal characteristic which all of his biographers agree in attributing to him is absent-mindedness, and his general principle of natural liberty seems to have been one of the things he was most absent-minded about. We have already seen that in his more systematic discussion of the functions of government, Smith made important concessions to the possibility of government promotion of the general welfare through public works and institutions. In stray but frequent moments of intimate contact with facts apparently hostile to the principle of natural liberty, Smith conveniently forgot the principle and went beyond the limits set in his formal discussion to the proper activities of government. In arguing for the duty of government to support educational institutions which promote the martial spirit of the people, Smith incidentally concedes that "it would deserve its most serious attention to prevent a leprosy or any other loathsome and offensive disease, though neither mortal nor dangerous, from spreading itself among them,"[89] from which it may reasonably be inferred that he would even more strongly support public action taken to prevent the spread of dangerous diseases, and thus would include public hygiene among the proper functions of government. In many instances Smith supported government restrictions on private initiative where neither justice nor defense was involved, and where the sole aim was to improve upon the direction which private initiative gave to the investment of capital, the course of commerce, and the employment of labor. He supported the compulsory registration of mortgages,[90] and he

[89] *Ibid.*, II, 272.

[90] *Ibid.*, II, 347.

wrote approvingly of colonial laws which promoted agricultural progress by checking the engrossing of land.[91]

To the great indignation of Jeremy Bentham, he approved of the prevailing restriction of the maximum rate of interest to 5 per cent, on the ground that if a higher rate were current, "the greater part of the money which was to be lent, would be lent to prodigals and projectors, who alone would be willing to give this high interest. . . . . A great part of the capital of the country would thus be kept out of the hands which were most likely to make a profitable and advantageous use of it, and thrown into those which were most likely to waste and destroy it."[92] We may be inclined to agree with Bentham that this is an inadequate defense of the usury laws, but what makes it significant for our purposes is that it involves an admission on Smith's part that the majority of investors could not be relied upon to invest their funds prudently and safely, and that government regulation was a good corrective for individual stupidity.

Smith also makes several concessions to the mercantilistic policy of regulation of the foreign trade. He admits that there are circumstances under which export restrictions on corn may be warranted;[93] he approves of a moderate export tax on wool on the ground that it would produce revenue for the government and at the same time would afford an advantage over their foreign competitors to the British manufacturer of woolens;[94] he favors moderate taxes on foreign manufactures, which would still give to domestic workmen "a considerable advantage in the home market."[95]

Smith recommended that rents in kind should be taxed more

[91] *Ibid.*, II, 73.

[92] *Ibid.*, I, 338.

[93] *Ibid.*, II, 41.

[94] *Ibid.*, II, 152.

[95] *Ibid.*, II, 367. Smith may, however, have supported such taxes as an alternative to the existing higher taxes and prohibitions of import, and not as preferable to free import.

heavily than money rents, because "such rents are always more hurtful to the tenant than beneficial to the landlord."[96] He would tax rent from leases which prescribe to the tenant a certain mode of cultivation more heavily than other rent, in order to discourage the practice of making such leases, "which is generally a foolish one."[97] He would tax at more favorable rates the landlord who cultivates a part of his own land, because it is of importance that the landlord, with his greater command of capital and his greater willingness and capacity to try experiments, should be encouraged to take an active part in agriculture.[98] He would penalize by heavier taxation the landlord who capitalizes a part of the future rent, because this is usually the expedient of a spendthrift, is frequently hurtful to landlord and tenant, is always hurtful to the community.[99] Shortly thereafter, however, Smith returns to laissez faire: "The principal attention of the sovereign ought to be to encourage, by every means in his power, the attention both of the landlord and of the farmer; by allowing both to pursue their own interest in their own way, and according to their own judgment."[100]

Smith gives a little support to the use of the taxing power as what would now be called "an instrument of social reform." He approves of a tax on the retail sale of liquor so adjusted as to discourage the multiplication of little alehouses,[101] and of a heavy tax on distilleries as a sumptuary measure against spirituous liquors, especially if accompanied by a reduction in the tax on "the wholesome and invigorating liquors of beer and ale."[102] He supports heavier highway tolls upon luxury carriages than upon freight wagons, in order that "the indolence and vanity of the rich [be] made to contribute in a very easy manner to the

[96] *Ibid.*, II, 316.
[97] *Ibid.*
[98] *Ibid.*
[99] *Ibid.*, II, 315.
[100] *Ibid.*, II, 318.
[101] *Ibid.*, II, 337.
[102] *Ibid.*, II, 375.

relief of the poor."[103] He asserts that "the gains of monopolists, whenever they can be come at [are] certainly of all subjects the most proper" for taxation.[104] The modern single-taxer finds support for his cause in Smith's argument for the special taxation of land values. "Ground-rents, so far as they exceed the ordinary rent of land, are altogether owing to the good government of the sovereign. . . . . Nothing can be more reasonable than that a fund which owes its existence to the good government of the state, should be taxed peculiarly, or should contribute something more than the greater part of other funds, towards the support of the government."[105] He lends mild support to the principle of progressive taxation: "It is not very unreasonable that the rich should contribute to the public expence, not only in proportion to their revenue, but something more than in that proportion."[106]

Though there is nowhere in Smith's writings a general discussion of the possibilities of voluntary co-operation, he makes clear that he did not hope for much good from it. Making a reasonable inference from past experience, but a bad forecast of the subsequent trend, he saw in the joint-stock company very limited promise even for money-making purposes.[107] It was his verdict that the corporate guilds had failed to promote good workmanship.[108] Exception being made for the Presbyterian church, he saw even in religious associations much to blame.[109] About the only types of voluntary association in which Smith saw a high degree of effectiveness in accomplishing their purposes were associations of merchants and manufacturers to exploit the consumer and of masters to exploit the worker.

Adam Smith was not a doctrinaire advocate of laissez faire.

[103] *Ibid.*, II, 216.

[104] *Ibid.*, II, 377.

[105] *Ibid.*, II, 329.

[106] *Ibid.*, II, 327.

[107] *Ibid.*, II, 246.

[108] *Ibid.*, I, 131.

[109] *Ibid.*, II, 273 ff.

He saw a wide and elastic range of activity for government, and he was prepared to extend it even farther if government, by improving its standards of competence, honesty, and public spirit, showed itself entitled to wider responsibilities. He attributed great capacity to serve the general welfare to individual initiative applied in competitive ways to promote individual ends. He devoted more effort to the presentation of his case for individual freedom than to exploring the possibilities of service through government. He helped greatly to free England from the bonds of a set of regulatory measures which had always been ill advised and based on fallacious economic notions, but he did not foresee that England would soon need a new set of regulations to protect her laboring masses against new, and to them dangerous, methods of industrial organization and industrial technique. Smith was endowed with more than the ordinary allotment of common sense, but he was not a prophet. But even in his own day, when it was not so easy to see, Smith saw that self-interest and competition were sometimes treacherous to the public interest they were supposed to serve, and he was prepared to have government exercise some measure of control over them where the need could be shown and the competence of government for the task demonstrated. His sympathy with the humble and the lowly, with the farmer and the laborer, was made plain for all to see. He had not succeeded in completely freeing himself from mercantilistic delusions, and he had his own peculiar doctrinal and class prejudices. But his prejudices, such as they were, were against the powerful and the grasping, and it was the interests of the general masses that he wished above all to promote, in an age when even philosophers rarely condescended to deal sympathetically with their needs. He had little trust in the competence or good faith of government. He knew who controlled it, and whose purposes they tried to serve, though against the local magistrate his indictment was probably unduly harsh. He saw, nevertheless, that it was necessary, in the absence of a better instrument, to rely upon government for the performance of many tasks which individuals as such would not do, or could not do, or could do only badly. He did not believe that laissez faire was always good, or always bad. It depended on circumstances; and as best he could, Adam Smith took into account all of the circumstances he could find. In these days of contending schools, each of them with the deep, though momentary, conviction that it, and it alone, knows the one and only path to economic truth, how refreshing it is to return to the *Wealth of Nations* with its eclecticism, its good temper, its common sense, and its willingness to grant that those who saw things differently from itself were only partly wrong.

CHAPTER VI

ADAM SMITH: MORALIST AND PHILOSOPHER

GLENN R. MORROW

Once upon a time there was a man who read the *Wealth of Nations;* not a summary, nor a volume of selected passages, but the *Wealth of Nations* itself. He began with the Introduction, he read the famous first chapter on the division of labor, the chapters on the origin and use of money, the prices of commodities, the wages of labor, the profits of stock, the rent of land, and all the other well-known economic portions of the first book, not omitting the long digression on the fluctuation in the value of silver during the last four centuries, and the statistical tables at the end. Having completed the first book he went on to the second, not deterred by the fact that it is supposed to contain an erroneous theory of capital and an untenable distinction between productive and unproductive labor. In Book III he found an account of the economic development of Europe since the fall of the Roman Empire, with digressions upon various phases of medieval life and civilization. In the fourth book he came upon extended analyses and criticisms of the commercial and colonial policies of European nations, and a whole battery of free-trade arguments. Finally he attacked the long concluding book on the revenue of the sovereign. Here he found even more varied and unexpected matters: an account of the different methods of defense and of administering justice in primitive societies, and of the origin and growth of standing armies in Europe; a history of education in the Middle Ages and a criticism of eighteenth-century universities; a history of the temporal power of the church, of the growth of public debts in modern nations, of the mode of electing bishops in the ancient church; reflections upon the disadvantages of the division of labor, and—what is the main purpose of the book—an examination of principles of taxation and of systems of public revenue. Time is too short to enumerate all that he found here before he finally came to the concluding paragraphs, written during the opening events of the American Revolution, concerning the duty of colonies to contribute toward the expenses of the mother-country.

Now of course I may have exaggerated somewhat. There probably never was any such man. But what I have said remains hypothetically, if not categorically, true. If there had been such a man, with the leisure and the industry, with the dogged perseverance and the freedom from doctrinal obsessions to follow the work of this great thinker to the very end, he would have found all that I have described. And at the conclusion of his reading he would have paused to reflect: This an economic work? It is far more than that; it is a history and a criticism of all European civilization.

And I think he would have been right. How absurd to think of the author of the *Wealth of Nations* as interested only in the wealth of nations! Adam Smith's great work is more than a treatise on economics; it is a philosophical work, in that sense of the word "philosophy" which has almost passed out of usage in the last hundred years. It is a philosophical work in that it deals with broad problems of human welfare, and deals with them in a reasoned and unprejudiced manner. Adam Smith had a tremendous breadth of interest, and his attention is attracted by the most diverse and seemingly the most insignificant facts. But this is not all. It takes more than breadth of interest, or variety of facts, to make a philosophy. Facts must be bound by the tie of the cause, as Plato says; they must be systematized; they must be held, not for their own sakes, but for the principles they disclose; only then do they constitute true knowledge, whether scientific or philosophical. Adam Smith does not obtrude his principles, he does not expound them dogmatically and abstractly, he does not let them override his facts; but the principles are there just the same—economic principles, ethical principles, principles of jurisprudence, even principles of theology. A candid and comprehensive inquiry, enlightened by principles and inspired by concern for human welfare, the *Wealth of Nations* has every claim to be called a philosophical work.

I want to formulate briefly here some of the philosophical principles which run through the *Wealth of Nations*. I wish I had the skill of Adam Smith himself, so that I could present them in his own empirical persuasive fashion. But lacking that, I must necessarily present them somewhat bluntly and abstractly, in all their skeletal bareness, and it will be something, I suppose, if we succeed in distinguishing the members and finding the articulations without blundering.

Adam Smith was no metaphysician. The eighteenth century was not a metaphysical one, and Adam Smith was one of the least metaphysical persons of his century. Perhaps, however, we should only say that he avoided metaphysics in his two great works; for, like Socrates with respect to physical science, he was himself not unversed in these inquiries which he avoided. His first appointment at the University of Glasgow was to the chair of logic and metaphysics, and a part of his inaugural address is still preserved;[1] it bore the title "De Origine Idearum," and was concerned, among other things, with an examination of the Platonic doctrine of ideas. But Smith was shortly transferred to the chair of moral philosophy, and there is no reason to doubt that

[1] In the essay, "The History of the Ancient Logic and Metaphysics," in the posthumous *Essays on Philosophical Subjects*.

it was a transfer thoroughly to his liking. This latter position he held for twelve years. We know something of the way he conceived and taught moral philosophy during this period. His predecessor and former teacher, Francis Hutcheson, had divided moral philosophy into four branches, viz., natural, theology, ethics, jurisprudence, and political economy; and Adam Smith, so his earliest biographer tells us, followed this same classification in his university lectures. The two works on which his fame chiefly rests, the *Theory of Moral Sentiments,* and the *Inquiry into the Nature and Causes of the Wealth of Nations,* are the fruit of his studies in two of these divisions; the *Moral Sentiments* probably contains the content of the lectures on ethics, while the *Wealth of Nations,* contains the material of the fourth part of his lectures, elaborated, developed, and enriched by the reflections of seventeen years of travel and retirement. In the later years of his life he was also reported to be engaged upon another work, which, judging from some hints in the *Moral Sentiments,* was probably a treatise on jurisprudence after the manner of Montesquieu; but the materials which he had collected for this work were destroyed at his own order shortly before his death.

That there was a unity of spirit and aim in Adam Smith's treatment of these separate divisions of moral philosophy cannot be doubted. He had no use for the kind of moral philosophy taught in the medieval universities and still persisting in some quarters in the eighteenth century. This philosophy, as he saw it, was chiefly concerned with the rewards and penalties of a future life, and looked upon virtue as inconsistent with happiness in this world; it was casuistical in its method and ascetic in its aim—in short, a thoroughly perverted form of moral philosophy. It was a form of moral philosophy, moreover, which was hard to reconcile with the material prosperity that the European nations were beginning to enjoy. The famous Dr. Mandeville, in his *Fable of the Bees, or Private Vices Public Benefits,* had made much of this opposition between the moral standards which the modern world had inherited from the Middle Ages, and the practices by which it got its wealth. The vices of men, said Mandeville—luxury, ambition, desire for worldly gain in all its forms—are the causes of the wealth of modern times. Self-denial, which is the only true virtue, is generally acknowledged, but fortunately not generally practiced; for if it were, the present era of material progress would soon come to an end. The *Fable of the Bees* made a great stir in the eighteenth century, and was thought worthy of an answer by Bishop Berkeley, and William Law, and by almost every other writer of importance in the century. Adam Smith sees with Mandeville the conflict between an ethics of complete self-denial and the material prosperity of modern times. But he insists that the moral philosophy which would make virtue consist in complete self-denial is a perversion of the true doctrine. The true moral philosophy is concerned with human happiness and welfare in this world, and it conceives of no opposition between the demands of this world and the demands of perfect morality. Its object is to determine "wherein consists the happiness and perfection of a man, not only as an individual, but as a member of a family, of a state, and of the great society of mankind."[2] In this fine and inclusive statement, Adam Smith's moral philosophy exhibits its sharp divergence from all ascetic theories, and its willingness to cope with the problems of human welfare in all the concrete conditions of the modern world.

There are other elements in Adam Smith's moral philosophy which differentiate it sharply from the orthodox moral philosophy of preceding centuries. The eighteenth century may be said to mark the culminating point in the movement of the modern

[2] *Wealth of Nations,* II, 259. This and the following references are to the edition of Edwin Cannan, London, 1904.

world away from the social and moral order of the Middle Ages. It was an age of criticism, consciously and ruthlessly directed against the lingering structures of the medieval system. The political liberalism, the religious liberalism, and the economic liberalism of the eighteenth century were merely separate manifestations of one and the same attempt to break down the older institutional forms and set free human energies and allow satisfaction to human aspirations that could no longer find expression in those forms. Liberalism in all its manifestations was essentially a doctrine of the rights of the individual, and a criticism of the claims of existing institutions to regulate his activity. Individual liberty, in politics, in religion, in industry, was felt to be the first and sometimes the only thing necessary for the introduction of a better social and political order. Other ages have perhaps appreciated more fully the meaning of individuality, but no age ever desired or fought for it with greater zeal than the century of Voltaire, Rousseau, and Adam Smith.

This individualism characteristic of the century finds a prominent place in Adam Smith's moral philosophy. It appears in the *Wealth of Nations* not only as a protest against the system of government regulation in industry and an appeal for freedom of trade and commerce; but also in another guise which has frequently caused much concern to moralists, viz., in the emphasis which Adam Smith places upon the activity of self-interest in the economic order. The prosperity of a nation can best be advanced, according to Smith, by allowing each individual to pursue his own interests as he sees them. The strongest and the surest motive operating in economic relations is this "uniform, constant, and uninterrupted effort of every man to better his condition." "It is not from the benevolence of the butcher, the brewer, or the baker that we expect our dinner, but from their regard to their own interest. We address ourselves, not to their humanity, but to their self-love, and never talk to them of our own necessities, but of their advantages."[3] Here we have the theme which is elaborated and developed and repeated with variations throughout the *Wealth of Nations*. Of course Adam Smith does not intend to represent self-love or self-interest as the only motive which ever actuates men. He recognizes in the *Wealth of Nations* other "passions" as occasionally responsible for economic conditions. He recognizes also that self-interest is stronger in some men than it is in others, and that all men may misconceive their interests and act contrary to them. But with these reservations, Adam Smith regards self-interest as the basis of the economic order, and as the main psychological factor in industrial prosperity.

This seeming glorification of self-love has been a stumbling-block to many admirers of Adam Smith, who have tried to minimize the extent to which he relied upon this explanatory principle in his economic work. It is sometimes necessary to know the truth, however, even about our heroes; and if we examine the *Wealth of Nations* with this question in mind, we shall find that Smith applies this principle of explanation almost universally, both to the fundamental traits of the economic order and to the variety of detail. The two main causes of the productivity of modern industry are the division of labor and the accumulation of capital. Self-interest is the explanation of both these key facts. The individual finds it more to his interest to exercise his strength and develop his skill in one occupation and exchange the surplus of what he produces for the products of other men's skill than to attempt to supply all his various needs by the labor of his own hands; hence the division of labor. Likewise the accumulation of capital: "The principle which prompts to save is the desire of bettering our condition, a desire which, though generally calm and dispassionate, comes with us from the womb and never leaves us until we go into the grave."[4] Thus

[3] *Op. cit.*, I, 16.

[4] *Op. cit.*, I, 323.

by following his own interest, as the individual sees it, he is furthering the progress of his neighbors and his nation toward wealth and prosperity. Directly growing out of the division of labor are all the facts of exchange. The invention of money, the variations in the price of labor, of rent, and of commodities are all explained by the higgling of self-interested individuals, each unwilling to pay more than is necessary for what he wants, or to sell for less than he can get. So when capital has been accumulated, its employment is regulated in every case by the prospective profits to the owner, and not by any concern for the public welfare.

But I need not multiply illustrations from these familiar economic doctrines. Other more striking cases can be found in which Adam Smith introduces the principle of self-interest as an explanation of facts usually regarded as outside the sphere of economic rivalry. England had an admirable system of justice in the eighteenth century—at least so Adam Smith thought—and the cause of its efficiency, he says, is the ancient system of maintaining the courts by fees collected from the parties at law; for under this system of competition "each court endeavored, by superior dispatch and impartiality, to draw to itself as many cases as it could."[5] In contrast with the courts, the English universities of the eighteenth century were centers of indolence and intellectual apathy, and had almost ceased to function as educational agencies. The cause of this deplorable state of affairs, which Smith had abundant opportunity to observe during his six years at Oxford, was the presence of great endowments and the lack of competitive conditions to stimulate the activity of self-interest among the professors.

It is the interest of every man to live as much at his ease as he can; and if his emoluments are to be precisely the same, whether he does or does not perform some very laborious duty, it is certainly his interest, at least as

[5] *Op. cit.*, II, 212.

interest is vulgarly understood, either to neglect it altogether or, if he is subject to some authority which will not suffer him to do this, to perform it in as careless and slovenly a manner as that authority will permit. If he is naturally active and a lover of labor, it is his interest to employ that activity in any way from which he can derive some advantage, rather than in the performance of his duty, from which he can derive none.[6]

Contrast with this the efficiency of the teachers in ancient Greece, whose talents were developed through the effort to attract as many students as possible. Likewise, Adam Smith thinks that the industry and zeal of the inferior Catholic clergy are in most cases superior to those of the Protestant clergy, for the reason that they depend upon the voluntary contributions of their hearers rather than upon a fund provided by the state or upon endowments.[7] Here, then, are three classes of men—the judge, the university professor, the priest—in whom the motive of self-interest is in general more efficacious than the sense of duty. It sometimes seems as if Smith could see no other real explanation of human activity. When the Quakers of Pennsylvania set free their slaves, we can be sure, Smith says, that the number of these slaves was not very great. Had they made any considerable part of their property, such a resolution could never have been agreed to. And even then they were set free only because slave labor was unprofitable in that corn-growing colony.[8]

This is not all. Adam Smith not only represents self-interest as the usual and most powerful motive in economic activity, but by showing that economic institutions arise naturally, i.e., spontaneously, through the operation of this principle in human nature, and that they are socially useful in proportion to the degree to which they have been allowed to arise naturally, i.e., through the operation of self-interest, he represents self-interest as the motive which *should* actuate men in their economic rela-

[6] *Op. cit.*, II, 250. [7] *Op. cit.*, II, 274, 275. [8] *Op. cit.*, I, 365.

tions. He even deprecates reliance upon any other motive. "I have never known much good done," he says, "by those who affected to trade for the public good. It is an affectation, indeed, not very common among merchants, and very few words need be employed in dissuading them from it."[9]

In view of these passages we can understand why Ruskin referred to Adam Smith as "the half-bred and half-witted Scotchman who taught the deliberate blasphemy: 'Thou shalt hate the Lord, thy God, damn his law, and covet thy neighbor's goods.' " Other critics, with less talent for denunciation and more concern for understanding Smith, have pointed out that the picture of human nature presented in the *Wealth of Nations* is seemingly inconsistent with the viewpoint of his other great work, the *Theory of Moral Sentiments.* In this work, published seventeen years before, Smith aligns himself with Hutcheson and Shaftesbury, the "benevolent" moralists, in opposition to the egoistic ethics of Hobbes and Mandeville, who asserted that the only motive of human activity is self-love. Consequently it has been maintained that the two works represent different stages of Adam Smith's own development: the *Moral Sentiments* an earlier, altruistic stage; the *Wealth of Nations,* a later, cynical, materialistic stage, in which altruism has been replaced by selfishness, and virtue by material wealth. Those who found this explanation satisfactory also found no difficulty in assigning the cause of this change to Smith's residence in France during the years 1764–66. According to this ingenious view, these three years in France not only gave Smith his most important economic ideas, through his contact with Turgot and the Physiocrats, but also, through his friendship with Voltaire, Diderot, d'Alembert, and other leaders of the French Enlightenment, changed him from an idealist to a materialist. Unfortunately for this theory, which was quite popular in the later nineteenth century,

[9] *Op. cit.,* I, 421.

there was discovered some thirty years ago a manuscript copy of a set of notes taken down by a student of Smith's at Glasgow in the year 1763, the very last year of his professorship. These notes of Smith's lectures enable us to ascertain definitely the economic doctrines taught by him before he came in personal contact with the Physiocrats, and to determine the precise nature of his indebtedness to the French thinkers. Cannan, who edited these lecture notes, has made quite clear, in the introduction to this volume and in the introduction to his edition of the *Wealth of Nations,* the elements of Smith's economic theory which he owed to the Physiocrats. In general, this indebtedness is much less than was formerly supposed. The theory of stock or capital in Book II, the theory of unproductive labor, and perhaps the doctrine of distribution, were borrowed from Physiocratic theory; but his economic liberalism, his doctrine of the division of labor, and—what is most to the point here—his view of the primary rôle played by self-interest in the economic order —these doctrines were taught by Smith before going to France. It is therefore impossible to suppose that he underwent a radical change of view between the period of the professorship at Glasgow and the appearance of the *Wealth of Nations.*

In fact, if those who believed there was a discrepancy between the *Moral Sentiments* and the *Wealth of Nations* had but taken the pains to consult the former work thoroughly, a great deal of this alleged discrepancy would have disappeared. It is true that in the *Moral Sentiments* Adam Smith opposes the egoistic doctrine that man acts only from self-love, and exalts benevolence as the highest virtue. But there are other, inferior virtues recognized, such as prudence, frugality, industry, self-reliance. These virtues must be restrained and regulated by justice, but when so regulated they are conducive to the welfare of the general public as well as of the individual. The important consideration is that these self-interested activities must be regulated by justice. Very little is said in the *Wealth of Nations* about the principles of justice (that was to have been the subject of Adam Smith's projected work on jurisprudence); but justice is of course always presupposed as necessary for the existence of nations at all, especially of wealthy nations. Justice is, in fact, so very important that its administration is one of the three duties which Smith intrusts to the sovereign. In short, unregulated self-interest is no more advocated in the *Wealth of Nations* than it is in the *Moral Sentiments,* whereas in the latter work the moral value of the inferior virtues, when properly regulated, is fully recognized.

Adam Smith's employment of self-interest in the *Wealth of Nations,* then, does not mean either that he regarded self-love as the only actuating principle in human nature, or that he recommended unrestrained selfishness as the best means of promoting public wealth. It merely means that Smith was preaching, in the economic world, the same gospel of individual rights and individual liberty which in one form or another was the burden of eighteenth-century social thought. It expresses his faith in the value of the individual and in the importance of freeing the individual man from the fetters of outworn economic institutions. If Smith had lived to complete his work on jurisprudence we might have seen a similar application of his individualistic principles to the subject of law and political institutions. As it is, we have evidence of his warm sympathy for the political and religious liberalism of the Continent. He was ever a devoted admirer of Voltaire, and he followed the development of Rousseau's thought with the greatest interest. He was far from sharing the political conservatism of the French Physiocrats, with whose economic liberalism he was, of course, in entire sympathy. They were distinctly of the old régime, and believed that the *ordre naturel* could only be instituted and maintained in operation through the absolute power of an enlightened few. But

Smith was as convinced a believer in equality as any revolutionary leader. "The difference between the most dissimilar characters, between a philosopher and a common street porter, for example, seems to arise not so much from nature as from habit, custom, and education."[10] In the main, it is dissimilarity of occupation which occasions the diversity of character. Plato, it will be remembered, had precisely the opposite opinion: it is difference of nature which makes possible the division of labor and the dissimilarity of occupation. Plato's view is probably the truer, but Adam Smith's is more characteristic of his century. It is this natural similarity and equality of all individuals that furnishes the basis for one of the theories of value found in the *Wealth of Nations*. If all individuals are naturally alike, it follows that "equal quantities of labor, at all times and places, may be said to be of equal value to the laborer." Hence "labor is the real measure of the exchangeable value of all commodities."[11] Smith seems to have felt, like the writers of the Declaration of Independence and the Declaration of the Rights of Man, that in the conception of abstract individuals he had reached entities as absolute and irreducible as the atoms of the physical world were then thought to be.

There is another element besides individualism involved in Adam Smith's doctrine of self-interest. This is the conception of a rational or natural social order, in which there is a complete reconciliation of the interests of the individual and the interests of the society. This natural order is not merely an ideal for future realization, but an order which Smith conceived of as actually existing in every society, though not fully realized in his day because of the unwise restrictions of governments. To realize the natural order in its fulness it is necessary only to remove these restrictions, and restore the conditions of free competition, the system of natural liberty. "All systems of prefer-

[10] *Op. cit.*, I, 17.

[11] *Op. cit.*, I, 32, 35.

ence or of restraint, therefore, being thus completely taken away, the obvious and simple system of natural liberty establishes itself of its own accord."[12] In calling this order "natural," Smith means to say that it is superior to human contrivance, and expresses the ultimate and rational foundation of things. It may be hindered by the unwise tinkering of governments; but it can never be completely destroyed.

> In the political body the natural effort which every man is continually making to better his condition is a principle of preservation capable of preventing and correcting, in many respects, the bad effects of a political economy in some degree both partial and oppressive. In the political body the wisdom of nature has fortunately made ample provision for remedying many of the bad effects of the folly and injustice of man, in the same manner as it has done in the natural body for remedying those of his sloth and intemperance.[13]

Adam Smith's reasons for believing in the reality of this "natural order" were partly empirical, but mainly, it is safe to say, a priori. Experience shows many instances of the socially beneficent results that come from individual enterprise carried on without any thought of public gain: the employment of stock in the production or procurement of the commodities most needed; the diversion of labor into occupations most highly paid and therefore most in demand by the society; and, underlying all these exchange aspects of the economic order, the primary impulse to appropriate and utilize the material goods and the forces of nature for the satisfaction of human desires. But Adam Smith clearly saw the reverse side of the medallion: the cases in which the interests of certain groups, e.g., the merchants and manufacturers, are contrary to the public interest; and those cases of enterprises necessary for the public good, such as the maintenance of justice and the construction of public works, "which it can never be for the interest of any individual,

[12] *Op. cit.*, II, 184.

[13] *Op. cit.*, II, 172.

or small number of individuals, to erect and maintain."[14] The empirical evidence is therefore far from conclusive. The real foundation for Adam Smith's faith in the ultimate harmony of the conflicting interests of individuals is to be found in his theology. As I have said before, natural theology constituted the primary division of moral philosophy as it was taught at Glasgow by Smith. We have no systematic exposition of this part of his lectures, nor have we any indication that he ever contemplated writing on the subject at all. About all that we know of him in this connection is the statement in Dugald Stewart's memoir of Smith that in these lectures he considered the proofs of the existence and attributes of God, and those principles of the human mind on which religion is founded. We can supplement this meager description both with fragmentary passages from Smith's works and with what we know to have been characteristic of natural theology in the eighteenth century. Natural theology, as then conceived, dealt with those universal religious truths which underlie all positive religions and can be discovered by the human reason independently of a divine revelation: such truths, for instance, as the existence of God and the moral government of the world. The chief concern of natural theology was to furnish a foundation for morality independent of positive religion; with religion in the popular sense it had nothing to do. Like most of his contemporaries, we find Adam Smith, in the *Moral Sentiments*, relying upon natural theology as a support for moral principles, and at the same time deprecating anything that savors of religious zeal or enthusiasm as excrescences upon, or perversions of, the true religion. Smith was by no means a sectarian. The public interests, he thinks, are best promoted by an equal and impartial toleration of all sects; for the competition of these different sects with one another will "probably reduce the doctrine of the greater part of them to that pure and rational

[14] *Op. cit.*, II, 185.

religion, free from every mixture of absurdity, imposture, or fanaticism, such as wise men in all ages of the world have wished to see established."[15]

In accordance with this theology, Adam Smith looks upon social and economic institutions as the product of a power beyond human power, of a reason which human reason can fathom but cannot imitate. He speaks with awe of "the great, the immense fabric of human society, that fabric which to raise and support seems in this world, if I may say so, to have been the darling care of Nature."[16] (Nature, spelt with a capital *N*, equals God.) He sees the working of an invisible hand in the action of self-interested individuals. Providence divided the earth among a few lordly masters, and these are "led by an invisible hand to make nearly the same distribution of the necessaries of life, which would have been made had the earth been divided into equal portions among all its inhabitants; and thus, without intending it, without knowing it, advance the interests of society."[17] Likewise the capitalist, in preferring domestic to foreign industry, and in directing that industry most profitably, is "led by an invisible hand to promote an end which was no part of his intention," viz., the public good.[18]

This reliance upon the invisible hand, this appeal to a natural order which maintains itself in and through the activity of self-seeking individuals, has frequently been regarded as a defect in Smith's thought, at least in his scientific thought. Certainly it is an expression of the eighteenth-century faith in the beneficent harmony and the ultimate rationality of things. But besides expressing in concrete form this faith in the processes of nature, Adam Smith's doctrine has great significance in another direction: it is an effort to think of the social order as a

[15] *Op. cit.*, II, 278.

[16] *Moral Sentiments,* Pt. II, Sec. II, chap. iii.

[17] *Ibid.*, Pt. IV, chap. i.

[18] *Wealth of Nations,* I, 421.

genuine organic unity, with principles of structure and functioning which maintain themselves independently of the wills of individuals. It expresses, to use technical terms, a realistic, as contrasted with a nominalistic, conception of society. In considering the relation between the individual and the social order, we may proceed in one of two ways. We may start from the individual and attempt to interpret the institutions and the phenomena of society as the results of instincts, or characteristics, which are found in the individual man; or we may start from the concrete historical order and interpret the nature of the individual man through the social forces which have moulded him. The first way of proceeding makes society a derivative of the individual; the second shows the individual to be a product of society. Both ways of proceeding are legitimate, for each brings out one side of the complex organic relation between the individual and the institutions and social observances among which he lives. Adam Smith is employing the former method when he attempts to show how specific economic institutions arise from certain human traits, e.g., the division of labor from the instinct to barter; or when he constructs the whole economic order upon the activity of individual self-interest. This interpretation of social facts in terms of individual traits was, in fact, the more common procedure of the eighteenth century; and the almost universal employment of this individualistic method is one of the defects of eighteenth-century thought. The concrete social environment must also be taken into consideration in explaining the nature of the individual man, and Adam Smith is one of the very few thinkers of his time who had any realization of this complementary point of view.

This concrete social point of view is best expressed, not in the *Wealth of Nations,* but in the *Theory of Moral Sentiments.* This work has by no means been as influential in the history of thought as was its illustrious successor. Few people ever read it now, except antiquaries of thought and persons celebrating the sesquicentennial of the *Wealth of Nations*. Its own sesquicentennial was not observed. And yet it was one of the most popular books of the eighteenth century; it procured its author immediate fame, not only in England and Scotland, but even in France, where Smith became almost as popular in the salons of Paris as Hume had been. During Smith's lifetime it went through six English editions and was published in at least three French versions. The oblivion in which it now rests is due partly, no doubt, to the greater success and influence of the *Wealth of Nations;* but also to intrinsic faults. Its rhetoric, so much admired in its day, now rather palls; and its treatment of the moral experience seems at times superficial, even insincere. And yet in its fundamental doctrine, the doctrine of sympathy, Adam Smith develops a highly original theory of the moral consciousness, one which is far ahead of the current individualistic doctrines of his contemporaries.

Like the natural theology of the seventeenth and eighteenth centuries, the English ethics of this period was concerned with finding a rational foundation for morality, a foundation independent of theology or ecclesiastical authority. As ethical inquiry proceeded, two problems soon began to stand out as distinct from one another: the problem of the content of morality, or the nature of right, and second, the problem of the moral faculty by which we distinguish between right and wrong. The latter question, at the time at which Smith wrote, proved the more absorbing of the two, and this is the question with which Smith is chiefly concerned in his *Moral Sentiments*. This work is therefore not so much an attempt to determine the nature of morality as an ingenious theory of how we come to judge certain actions good and certain characters virtuous. This is not to say that it ignores altogether the question of the nature of virtue; but Smith's answer to this question involves nothing more distinctive than an effort to unite in one comprehensive view the diverse answers given by preceding moralists. He finds virtue to consist, not in benevolence alone, but in benevolence, justice, and certain inferior virtues summed up under the name of prudence. Besides these three, he borrows from ancient ethics a fourth constituent, propriety. Clearly this conception of virtue is to be praised more for its breadth of view than for its logical clearness and consistency. But after all, the whole theory of the nature of virtue is in the main incidental to the real inquiry which Smith has in mind. The more important, and by far the larger, portion of his work is given over to the development of a psychological theory of the origin of the moral judgment. This portion of the *Moral Sentiments* is unique; it may be said to have anticipated, in some important respects, the results of later social philosophy and psychology with respect to the origin of the moral consciousness.

The primary factor in the development of the moral sentiments is what Smith calls sympathy, or the capacity which we have of entering into the situation of another and experiencing an emotion similar to what we would feel if in his situation. The misery and misfortunes of others excite emotions in us similar to the emotions the sufferers themselves feel; and likewise we take pleasure in beholding their happiness. When we see a stroke aimed at the leg or arm of another we instinctively draw back our own as if it were threatened. In watching a tight-rope walker we ourselves feel a sense of relief when he has reached the platform at the end. Any passion whatever of which the human mind is susceptible may be reflected in the sentiments of the attentive bystander. Furthermore, there is a distinct pleasure when our own sentiments accord with those of our fellowmen. Nothing pleases us more than to observe in other men a sympathetic echo of our own emotions; and nothing chagrins us more than an appearance of the contrary; as when a man, after having endeavored to divert the company, looks round and sees that nobody laughs at his jests but himself. Now this pleasure which arises from a mutual accord of sentiments, and the disagreeable feeling aroused by this disproportion, is the ultimate basis of the moral judgment. Briefly stated, when we approve of the actions or emotions of another we do so because we perceive that we fully sympathize with his sentiments, i.e., that we would feel the same in his place, and even now feel something of what he feels. When we sympathize we approve; and by approving we judge the sentiment in question to be appropriate, or suitable, or just, with respect to the given situation.

This is really all there is in the theory, though the detailed application of this simple principle to the various forms of moral judgment is most interesting and ingenious. The simplest cases are those in which we approve of the sentiments of another as being suitable or proportioned to the exciting cause. These are what Smith calls judgments of propriety. More complex cases are judgments of merit or demerit, in which our sympathy or lack of sympathy with the person in question is joined with or supplemented by our sympathy with the person affected by his action or emotion. The sense of merit is then a compound sentiment, consisting of a direct sympathy with the sentiment of the man who has conferred the benefit, and an indirect sympathy with the gratitude of the recipient. Likewise, the sense of demerit is compounded of a direct antipathy to the sentiments of the agent, and an indirect sympathy with the resentment of the sufferer. As for gratitude and resentment, they are instinctive feelings which the theory of sympathy presupposes; they are principles with which Nature (again with a capital *N*) has endowed mankind for the preservation and welfare of society.

But what is the foundation of our approbation or disapprobation of our own actions? This is a case of reflected sympathy. We approve or disapprove of ourselves by identifying ourselves in imagination with the spectators of our actions, and perceiving whether under such conditions we can or cannot sympathize with our own conduct. In other words, we judge ourselves through the approbation or disapprobation of others. Society is a mirror which shows us ourselves. Our first moral criticisms refer to the characters and conduct of other persons, and only later do we learn to judge our own conduct and character by considering how they appear to our neighbors. A human creature who should grow up in some solitary place, without any communication with his kind, would have no idea of virtue or vice. It may be objected that our moral consciousness demands not so much that we receive the approval of our fellow-men as that we be worthy of their approval. There are cases in which our conscience approves of our conduct in spite of the disapproval of our fellow-men. Such cases are explained by Adam Smith in the following way. Our observation of the conduct of others insensibly leads us to form certain general rules concerning what is fit and proper either to be done or to be avoided. Actions which we have observed to shock all our natural sentiments and to arouse the detestation of all our fellow-men we resolve to avoid, and make a general rule to that effect. Thus are formed the general rules of morality, which in their entirety constitute the moral conscience; they are ultimately derived from our experiences of the approval or disapproval of men, but are capable of resisting in special cases the force of our own passions or the temporary disapproval of our fellow-men. We appeal, in other words, not to the judgment of our immediate companions, but to the impartial spectator, who is freed from the limitations of their knowledge and experience. These general rules which have been distilled from social experience may even be looked upon as the ultimate foundation of what is just and unjust in human conduct, and as having their foundation in the command of God. Thus the morality of sympathy and social experience leads up ultimately to the same theological world-view which we found supporting Smith's belief in the natural order of economic liberty.

These are the essential parts of the *Theory of Moral Sentiments*. It is a theory which omits some of the important problems of ethics and deals sometimes rather superficially with the problems it touches. Yet it has the merit of opening what was practically a new line of inquiry in eighteenth-century thought. It looks for the origin of the moral judgment, not in an innate individual source of insight, but in social experience. The individual's moral consciousness with its judgments of approval and disapproval is a reflection, or a derivative, of the social consciousness; it grows through experience in society, and represents the demands of his fellow-men upon the individual. This theory, therefore, looks upon the individual not as an absolute and irreducible entity existing prior to social experience, but as a product of his social environment. It is true there are certain absolute elements that are supposed to exist in the individual, such as gratitude and resentment, pleasure and pain; but Smith's larger purpose in the *Moral Sentiments* is to show how these original passions develop into the moral consciousness through the working of sympathy in social experience. This was a relatively new line of thought for the eighteenth century. It is a noteworthy abandonment of facile abstractions in favor of a more concrete and positive method of inquiry. Obviously the theory of the social origin of the moral judgments goes far toward explaining the variations in moral standards that have taken place in the course of history. In one section of the *Moral Sentiments,* Adam Smith actually employs it for this purpose, and so points the way toward the same kind of treatment of ethics as Montesquieu had already given to laws, and as he himself had already employed with respect to economic phenomena in the historical passages of the *Wealth of Nations*. The point of view here presented in the *Moral Sentiments* and in the historical portions of the *Wealth of Nations* is an anticipation of the concrete historical outlook of the nineteenth century.

May I suggest also that this ethical theory is of great importance for understanding the doctrine of the economic harmony between the interests of the individual and the interests of the public which we found maintained in the *Wealth of Nations?* These various forms of self-interested activity upon which the economic order depends, i.e., desire for place, and conveniences, and honor, are motives which have been instilled into the individual, partially at least, through his social experience. As a product of society the individual is necessarily interested in securing those ends of which his fellow-men approve; and we here have an internal principle of regulation and adaptation sufficient in time to bring about that general harmony between the interests of each and the interests of all which the *Wealth of Nations* posits. It might almost be said that the doctrine of sympathy is a necessary presupposition of the doctrine of the natural order expounded in the *Wealth of Nations.* At least it seems quite probable that Adam Smith had this earlier theory in mind as a covering for the naked economic individualism which he expounds in the later work, and that it furnished him with an additional reason for believing in the absolute value of individual liberty. It is because the individual is in his very nature socialized, a product of the social environment, that he can in general be left without external interference to act in accordance with the demands of his individual nature.

Thus we arrive, by way of the *Moral Sentiments,* at a deeper understanding of that individualism which is presented in the economic liberalism and laissez faire of the *Wealth of Nations.* It was an ethical, and not merely an economic, individualism which Adam Smith held up as an ideal. The apocryphal personage mentioned at the beginning of my lecture who is supposed to have read the *Wealth of Nations* in its entirety—may his tribe increase!—could testify that Adam Smith looks at the economic prosperity of a nation in the broadest way possible; he sees its causes in human nature and in history, its effects, beneficial or otherwise, upon the individual and the society; and he by no means regards it as the supreme concern, either of moral philosophy or of human endeavor. But he was too canny to despise wealth, too wise not to recognize that the new era of material enterprise has possibilities for the advancement and perfecting of the human species which no other period ever possessed. Perhaps he was not sufficiently alive to other less glowing possibilities of the present age, but I am inclined to think that the effective moral philosophy of the future will be that which accepts, with Adam Smith, the material resources of the modern world, and the human traits which have created it, and attempts to determine under these conditions "wherein consists the happiness and perfection of a man, not only as an individual, but as a member of a family, of a state, and of the great society of mankind."

CHAPTER VII

THE INTRODUCTION OF ADAM SMITH ON THE CONTINENT

MELCHIOR PALYI

I

An attempt to trace the influence of Adam Smith on Continental economic thought involves in a striking degree the main kinds of difficulties which face the historian of the social sciences. The first difficulty arises from the fact that the influence may not have resulted simply from the development or propagation of certain ideas initiated by the hero. The influence of Smith's own ideas may have been, and, in the opinion of some, was, limited; in fact his fame was probably in part due to ideas not altogether his own. Who could dare to say exactly how much of his apparent influence on the Continental free trade movement was in reality due to other liberal thinkers? The second difficulty is the task of separating the practical influences from the scientific. Economic, like political, thought affects both science and practice; we have to confine ourselves here to purely literary tests. Furthermore, in the case of Adam Smith it would be very difficult indeed to state explicitly what proportion of his tremendous influence on the Continent was due to his *ideas,* and to what degree his *style* and the charming personality it expressed were responsible at least for his initial success. How far did his book merely present views which were already in the minds of the most prominent men of the time; how far was it only the expression of the trend which needed a formal statement of just this kind? At any rate, he was the "man of the moment." His style appealed to the scientist and the general reader, the practical statesman and the business man of broader view, and to the most orthodox exponent of any kind of "natural law." He was also the representative of the English, who, to the Continental peoples, embodied during the revolutionary and Napoleonic wars the opposition against imperialistic France. Important also was the extra prestige and persuasiveness for Continental readers which English writers on economic questions derived from the English leadership in economic practice and in the evolution of a more effective organizaton of industry.

His success on the Continent has to some extent, therefore, roots similar to those of his contemporary, Edmund Burke, although their ideas, their methods, even their problems were decidedly different, as different as the men themselves and their personal careers. The Continentals who were looking for spiritual allies against the French supremacy, and even the French opponents to the great Revolution, found in Burke and Smith the kind of allies they wanted. It is very enlightening, for instance, to follow the letters of vom Stein, the great reformer of Prussia, or of Frederic Gentz, the intimate friend and political adviser of the Duke of Metternich; the semi-liberal aristocrat Stein and the semi-conservative bourgeois Gentz, the two leading representatives of political thought in Germany during the Napoleonic period, were united in their admiration for Adam Smith and for Burke. And such was true also of their followers at that time in Italy and Russia, as well as in Central Europe. Just as Burke's traditionalism became the doctrinal foundation, on which many kinds of political theories opposed to French revolutionary ideas could be built up, so the liberalism of Smith supplied an arsenal of arguments against the Napoleonic system of Continental blockade (1805–14).

But, of course, his fame was based on a more solid foundation than the short-run international situation created by the Napoleonic wars. The historian may be inclined to divide the

150 years since 1776 into three main parts. The first period (1776–1830) may be called the one of the introduction and scientific triumph of the *Wealth of Nations*. The second period (1830–70) was that of its final diffusion; it was the time during which the practical teachings of Adam Smith had their glorious days of actual application to policies in England as well as on the Continent. From the beginning of the reaction against the theory and practice of free trade to the present day may be regarded as the third period. This last period was characterized also by a struggle for dominance between the influence of Adam Smith and three sets of rival economic doctrines: the post-Smithian English classical economists, and especially David Ricardo; the historical school; and the neomercantilists. During this third period the position of Adam Smith in economic thought and economic policy of the Continent has shown various and divergent features. The three periods are, to be sure, rather artificial and overlapping temporal units, which cannot be sharply marked off from each other; neither do the characteristics here attributed to them account for every line of movement relating to our problem. But for purposes of general orientation they will serve, even though the third may be characterized more accurately by lack of uniform trend than by any other single feature. It is the first, mainly, with which we have here to deal.

II

The eighteenth century has been called by Hegel the "excited century" and rightly so, for at least the second half of it is filled with an atmosphere of intellectual activity and intellectual excitement which has few parallels in human history. The whole civilized world seemed to be in the grip of an extremely intense feeling that the very foundations of society, its organization, and all its important functions were in a state of transition. The goal of this tremendous evolution, if not revolution, was considered by some as uncertain, by others as some kind of utopian community with unchecked future development of mankind. Still others recognized it as a more moderate but decidedly profound turning of history, evidenced by the beginnings of the technical revolution, by the overthrowing of feudal state and class organization, and by similar developments.[1]

This state of mind, which found its most expressive outburst in the French Revolution and which during the whole nineteenth century continued in many ways, may also explain the remarkable intellectual interconnection between the European countries of the time. In spite of the poor communications, intellectual influences spread more easily and international scientific relations were, generally speaking, probably better developed than at present. Nationalistic feeling was of course much less pronounced in the atmosphere of the aristocratic eighteenth century than of the democratic twentieth. In the former period, social science in each nation was less self-sufficient and more interested in external development. Undoubtedly, the number of foreign scientific books annually translated into German, French, or Italian, was at that time much larger than at present. At any rate, people on the whole Continent read the English and even the American literature of the day with a keen interest strikingly opposed to the trend of isolation so typical of the present. Alexander Hamilton's report presented to the American Congress on January 19, 1795, was a year later commented on and discussed

[1] Cf. Léonce de Lavergne, *Les économistes français du 18e siècle* (Paris, 1870), pp. 465 f.: "Les derniers mois de 1788 et les premiers de 1789 furent l'apogée ... de toute chose. Les meilleurs esprits se laissaient aller à un véritable enivrement; on rêvait un avenir indéfini de liberté, d'égalité, de paix, de travail, de richesse, de bonheur universel. 'Ceux qui n'ont pas vecu dans la société française aux approches de 1789,' disait longtemps après M. de Talleyrand, 'ne connaissent pas le plus grand charme de la vie.' "

in detail by the German professor Sartorius of Goettingen.[2] The technical discussions on the problems of bank restriction in England and the report of the Bullion Committee of 1810 were followed with keen interest by Napoleon's *Moniteur* as well as by German political writers; as early as 1811 the *Report of the Bullion Committee* appeared in an anonymous translation. Pietro Verri's *Meditazioni sull' economia politica* (1771) were twice translated into German, three times into French, and got also a Dutch edition. These are just a few striking instances. It is not surprising under such conditions that the first French translation of the *Wealth of Nations* appeared in 1779 (by Blavet) and that one volume of the first German translation (by T. F. Schiller) came out in the same year as the *Wealth of Nations* itself. Before the century closed, this German translation had passed through three editions; meanwhile a second and much better translation, which the "popular philosopher" Christian Garbe brought out in 1786 had met with great success. In France not less than six editions of three different translations were available before 1801, the year in which the fourth French translation, that of Germain Garnier, appeared.[3] An early translation ascribed to the famous Abbé Morellet, never was printed.[4] The first Italian edition appeared in 1779 in Naples;[5] the first Span-

[2] *Handbuch der Staatswirtschaft zum Gebrauch bey akademischen Vorlesungen nach Adam Smith's Grundsätzen ausgearbeitet von Georg Sartorius* (Berlin, 1796), pp. xi f.

[3] Cf. E. Allix, "L'oeuvre économique de Germain Garnier, traducteur d'A. Smith et disciple de Cantillon," *Revue d'Histoire des Doctrines économiques et sociales*, 1912, pp. 1 f.; de Waha, *Die Nationalökonomie in Frankreich* (Stuttgart, 1910), p. 11.

[4] Cf. J. Rae, *Life of Adam Smith* (1875), p. 359. The "moral sentiments" of Adam Smith were already known to the French public by several translations: one by Blavet (in several editions), another by Condorcet; cf. *Biographie universelle* (Paris, 1825), XLII, 486.

[5] Cf. Tommaso Fornari, *Delle teorie economiche nelle provincie Napolitane dal 1735 al 1839* (Milano, 1888), p. 61.

ish (translated by J. A. Ortiz) in 1794;[6] the Russian, ordered by Tzar Alexander I, in 1802–06 (translated by N. Politkoffski);[7] and F. Dväbye brought out a Danish edition in 1779–80 in two volumes.

The mere number of translations and editions is a sign of public interest in the work of an author; Adam Smith had, in France at least, found followers from the very beginning, and this not only among economists in the technical sense of the word. As early as 1785 the Assemblé des Notables de Paris had publicly discussed his free-trade policy, and this discussion apparently attracted much attention. Yet even in France, the success developed slower than is usually assumed.[8] Before about 1800, the *Richesse des nations* was recognized as the important work of a distinguished foreigner; still it was a foreign book, the work of a patriotic son of France's traditional and greatest enemy. The physiocrats, of course, had little inclination toward an author who had treated them in a rather scornful way. Dupont de Nemours expressed their opinion in 1782, by calling the book a "livre estimable" which does not contain any truth unmentioned in Turgot's *Réflections;* all that Smith added lacks, he wrote, exactness and is no good.[9] The opponents of the physiocratic school, on the other hand, may have been at first tired of the purely theoretical discussion; the empirical spirit of the traditional mercantilism still prevailed, although it had been given a highly enlightened form of expression. Voltaire's *Dictionnaire*

[6] Cf. Palgrave's *Dictionary of Political Economy,* Vol. III., art. "Spanish School of Political Economy" by E. Castelot.

[7] *Ibid.,* art. "Russian School of Political Economy" by Ivan Miklachewsky.

[8] As did assume the next generation, at least; but even the excellent essay of Professor Allix speaks only of the "success" of Smith in France (*op. cit.,* pp. 2 f.) without mentioning the qualifications of this success during the first twenty-five years.

[9] Cf. G. Schelle, *Dupont de Nemours et l'école physiocratique* (Paris, 1888), p. 159.

Philosophique (art. "Patrie") calmly stated the mercantilistic preconception of the *Philosophes:* "Nous faisons autant de perte que l'étranger de gain." The *ancien régime* was before 1789 and especially after the failure of Turgot's ministry too much of a reality; the overwhelming importance of agriculture as the economic basis of the ruling feudal class too obvious[10] to allow, in "realistic" minds, for the pleasant but apparently paradoxical ideas of a free-trade and industrial philosophy. The revolutionary years again brought more urgent problems in the foreground; the political interest prevailed by far over the economic. Even leading economists like Mercier de la Rivière, who died an unregenerate monarchist in 1794, published nothing more than political pamphlets. Linguet's *Annales politiques civiles et littéraires du XVIIIe siècle* (until 1792) as well as the *Décades philosophiques,* the periodical of the *Philosophes* since 1794, in which young Jean Baptiste Say played a very active rôle, also show the prevalence of the same type of interest.[11] The kind of *Kriegswirtschaft* developing during those years could hardly promote the currency of a purely liberal economic philosophy. Only after the "conspiracy" of Baboeuf, when on the one hand the growing discontent with the "socialistic" trends of the Revolution[12] led to what Aulard calls the *République bourgeoise* (after 1795) and when the reaction against the strong

[10] J. Pecchio, *Histoire de l'économie politique en Italie* ..., trad. par L. Gallois (Paris, 1830), pp. 274 f., mentions already this underlying factor, quoting Ganilh as his own source.

[11] The analysis of the revolutionary periodicals in Vols. III–VII of Hatin's *Histoire politique et littéraire de la presse en France* (Paris, 1857 f.) does not take notice of those mentioned in the text. On the many-sided development of the *Décades* under Say's and P. L. Roederer's directorship, cf. Fr. Picavet, *Les idéologues* (Paris, 1891), pp. 86–100.

[12] V. F. von Hacke, *Züsammenbruch und Aufstieg des französischen Wirtschaftslebens 1789–99* (München, 1923), pp. 96 f., 109 f.; Guthrie, *Socialism before the French Revolution* (New York, 1907), chap. vii–viii; Lichtenberger, *Le socialisme et la révolution française* (Paris, 1899).

attempts of the landowners to control the state began to prepare the way for a revulsion in the liberal sense, did the situation change in a manner favorable to a widespread acceptance of Smith's doctrines and point of view.

Similarly slow were the beginnings in Germany and Italy. Italian economic writers in the second half of the eighteenth century, such as Genovesi and Galiani in the South, Ortes, Verri and Beccaria in the North, showed insights to fundamental issues of economic theory and policy which in many cases rivaled those of the English classical writers.[13] Cesare Beccaria's principle that "every economical operation may be reduced to the means of procuring the greatest possible quantity of labour and action" anticipated Smith's labor-value theory[14] as the population theories of Ortes and of Ricci foreshadowed the Malthusian doctrine. Gian Rinaldo Carli (1720–95) tried to prove as early as 1770 in his *Breve ragionamento sopra i bilanci economici delle nazioni* that the balance of trade with a single foreign country does not provide any measure of wealth; the prosperity of a nation depends on many other factors. Pietro Verri's book on the *Elementi del commercio* (1765) and his *Riflessioni sulle leggi vincolanti . . .* , published later (1796), are known for their inclination toward free trade, influenced probably by the physiocrats, whose intellectual influence may have been also responsible for the Grand-Duke Leopold's partial free trade in Toscana.

But, on the whole, the mercantilistic spirit still prevailed, combined with a greater or lesser amount of "modern" social

[13] Cf. Zuckerkandl, *Zur Theorie des Preises* (Leipzig, 1889), pp. 44 f., 200 f.; R. Kaulla, *Geschichtliche Entwicklung der modernen Werttheorien* (Tübingen, 1906), pp. 112 f.; Augusto Graziani, *Storia critica della teoria del valore in Italia* (Milano, 1889); especially also, M. Pantaleoni, *Pure Economics* (Macmillan, 1898), *passim.*

[14] *Discourse on Public Economy and Commerce by the Marquis Caesar Beccaria Bonesaria. . . . , translated from the Italian* (London, 1769), p. 8.

philosophy and adapted at any rate to the needs and desires of local ruling dynasties and aristocracies. An early historian of Italian economics, the count Joseph Pecchio, made the sensible observation that, during the period in question, the general trend of his countrymen depended on the interests of the Province: those from the seaside rather favored commerce, while the writers from interior countries preferred agriculture. "Thus the Toscans Paoletti and Bandini, the Lombards Beccaria and Corniani were in favour of agriculture; while Galiani, Palmieri and Genovesi, all Neapolitans, recommended rather external trade, and the Venetians Zanon and Algoretti, emphasized the importance of industry."[15] The generalization may be somewhat risky; the political dismemberment of the country with the consequent narrowness of autocratic policies and the nearly complete lack of modern industrial beginnings[16] explain however, partially at least, the lack in Italy of systematic attempts in economics comparable with the English or the French and the atmosphere of weak opportunistic compromise in matters of policy.

The *Wealth of Nations* could not, in this atmosphere, easily make a great impression; it was not recognized as "the" *organon* until some time after the revolutionary armies swept over the valley of the Po. It did not seem perhaps to display a greater amount of common sense than the writings of the leading Italian authors; it even appeared, in the mercantilistic milieu, as rather dogmatic and doctrinaire; on purely theoretical matters like value problems it was often less clear and less profound than the best of the Italian writings. Consequently, even the few contemporary free-traders hardly mentioned the book. The most influential of them, the Neapolitan Gaetano Filangieri, in his rather able eclecticism of physiocratic principles and mercan-

[15] Pecchio, *op. cit.*, p. 385.

[16] The economic backwardness of Piedmont, as compared with contemporary France or Germany, was characteristic almost of the whole country; cf. G. Prato, *La vita economica in Piemonte al mezzo del secolo XVIII* (Torino, 1908).

tilistic technics does not mention either Turgot or Smith, although his work came out in 1780; and e.g., his chapter x on the sources of wealth,[17] assigning co-ordinate rôles to agriculture, industry, and commerce, suggests some influence from the West. Still in 1787, Lodovico Ricci of Modena discusses extensively not only local but also general problems of public charity and of taxation without quoting Smith.[18] Even a comparatively pronounced free-trader like the Count d'Arco (1739–91) of Mantova does not seem to know him;[19] so also the Neapolitan Giuseppe Palmieri,[20] presenting in 1790 a cautious treatment of commercial policy, does not reveal any influence of Adam Smith; to him universal free trade or moderate protection were the debatable alternatives. The nearer we come however to the expansion of the great Revolution the more does the fame of Adam Smith seem to rise. In 1790, Giambattista Vasco,[21] in his somewhat critical appraisal of guilds and monopolies quotes him mainly as an authority on some historical details. Yet, this was a progress, since the same authors' philosophical *Mémoire sur les causes de la mendicité et sur les moyens de la supprimer* (written, 1778; published in 1790), dealing with unemployment in terms of changes in the ratio between population and means of subsistence, did not even do so much. And in 1792, Francesco

[17] Filangieri, "Delle leggi politiche ed economiche," *Scrittori classici italiani di economia politica* (Milano, 1804), XXXIX, 134 f.

[18] Ricci, *Dell'origine e de progressi degl'instituti pii* ..., reprinted in *Scrittori classici italiani, parte moderna,* Vol. XLI (Milano, 1805).

[19] His three post-Smithian dissertations on trade and production appeared first in 1770, 1780, and 1782, respectively; they are reprinted in *Scrittori, parte moderna,* Vol. XXXI (1804).

[20] "Osservazioni sulle tariffe ..." (*Scrittori,* XXXVIII, 5 f.). Palmieri's book *Della ricchezza nationale* of 1792 (reprinted *ibid.,* pp. 91 f.) discusses and, for their theory of wealth, dismisses the physiocrats but ignores Smith completely, as is the case in the same author's *Reflessioni sulla pubblica felicità* ... (1789) (reprinted in *Scrittori,* Vol. XXXVII).

[21] *Della Universita delle arti e mestieri dissertazione.* Cf. pp. 189, 222, 258, 289, of the reprint in *Scrittori,* Vol. XXXIII (1804).

Mengotti's[22] moderate attack on Colbertism, practically the first Italian approximation to the classical English liberal doctrine, quotes Smith already as a well-known authority, but still just only incidentally, together with so miscellaneous a company as Dutot and Locke, Ulloa and Ustariz, Mercier and Raynal, etc.; and finally (pp. 402 f.) decides in favor of the more "moderate" policies of *uomini saggi e benemeriti* like Hume, Melon, Genovesi, and Verri. The change from the position of a hardly quoted respectable author to that of a great thinker of wide influence was indeed an enormous one and must have occurred rather suddenly some time during the early Napoleonic years. In 1808, at any rate, even a purely technical pamphlet of a high official of the Kingdom of Italy, G. Tamassia's *Del fine delle Statistiche* (Milano, 1808, pp. 6 f.) could not do better than start out with a long citation from Adam Smith on the duties of sovereigns as the foundation on which the author bases his own *lezione*. When moreover, after 1810, the influence of Say and Tracy made itself felt, the leading Italian economists of the time, Michele Agazzini and Joseph Pecchio; the Roman Carlo Bosellini; the Neapolitans Nicola Porcinavi, Francesco Fuoco, and Samuele Cagnazzi; the Sicilians Sanfilippo and Paolo Balsamo, were competing with each other in admiration for Adam Smith and Say; while a smaller number of mercantilists, mostly from the northern provinces ruled by the Austrian bureaucracy, like G. D. Romagnosi and Melchiore Gioja, rejected or accepted only with serious reservations the economics or the philosophy of the *Wealth of Nations*.[23] On the whole, of course, "the importation of Smith's

[22] "Il Colbertismo ossia della liberta di commercio de'prodotti della terra dissertazione" in *Scrittori* XLVIII, 253–419. Smith is cited on pp. 262, 273 f., 286, 324, 350, 352, 362, 405.

[23] On Italian economics in the early nineteenth century, cf. M. Mohl, "Aperçu sur les productions les plus récentes des économistes du royaume de Naples" in *Journal des Economistes,* 1844, pp. 174 f.; Augusto Graziani, *Le idee economiche degli scrittori emiliani e romagnoli* (Modena, 1883); Fornari, *op. cit.;* L. Cossa,

doctrines, instead of acting as a stimulus to reflection, only evoked a number of second-rate compilations,"[24] and the reprinting of the older writers in Baron Custodi's grand series of Italian "classical" economists (1802–16) contributed largely to the temporary survival of mercantilist trends.

The parallelism of the Italian with the German development is a very striking one. There are, however, two important differences. In Italy as in Spain, Adam Smith became popular in large part through the influence of Say and other French writers; in Germany, the success was a more genuine one. In the second place, Ricardo influenced deeply the Italian thought from the early twenties;[25] while for the German economists, disregarding Thünen, Ricardo remained for at least another fifty years the originator of some rather curious *weltfremd* exaggerations and never became really influential. But these are later developments; for the first period, until the end of the eighteenth century, the parallelism prevails. It consists practically in a neglect, or at least a minimization of the significance of the *Wealth of Nations* by the German professors who at that time (and since) almost completely dominated and represented scientific opinion; the southern and especially Austrian feudal aristocracy asserted its mental independence, but was of course very little trained for economic problems. Friedrich von Gentz in letters to Smith's translator, Christian Garbe, and in other private writings had already strongly supported the doctrines of the Scotch master in the early nineties; but this support was hardly of more importance than the pseudo-revolutionary inclinations of the

Histoire des doctrines économiques (Paris, 1899), chap. xv; more recently, Antonio Mancarella, *Le dottrine di Ricardo e gli economisti italiani della prima meta del secolo XIX* (Napoli, 1906).

[24] Loria, art. "Italian School" in Palgrave's *Dictionary of Political Economy*, Vol. II.

[25] Cf. Mancarella, *op. cit.*

romantic crowd (the Schlegels, Schelling, etc.) at that time, although it lasted at least substantially longer.[26] Official Germany, however, simply ignored Adam Smith for about twenty years. A scholar like Roscher[27] could find before 1796 but five short reviews in three different periodicals, two of them written by men of physiocratic leanings; and all of them without any importance. This in a time of eager discussion of social issues (Sturm und Drang, French Revolution) and in spite of an overproduction of books and periodicals. More surprising even in a country where economics had long been an acknowledged part of the academic teaching of *Kameralwissenschaften,* while the first chair for political economy in Italy was the one inaugurated by Genovesi in Naples in 1754 and while France had practically no provision for the public teaching of economics until after the end of the eighteenth century.[28] But this very dominance of cameralist teaching, or better to say the spirit of the study it cultivated, was perhaps the greatest obstacle to the spreading of modern thought.

The German type of mercantilism, the so-called "cameralistic" study, practically ruled the universities;[29] physiocracy had

[26] On Gentz' economic and political ideas and their rôle, cf. R. Haym, art. "Gentz" in the *Allgemeine Encyklopädie* of Ersch and Gruber, vol. LVIII (1854); E. Guglia, *Fr. von Gentz* (1901). A recent American discussion of the same subject (P. F. Reiff, *Fr. Gentz, an Opponent of the French Revolution and Napoleon* [Urbana, 1912], pp. 30–52) mentions everybody from Cicero to Mallet du Pan who may have influenced Gentz, but omits the name of Smith.

[27] *Geschichte der Nationalökonomik in Deutschland* (München, 1874), pp. 598 f.

[28] Cf. A. Graziani, *Teorie e fatti economici* (Forino, 1912), p. 3; and E. Levasseur, "L'économie politique au Conservatoire des Arts et Métiers," *Revue d'écon. pol.*, 1905–6.

[29] F. H. Moshammer's *Gedanken und Vorschläge über die neuesten Anstalten teutscher Fürsten die Kameralwissenschaften auf hohen Schulen in Flor zu bringen* (Regensburg, 1782) gives a surprising list of institutions providing for cameralistic teaching.

exerted but a slight influence. Cameralism had its productive period in the seventeenth and early eighteenth century; in the second half of the eighteenth, at any rate, it was substantially different from contemporary mercantilism in Western Europe. It was, as to its economic content, a simple collection of more or less incoherent precepts for civil service officers, offering advice on every kind of service for the more or less enlightened local tyrant and his "servants." Cameralists themselves preferred to call their field the "science of police," and this indeed expressed its real meaning. The most important representatives of this science in the period under review, men like Justi, and the Austrian Sonnenfels, liked to couple it with definitions of the state, of the duties of different kinds of citizens, etc. They did so, in order to give a more scientific appearance to this body of unsystematic knowledge which, compared with contemporary French, Italian, and English mercantilism, had but slight touch with economic developments of the time. Nevertheless this kind of teaching characterized the universities, and the same spirit prevailed in most of the about 360 tyrannical governments with which at the time the German nation was blessed. It adhered to rather primitive theories of the balance of trade as a basis of commercial policy; while in Western countries writers for two centuries had discussed the quantity theory of money, the cameralistic literature hardly ever went deeper than to realize Gresham's law,[30] and an outsider like the mintmaster of Frederick II of Prussia, Graumann, showed deeper insight into monetary problems than most of the cameralists.[31] The economic policies advocated by

[30] The scattered statements of the quantity theory by Justi and Sonnenfels are gathered in A. E. Monroe's *Monetary Theory before Adam Smith* (Cambridge, Massachusetts, 1923), pp. 201, 250, 219; Justi's opinions on money, etc., are discussed at great length, but without realizing their inconsistencies, in Luise Sommer's book (cited below), p. 273–86.

[31] It is worth while to compare Graumann's technical discussion of contemporary coinage practices (*De la proportion entre l'or el l'argent, et des monnaies*

the writers in question were the type of police regulations interfering with practically every aspect of business management and even with private consumption, mainly under the dominance of incoherent technical and technological viewpoints often contradicting each other. The same Justi, in his *Grundsätze der Polizeywissenschaft* (3d ed., with notes from Joh. Beckmann [Göttingen, 1782]), advocates strongly low prices, including of course low interest rates, and wishes at the same time to prohibit the import of "foreign money"; the payment of interest, he argues (p. 201), would impoverish the country. It is hardly possible to find in this literature even confused beginnings of a theory of value or control, and the detached reader finds it difficult to understand the favorable reappraisal of cameralists initiated by Schmoller's historical school and spread since by Professor Small's well-known book.[32] It was not surprising that the cameralist professors whose textbooks were brought out in new editions even as late as in the 1820's, often preferred to disregard the *Wealth of Nations*. So did, for instance, Sonnenfels, even in the editions of his textbook after 1800, which remained the offi-

---

en France. Traduction libre des 4e et 11e lettres de M. Graumann, ..." [Berlin, 1762]) with Justi's lamentations about bad coinage (*Entdeckte Ursachen des verderbten Münzwesens in Teutschland* [Leipzig, 1775]).

[32] A. W. Small's *The Cameralists, the Pioneers of German Social Polity* (Chicago, 1909) is misleading by its title and general trend; cameralism had—in spite of an amount of social interest of the social welfare type it displayed—actually no connection whatever with modern social politics in Germany; there is, of course, some connection between old and modern bureaucracy in Germany, and cameralists were indeed strong supporters of a bureaucratic régime. Still, Small defines cameralism (pp. 591 f.) as "an administrative technology" and sees clearly its lack of systematic economic thought as well as its purely political meaning; while more recent German interpretations, inspired by Small's work, try more or less to bring cameralism into the same range with Western mercantilism. Cf. Zielenziger, *Die alten deutschen Kameralisten* (Jena, 1914); L. Sommer, *Die österreichischen Kameralisten,* Vol. II (Wien, 1925) (more cautious); E. von Philippovich, in *Grundriss der Sozialökonomik* I (2d ed.), 132 f.

cial textbook of cameralism in the whole Austrian Empire, practically until the revolution of 1848; his pupil, the Vienna professor von Kudler (1786–1853) did not have the courage until 1846 to pour a lot of Smithian spirit into the old stuff of his master.[33]

This is characteristic of the backwardness of the Austrian Empire during the so-called "Metternich régime." In the rest of Germany things changed sooner; but even there, at first, the cameralistic resistance to Smith was a very decided one. It had its ultimate foundation in the economic and social organization of the country.[34] Germany was very differently developed in her different portions: she included the Polish provinces of Prussia, which still were in purely feudalistic conditions, as well as the comparatively rich merchant cities of the northwestern coast; and the French influenced southwestern peasant and artisan communities. But on the whole, the country was still in the medieval stage. Agriculture was, with few exceptions, organized as it had been for many centuries, if not in an even more feudalistic way, for after the suppression of the peasant uprisings in the sixteenth century their position had become harder than ever before. The mass of urban population was made up of poor artisans strongly organized in the old fashioned guilds (*Zünfte*). The kind of bourgeoisie which was the main support of the new industrial economics in the Western countries was almost wholly absent in Germany, or else was completely tied up in the local monopolistic guilds. Security markets and similar capitalistic developments hardly played any rôle as yet in economic life.[35]

[33] G. von Kudler, *Die Grundlehren der Volkswirtschaft*, 2 vols (Wien, 1846). Cf. Lustkandl, *Sonnenfels und Kudler* (Wien, 1891).

[34] See an introductory survey of German economic conditions at about 1800 (with further references) in C. W. Hasek, *The Introduction of Adam Smith's Doctrines into Germany* (New York, 1925), chap. i.

[35] Cf. Kaulla, *op. cit.*, p. 111.

The first response to a liberalism of the Smithian type should have been, therefore, a very unfriendly one; and it is rather surprising, and at the same time a proof of the might of ideas even contrary to actual economic organization, that the resistance against the *Wealth of Nations* did not last longer than some twenty years and did not take a more active form. The opposition found later its most characteristic literary expression in writings of men like Buesch[36] and A. W. Rehberg (1754–1836), both under the influence of James Steuart. Both were opposed to the *Wealth of Nations,* though conceding some of its merits. The resistance was the result, especially with Rehberg, of the traditional point of view of the family father as an ideal guide and leader of economic activities; arising out of the political philosophy of a patrimonial, highly inefficient but, in mere details, extremely vigorous bureaucracy. The economic freedom of laissez faire was for men of this type not much different from complete social disorganization. It is specially interesting to observe that an author like the learned representative of the commercial interests of Hamburg, Buesch, allied himself with this position. Hamburg was at this time perhaps the most modern commercial city of Germany and at the same time a republic; but its ruling body of distinguished merchants was more mercantilistic and more conservative than some of the feudal potentates.

Furthermore, there was even a distinct literature which frankly stood for feudal interests. Justus Moeser (1720–94) was the best writer of this kind; later, during and after the Napoleonic wars, Adam Müller, Heinrich Luden, the poet Kleist, and von Haller joined him. They did not attack Adam Smith

[36] J. G. Büsch, *Sämmtliche Schriften* (Wien, 1913–18), 16 vols. (incomplete). His two volumes on money (*Abhandlung von dem Geldumlauf* [Hamburg, 1800]) are perhaps what may be labeled as the best product of German mercantilism.

himself; it was rather the French Revolution and Rousseau whom they had in mind. They only tried to discredit him—and they were partly followed in this later by the German historical school—by arguing that his system merely describes or generalizes specific conditions which may exist on the British Isles but which are—they thought—impossible for the Continent. Their admiration for the institutions of the medieval age (Moeser, for instance, attempted an economic justification for agrarian serfdom)[37] could not fail to have its consequences when economic interests which could be served by them became sufficiently strong.

III

It seems that in France, after the Revolution, the *Wealth of Nations* held undisputed sway over the scholars. The old state and its bureaucracy were gone; in the new one, whatever government may have come, a large amount of (at least internal) economic freedom was the logical outcome of the abolition of vested rights[38] and of the administrative unification of the country. Mercantilism lost in this milieu, from the first, its obviousness even for the most pronounced "realist"; contrary to the situation in Italy, Spain, and of course Germany, almost no mercantilist writer in the old sense survived the great "revaluation of all values." F. L. A. Ferrier is regarded usually as one of the rare post-revolutionary mercantilists in France (*Du gouvernement considéré dans ses rapports avec le commerce* [Paris, 1805]); he insisted on the advantages of a favorable balance of

[37] J. Möser, "Defense of Serfdom" in *Vermischte Schriften,* II (Berlin, 1797), 106 f. Cf. L. Rupprecht, *J. Mösers soziale und volkswirtschaftliche Anschauungen* (Stuttgart, 1892). On the economics of German romanticism further references in Palyi, "Romantische Geldtheorie," *Archiv für Sozialwissenschaft* (1916).

[38] Ganilh, *La théorie de l'Économie politique...,* (Paris, 1815), I, 22, emphasized already this effect of the Revolution.

trade and even more on those of "fiat money." More than his contemporary J. Blanc de Volx (*État commercial de la France* [Paris, 1803. 3 vols.]) and just as St. Chamans a generation later (1852), he was rather an inflationist than anything else; in many respects, these "neomercantilists" were also influenced by Smith and Sismondi.[39] Charles Ganilh, also, in his different popularizations,[40] tried to moderate what he considered as exaggerations in Smith; this was, however, from the point of view of the general reader, very little different from a more superficial rearrangement of the *Wealth of Nations*.

Neither did the apparent competition with the system of the physiocrats mean a substantial obstacle. The influence of the latter in France had been of course probably more intensive and more widespread than anywhere else. In the 1770's practically everybody in France interested in financial and similar matters joined them; even politicians of the type of Necker, who was brought up in the mercantilist atmosphere and who certainly had not too much of theoretical or doctrinal inclinations, was "disposed to grant them the farthest reaching concessions."[41] The tide turned very soon in the opposite direction; and the critics, who had long been waiting for their chance, captured public opinion after the tragic breakdown of Turgot in the very year 1776. The *économistes* had become to some extent an object of ridicule for the intelligentsia who were disgusted by the rigid

[39] Cf. G. Dionnet, *Le néomercantilisme au 18e siècle et au début du 19e siècle* (Paris, 1901).

[40] *Des systèmes d'Économie politique* (Paris, 1809; 2d ed., 1821) (the first history of economics); *Dictionnaire analytique d'Économie politique* (Paris, 1826); *La théorie* ... (cited above). Canard, originally a moderate Smithian, joined Ferrier later in his *Mémoire sur les causes qui produisent la stagnation et le décroissement du commerce en France* ... (Paris, 1826).

[41] René Stourm, *Les Finances de l'ancien régime et de la Révolution* (Paris, 1885), II, 7, 11.

sect-like behavior and orthodox zeal of the group.[42] But their keenest adversaries among the *encyclopédistes,* like Diderot, Voltaire, Galiani, d'Holbach, Raynal, as well as among the contemporary "socialistes," like Linguet, Mably, Graslin, Legros, Tifaut, de la Noue and others, attacking the physiocrats individually or as a group on many lines of detail and generally on account of their very dogmatic attitudes,[43] almost unanimously agreed with them on some fundamentals of the liberal philosophy which was, for economic purposes, only slightly different from that of Adam Smith.

As a matter of fact, the physiocrats helped to pave the road for the success of the *Wealth of Nations* while they lost the capacity to obstruct that success to any important degree. To some extent, at least, Adam Smith profited immensely by the general spread of their ideas, since what *he* offered was or worked itself out as the direct continuation and refinement of the physiocratic doctrine. It was often observed, and is very obvious indeed, that agrarian economics still plays a fundamental rôle in the *Wealth of Nations* and that its author does not conceal his sympathy for landowners. Agriculture appears there not only as a "basic" industry in the technical sense; labor itself, the source of wealth, is in the first place agrarian labor. Furthermore, the ambiguity of the Smithian value-notion, the idea of using wheat as the standard in which to measure labor-value, may have easily impressed the contemporary reader as a fundamentally physiocratic concept.[44] No wonder, then, that the declining physiocratic movement, after having ignored the *Wealth*

[42] Cf. Allix, *op. cit.,* pp. 2 f. Dupont de Nemours (Schelle, *op. cit.,* pp. 182 f.) described frankly, during the Revolution, this situation of his friends.

[43] Cf. Weuleresse, *Le mouvement physiocratique en France,* II (Paris, 1910) 626–82; André Lichtenberger, *Le socialisme au 18ᵉ siècle* (Paris, 1895), pp. 276 ff; F. Blei, *Galiani und die Physiokraten* (Bern, 1895).

[44] H. Denis, *Histoire des systèmes économiques et socialistes,* I (Paris, 1904), 258 ff., mentions the agricultural bias of Smith also.

of Nations at first,[45] later tried to capitalize its influence by combining its doctrines with the dialectic of the *produit net.* This was not simple opportunism; the school developed to some extent under the genuine influence of Gournay and Turgot, and especially with Morellet in a direction similar to the classical English line.[46] But, of course, it was at the same time dictated by the desire to participate in the rapidly rising fame of the new system. A literature of a purely eclectic type arose, starting perhaps with Germain Garnier's *Abrégé élémentaire des principes de l'Économie politique* (Paris, 1796), followed by Peuchet's voluminous compilation (*Dictionnaire de géographie commerçante* [5 vols. Paris, 1799–1800]), by J. Dutens', *Analyse raisonnée des principes fondamentaux de l'économie politique* (Paris, 1804), and to some extent also by de Hauterive (1825) in France, the Swiss Isaac Iselin, the Germans Schmaltz, Karl Fulda, Leopold Krug, etc.; but it has only historical interest by marking the period of transition toward the ultimate victory of Smith. It shows also the transition to a new period of economic history which necessarily provides for the success of a new viewpoint just as the wide circulation of the *Physiocratie* at its time had been founded on the feudal and agrarian character of the period.[47]

The Smithian doctrine overcame the physiocrats for a reason much more important than a matter of purely scientific discussion. The same Garnier who had translated Smith and who, in the meantime, had practically left the physiocratic ranks,

[45] Thus Grivel, as late as 1794–98, in the dictionary *Panckoucke,* quoted by Allix, p. 5.

[46] As Weuleresse (*op. cit.* II, 723) pointed out.

[47] On the overwhelming agrarian economic interests backing *Physiocratie,* cf. Weuleresse, *op. cit.*, p. 719, and St. Bauer, "Zur Entstehung der Physiokratie" in *Jahrbücher für Nationalökonomie,* Neue Folge, vol. XXI (1890). *Vide* also Léon Cheinisse, *Les idées politiques des physiocrates* (Paris, 1914).

tells us in the Preface to his translation[48] how his former friends happened to attract the full hatred not only of all kinds of vested interests but also of the commercial and industrial middle classes. These classes were of course not yet very far in their development; the industrial revolution, however, although much slower in France until 1830 than in England, was on the way; without having yet produced so striking results in industrial progress and concentration, the fundamental change of the economic organization of the country was already, as Henri Sée's analysis of the restoration period shows, in full development.[49] This is especially true for the Napoleonic years; the data collected by a contemporary writer, Chaptal, show a partial transformation of the leading industries during those years and a consequent multiplication of the French production of wool and cotton goods, of coal, iron, and steel, chemicals, etc.[50] It was sufficient, at any rate, to raise the number and relative weight of the industrial and commercial middle classes. Their political weight, based as it was largely on the control of the financial and "intellectual" resources of the country, was substantially greater than the mere grade of progress in *machinisme* and industrial concentration would suggest.

The physiocrats, however, even thôse surviving after 1789, stood decidedly for the "landed interest." Weuleresse[51] holds them partly responsible for the Revolution: the attempt of the *seigneurs* which they fomented to get a share in the rise of revenues of the peasants had substantially contributed to evoke the hatred of the peasant population against fedual rights. The point is, of course, very controversial. Professor Allix has how-

[48] *La richesse des nations* (ed. Blanqui, Paris, 1843), p. xliv.

[49] *Sée* "Esquisse de l'évolution industrielle de la France de 1815 à 1848" in *Revue d'hist. écon. et sociale,* 1923, pp. 473 ff.

[50] Chaptal, *De l'industrie française* (Paris, 1819. 2 vols.).

[51] *Op. cit.,* p. 717.

ever recently, in a keen analysis of the political backgrounds of the later physiocrats, elucidated some of the interconnections.[52] A school, indeed, the best representatives of which, like Turgot, stood frankly for the thesis that *quoiconque n' a pas de terre n' a pas de patrie,* or, like Condorcet, denied full citizenship to anybody who was not a landowner, could hardly stand the intellectual storm brought out by the new "industrial system." The antagonism against this agrarian direction and its political representatives was certainly one of the main sources out of which the Smithianism of Say as well as the industrialism of Saint-Simon drew their original impetus. It was in the light of this fundamental political antagonism of the leading social classes that Say's work appeared to the contemporaries; it helps, indeed, to explain the success of Say which, on the Continent, in its turn contributed so greatly to the fame of Adam Smith.

A country with strong national self-consciousness and with aspirations toward political or at least cultural domination of the world does not easily accept the leadership of a foreigner; except when he gets "assimilated" through the work of an indigenous writer. Shortly after 1800, three French books appeared almost at the same time with the more or less avowed purpose of rearranging the *Wealth of Nations.* The first was the *Principes d'Économie politique* (Paris, 1801) of an engineer, N. F. Canard; it got the prize of the French Institut as the best reply—perhaps only by default of a better one—to the question whether, in an agrarian country, the landowners necessarily bear the burden of all taxes. The categorically negative reply indicates the break with physiocratic tradition; Canard's famous argument against *le frottement et les fluctuations qui sont une suite du défaut d'équilibre que l'établissement de l'impôt a rom-*

[52] "La rivalité entre la propriété foncière et la fortune mobilière sous la révolution," *Revue d'hist. écon. et sociale,* 1913, pp. 298 ff. Cf. also B. Minzès in *Revue d'écon. politique,* 1893.

pu (p. 186) is just as characteristic of the French bourgeois attitude as was Napoleon's almost simultaneous advice to the new Banque to keep the interest rate steady. But this first attempt on the Continent to build a new theory on Smithian foundations by casting his economic order into algebraic equations completely failed. It was just a short essay without sufficient elaboration; and the attempt to express a rather primitive labor-value theory in arithmetic form was an echo, in its artificial assumptions and its naïve mathematics, of the worst aspects of the *Tableau économique.* In spite of some of its merits (it gives an excellent statement of the equation of exchange on pp. 67 ff., and of price-determination by what the Austrians later called "marginal pairs"; it analyzes on pp. 182 ff. the incidence of taxation under the viewpoint of reactions on the demand side to price-changes, etc.), it was soon forgotten, and later, by the mathematical school (Cournot), dismissed.[53] The Bohemian aristocrat and enterpriser, Count Georg von Bouquoy (*Theorie des Nationalreichthums* [1816]), who first applied the calculus to economics, may be regarded as one of the few followers of Canard.

Smithianism ultimately starts in France in 1803 with Sismondi and Say. What considerations led these two very independent men to become—the first of course only temporarily—followers and popularizers of the *Wealth of Nations?* What was their own contribution toward the conquest of the Continent by Adam Smith? Just a few remarks on these may be allowed; the life-work of the two great French thinkers—both were, by the way, of *huguenot* descent—cannot be discussed here.

J. C. L. Simonde de Sismondi had been living at the end of

[53] Cf. G. Moret, *L'emploi des mathématiques en économie politique* (Paris, 1915), pp. 70 f.; Wl. Zawadsky, *Les mathématiques appliquées a l'économie politique* (Paris, 1914), pp. 31 f. For a more impartial, although still incomplete analysis, cf. Allix' art. on Canard in *Revue d'hist. écon. et sociale,* 1915, pp. 38 ff. Sismondi (*De la richesse* ... [1803], pp. 65 f., 129 f.) criticized Canard severely.

the 1790's, as a political refugee in Italy, devoting himself to agriculture. The result was his first economic essay, the *Tableau de l'agriculture toscane* (Paris, 1801), in the main a technical study influenced by physiocratic ideas.[54] Then came the two volumes: *De la richesse commerciale, ou principes d'économie politique appliqués à la legislation du commerce* (Genève, 1803). They are, together with Jean Baptiste Say's *Traité d'économie politique ou simple exposition de la manière dont se forment, se distribuent et se consomment les richesses,* which appeared in Paris at the same date, the first literary expressions in France of the "new" economic spirit, the spirit of commercialism and industrial progress.[55] Both offer a "reorganization" of the Smithian doctrine, trying to bring it into a more systematic shape and avoiding some of its apparent inconsistencies; both are keenly opposed to mercantilist prejudices and physiocratic bias; but Say became the real leader of the school and, it may be expressed thus without exaggeration, a partner in the glory and honor attributed on the Continent to Adam Smith. Say's *Traité* appeared in his own lifetime in six editions (the last one in 1829); it was expanded without change in the substance to almost double size in his several times reprinted *Cours complet d'économie politique* (Paris, 1828–30); an extract of it, the *Catéchisme*

[54] Cf. A. Aftalion, *L'oeuvre économique de S. de Sismondi* (Paris, 1899).

[55] Disregarding articles in the *Décades,* the colorless lectures of Roederer in 1800–1801, which appeared later as *Mémoires sur quelques points d'économie politique* (Paris, 1840), and such pamphlets without any intellectual merit like *De l'influence du gouvernement sur la prospérité du commerce* by Vital Roux (Paris, 1800). Cf. Allix, "J. B. Say et les origines de l'industrialisme" in *Revue d'économie politique,* 1910, pp. 303 f. Say's early work: *Olbie ou essai sur les moyens de réformer les moeurs d' une nation* (Paris, 1800) was not available for examination. A good bibliography of Say and his work is to be found in the book of E. Teilhac, *L'oeuvre économique de J. B. Say* (Paris, 1927), which appeared after this article was put in type. Teilhac also mentions some more contemporary writers of a more or less eclectic attitude like de Lamoillardière (1800), d'Arnaud de Vitrolles (1801), etc.

d'économie politique, came out in 1817 and was republished for the fourth time in 1834.[56] Sismondi's book had, in spite of the literary fame of the author, but little resonance; his position in the history of economic doctrines is usually connected with his later works which, since 1817, offered one of the very first and famous "socialistic" attempts toward a fundamental criticism of capitalistic society. But the earlier work remained almost unknown outside of France;[57] while every great European nation has provided for a translation of at least one of Say's works; one of the American editions of the *Treatise* (by C. R. Prinsep) appeared in 1824 in Boston.

It is obvious however that even during the period before his turning against *machinisme* Sismondi could not compete with Say for leadership among economic writers. Say's famous division of the whole subject into the three main fields (production, distribution, consumption) was comprehensive and became the standard type of organization in textbooks. Sismondi wrote an essay on commerce, with valuable contributions to the theory of international trade and of taxes, rather than a general treatise, although his introductory chapters tried to cover all aspects of value-theory. They did it by pointing out two of the fundamentals of the Smithian theory: the cost-value concept in the theory of prices and distribution; and the concept of consumers' satisfaction as underlying the doctrine of welfare. The very fact

[56] For a short and very able presentation of Say's main doctrines, cf. his *Lettres à M. Maltus sur différens sujets d'économie politique* (Paris, 1820). He emphasizes here that the "loi des débouchés" only holds true under perfectly free competition and under the assumption that the expansion of production is not checked by absentee ownership (in agriculture), lack of transportation facilities, etc. (pp. 87 ff.).

[57] It was so much forgotten until recently—in spite of the fame of Sismondi's later works—that in 1889 the learned Professor Zuckerkandl fully ignored it. The significance of the work (Book I, chap. v) for the theory of international trade is recently emphasized by Jacob Viner (*Journal of Political Economy*, 1926, pp. 601, 622).

of Sismondi's logical juxtaposition of the two concepts and his analysis of the *prix intrinsèque* on the side of the seller based on the three "revenues" (not real costs) and of the *prix relatif* of the buyer which between them tend to equality, was certainly no great advance on Smith's exposition, and it was too technical and, in its terminology, too ponderous for a time more interested in immediately applicable doctrines than in "academic" discussions. Say, on the contrary, offered the "plain common sense" of supply-and-demand mechanism; dealing with costs he came much closer to the concept of "real cost," assuming, of course, that prices under free competition offer a perfect measure of real costs as well as of utilities. Nobody before brought out as clearly one possible meaning of Smith's price theory: supply-and-demand determining prices, but being, in their turn, determined by the prices leaving costs of production as the ultimate factor of what Say called the *prix réel.* And he brought out better than anyone before had, the connecting link between cost and revenue by emphasizing the productive rôle of each factor. Of course both, Sismondi and Say, were more interested in "welfare economics" than in value theory; both followed strictly Adam Smith by considering consumers' interests (satisfactions) as the ultimate standard of economic policies. But while Sismondi did not as yet go farther than to insist on this point—his attitude in the latter socialistic writings does not interest us here—Say's real emphasis was on the producer and on the technical productivity of the factor "capital." Sismondi still thought in terms of agrarian and artisan communities, underlining the importance of international division of labor for them; his instances were mainly based on his agrarian experience. Say, on the contrary, saw clearer than Adam Smith ever did, the two new forces ruling the new century: the machine as the realization of capital and the entrepreneur, whose rôle he started to emphasize, as the personal factor behind it; in better accordance with the technical spirit and interest of the time,[58] his own interest was on the side of progress in industrial technique. Both are sons of the eighteenth century and of its fundamentally optimistic spirit; but with Sismondi this took the form of a purely abstract "balance" between production and consumption, while Say made out of it the magnificent picture of limitless accumulation of the factor capital with unlimited productivity in a world of perfect harmony between production and purchasing power, between industrial progress and improvement of consumption.

The similarities of the two imitators of Smith are far greater than their differences. Yet, as to their general attitude, the one remained in the transitory stage so characteristic of the master himself, while Say idealized with prophetic clearness the spirit of "industrialism" and of "saving" as the foundations of economic society, which was evolving rapidly on both sides of the Channel. It was Say's emphasis on industrial progress and on the rôle of the entrepreneur which gave the basic suggestions to Saint-Simon, who frankly admitted this dependence,[59] and to Saint-Simon's pupils as well as to the younger economists grouped around the *Censeur* after 1814. It was his idea of "productivity" which first, with Destutt de Tracy,[60] led to the distinction of the *classe*

[58] For the vast amount of interest in purely technical problems on the part of the "idéologues," cf. Picavet, *op. cit.*, Introd. and chap. i. On the prevalence of the spirit of natural sciences at the time, see: Taine, *The Ancient Régime*, Bk. III, chap. iii–iv; Bk. IV, chap. i. Say's *Traité* has an entire part devoted to the "Application des principes de l'économie politique aux diverses industries," dealing mainly with techniques; whereas only a short chapter deals with the monetary problem. Chapter xxi of Part V and chapter v of Part VII in his *Cours* hardly conceal his belittling of the importance of agriculture.

[59] Cf. Allix, *Revue d'économie politique*, 1910, pp. 357 f.; also E. Halévy, *Revue du Mois*, December 10, 1907, and July 10, 1908.

[60] *Eléments d'idéologie* (Paris, 1815), Parts IV and V; in the second edition these parts appeared as a separate *Traité d'économie politique* (Paris, 1823). Tracy's rôle as literary initiator of the "conflict" between creditors and debtors in capitalistic society was first approached by Karl Marx; Picavet's lengthy dis-

productive as opposed to the *oisifs* enjoying "unearned" revenues —the basic elaboration of the conflict between the entrepreneur and the *capitaliste*. It was the same mental attitude, expressed in political terms, underlying, after the end of the Empire, the liberal opposition of Dunoyer, Charles Comte, Benjamin Constant, and Thierry.[61] It was the same productivity idea which, combined with the influence of Ricardian analysis, gave the impetus to Thünen's notion of marginal productivity on the one hand and to the socialist development of labor-value theory on the other, and which, since the 1820's, was provided with an ethical sanctification by the narrow kind of moralism introduced by Charles Dunoyer and used since by typical exponents, conscious and unconscious of capitalistic interests.[62]

IV

Sismondi, as an economist, in his Smithian period had practically no influence; besides, during the Napoleonic years, he was again in exile. Say, in 1803, refused Napoleon's offer to co-operate with him, lost his position as member of the governing *tribunat*, and had to earn his living for a couple of years as an entrepreneur who was among the first ones to introduce the spinning jenny into France. But already under the Empire the influence of Smith on public policies became apparent. The French revolution had to some extent realized the liberal doctrine by

---

cussion (*op. cit.*, chap. v., especially pp. 377 f.) and even Allix' article on "D. de Tracy, économiste" in the *Revue d'économie politique*, 1912, pp. 424 ff., disregard this aspect of Tracy's work.

61 This political turning of economic liberalism is well described by Albert Schatz, *L'individualisme économique et social* (Paris, 1907), pp. 196 ff.

62 A Catholic writer, Charles Périn (*Les doctrines économiques depuis un siècle* [Paris et Lyon, 1880], pp. 80 ff.), was among the first ones to see the straight line of thought from Say's restriction of economics, suggested of course by Smith, to purely "economical" issues dismissing ethical and political questions, to Dunoyer's ethical glorification of the capitalistic system.

destroying the remnants of agrarian feudalism and of the guild system. As to financial matters, Napoleon's policy—he had read the *Wealth of Nations,* as well as Filangieri and Necker, in the military school in Paris[63]—of sound money and a stable interest rate, his severe economy in public expenditure, his disinclination against public debts of other than an emergency-character, and especially his decided attitude against every kind of direct state participation in trade, may have been suggested, partly at least, by Smith and his French followers. The *restauration* period gave the new school the chance to convert public opinion by combining industrial with the political liberalism; under the "bourgeois kingdom" of Louis Philippe the victory was so complete that liberalism had already to defend itself against the growing popular movements with socialistic trends. Official "science" at any rate, represented not only by Say's political partisans but also by the textbook-literature of the time (Joseph Droz, Dunoyer, Blanqui, and Carrion-Nisas *fils*[64] in the twenties and thirties; Pellegrino Rossi's *Cours d'économie politique* in 1840, etc.), stood firmly on Smithian grounds; it was of course Bastiat's *Harmonies économiques* (1850) which ultimately, by substituting a keen refutation of socialism in the place of Say's anti-mercantilism and anti-physiocracy, hammered the doctrine of laissez faire and of the natural division of labor into the capitalist minds of the whole Continent.

The story of the introduction of Adam Smith was perhaps more dramatic in Germany than anywhere else. Thanks to the painstaking scholarship of Wilhelm Roscher, it has long been known and has recently been retold.[65] The cameralistic resistance

[63] Cf. August Fournier, *Napoleon the First,* translated by Bourne (New York, 1904), p. 13.

[64] A. de Carrion-Nisas fils, Principes *d'économie politique* (Paris, 1825); J. Droz, *Économie politique* ..., (Paris, 1829).

[65] *Op. cit.*, pp. 593 ff. A more detailed history of the early introduction of Smith by Roscher is to be found in *Berichte über die Verhandlungen der kgl.*

has already been mentioned. It was suddenly broken by the energetic action of a number of professors who, though they did nothing but rewrite it and comment on it, must be credited for the initial success of the *Wealth of Nations* in Germany. It was of course largely facilitated by the fact that one of the leading German universities, Göttingen, came under English influence. Göttingen was the university of the Kingdom of Hanover, the Continental possession of the English dynasty. The official scientific paper of this university brought out the first German review of the *Wealth of Nations*. This university, thanks to the English influence and to the lack of immediate control by a narrow-minded ruler, was the most respected German school of social sciences of the time. Some of the best theorists of law, like Hugo, A. L. Schloezer, and Puetter, were teaching there. It was here that Professor Sartorius published in 1796 a textbook of economics which was really a summary of Adam Smith's principles, "for use with academic lectures" as the title remarked, and expounded the same subject further in another book ten years later.[66] From that time the *Wealth of Nations* became the main

sächsischen Gesellschaft der Wissenschaften, XIX (1867), 1–74, under the title "Die Ein- und Durchführung des Adam Smith' schen Systems in Deutschland." The numerous biographic articles of the *Handwörterbuch der Staatswissenschaften* (mostly by Meitzen) simply repeat Roscher's remarks, with some additional references. Carl William Hasek's *Introduction of Adam Smith's Doctrines into Germany* (New York, 1925) is in the main confined to the time about 1810, without trying to exhaust even that limited period. It deals only with part of the works of Garve, Sartorius, Kraus and Lueder, disregarding all other publications, even previous to 1810. Its merit lies in the analysis of Smith's influence on the Stein-Hardenberg reform work, elaborating the work done by historians like E. Meier (1881) and M. Lehmann (1902–5). A collection of essays dealing partly with our subject and not mentioned by Hasek is contained in the symposium *Die Entwicklung der deutschen Volkswirtschaftslehre im 19. Jahrhundert,* 2 vols. (Leipzig, 1900), cited in the following as "Schmoller-Festschrift."

[66] *Von den Elementen des Nationalreichthums, und von der Staatswirtschaft, nach Adam Smith* .... (Göttingen, 1806). Later, a disciple of Sartorius, Oberndorfer, brought out a revised presentation of the same kind under the title,

subject of economic teaching in Göttingen. Christian J. Kraus followed soon in the Prussian university of Königsberg;[67] Lueder,[68] first in Göttingen, then in another leading Prussian university, Halle (1816–17). By the force of competition the other universities, with the exception of the Austrian and a few more, followed suit. As the new century opened, the German universities, one after the other, offered chairs of economics to men of the new point of view, while cameralism gradually developed into a specialized study of "positiv" (as opposed to "natural") law and of administration.

The students of Sartorius, of Lueder and of Kraus, entering the Prussian civil service about 1800, laid the legal foundations of a modern Germany by the reform work of Stein and Hardenberg; in this indirect influence on policies—to be dealt with later—rather than in their own intellectual merits is to be sought the real basis for the fame of the early German Smithian writings. They only paraphrased the *Wealth of Nations,* adapting it to local needs of administration (Kraus) and to educational purposes; Sartorius emphasized the historical implications; while Lueder's book mainly collected additional statistical and descriptive data. This could not, of course, in the long run, be regarded as adequate. The same Sartorius, in 1806, started out in a new book[69] to supplement the economics of Adam Smith by additional emphasis on moral aspects, and to "moderate" the so-called "exaggerations" of the free-trade doctrine, without sub-

System der Nationalökonomie, aus der Natur des Nationallebens entwickelt (Landshut, 1822).

[67] His *Staatswirtschaft,* 5 vols. (Königsberg, 1808–11), appeared after his death. Cf. E. Kühn, *Der Staatswirtschaftslehrer Christian Jacob Kraus und seine Beziehungen zu Adam Smith* (Königsberg, 1902).

[68] August Ferdinand Lueder, *Über Nationalindustrie und Staatswirtschaft,* 2 vols. (Berlin, 1800–1802).

[69] *Abhandlungen, die Elemente des Nationalreichthums und die Staatswirtschaft betreffend,* Vol. I (Göttingen, 1806).

stantially deviating from the economic teachings of the master. This additional element in the early German Smithianism, similar to some extent to the humanitarian moralism of the later works of Sismondi, was, partly at least, due to the great interest in fundamental ethical issues raised by the Kantian philosophy, and especially also by Fichte. This combination of German "pure" ethics and Scotch economics may explain, at least in large part, the combination of a clear labor-value theory with a utopian system of distribution in Fichte's book *Der geschlossene Handelsstaat* of 1800; its best expression was, two decades later, the searching analysis of free competition and of other integral assumptions of the classical doctrine in the *Handbuch der Staatswirtschaftslehre* of J. F. E. Lotz (Vol. I [Erlangen, 1821]), with the resulting although carefully hidden claim (pp. 327 ff.) for equality of incomes as an essential condition for fair competition. In an earlier Book (*Über den Begriff der Polizei und den Umfang der Staatspolizeigewalt* [1807]) he defined as the purpose of economic policies (p. 11) the (ethical) perfection of the individual through the co-operation of all.

The "ethical" color in the academic economic teaching did not disappear even under the influence of Say's attempt at systematization, which however gave the direction to the thought of the next generation. L. H. Jacob, professor in Halle, claimed in 1805 that he was the first to try to bring the teachings of Smith into the form of a "scientific" system.[70] Indeed, the book presented by Smith was called even by Say a vast chaos of ideas and facts;[71] it was essentially a series of essays without definite systematic structure as a whole, with "hundreds of pages badly

[70] Ludwig Heinrich von Jacob, *Grundsätze der Nationalökonomie* (Halle, 1805). He also published (1807) a German and (later) a Russian translation of Say's *Traité*. His claim to the first systemization is in the third edition of his book, (Halle, 1825), I, iv f.

[71] In the first edition of the *Traité*, cited by Gide et Rist, *Histoire des doctrines économiques* (2d ed., Paris, 1913), p. 125.

arranged" (Patten); the one presented by Say organized the problems with regard to their respective relations, the whole presentation centered around the thesis of the equality, or better to say the perfect identity between producers' output and consumers' demand. It was the Smith-Say combination rather than Adam Smith alone which, for the following generation in Germany, as all over the Continent, served as the basis of economic thought. The main effort of the German writers in the first half of the nineteenth century was thus diverted toward the systematization of the "classical" doctrine. This trend covers, of course, different types of efforts. On the one hand, it was a purely methodological attempt, started with Hufeland's arguments about the definition of "goods," the nature of money, etc.;[72] it was continued especially with Soden's abstruse and often confused analysis of fundamental concepts,[73] followed by Murhard[74] and further developed by Lotz, ultimately leading to such terminological hair-splitting as lengthy discussions of the different kinds of riches and of poverty, of abstract and of concrete value, etc., in the leading textbook of the time, in K. H. Rau's *Grundsätze der Volkswirtschaftslehre* (8th ed., I [Leipzig, 1868], 94 f., 115 f.); even Lotz, certainly the best man of the group, confined his efforts partly to almost purely verbal issues like the definition of the words "cheap" and "expensive" and of the "right price" as

[72] Gottlieb Hufeland, *Neue Grundlegung der Staatswirtschaftskunst durch Prüfung und Berichtigung ihrer Hauptbegriffe von Gut, Werth, Preis, Geld und Volksvermögen,* Vol. I (1807), Vol. II (1813). The "new foundation" (mainly in the first volume) consists, as the title indicates, in the formal revision of the terms used by Smith and Say.

[73] Even a contemporary writer like Lotz (*Handbuch,* I, 137 f.) found the many-sided Count Julius von Soden too "metaphysical." But Lotz himself, as well as the rest, was influenced by the same "metaphysics" or rather "scholasticism"!

[74] Even the humorless Roscher (*Geschichte,* p. 847) could not help but be ironical about the ridiculous terminological innovations in Karl Murhard's *Theorie des Geldes und der Münze* (1817).

the mean between them.[75] Adolf Wagner, the re-editor of Rau's textbook half a century later, and Knapp, in his *State Theory of Money* (1903), still show the prevalence of the same spirit of terminological issues.

On the other hand, the systematic attempt went also in the direction of value-theory. Until the late seventies, when the unrestrained glorification of bureaucratic methods by the historical school captured the universities, a strong tradition of theoretical analysis prevailed, of course mostly in the sense of the Smith-Say type of approach; Thünen and Mangoldt were, as Ricardians, rather exceptions. Lotz tried occasionally, unfortunately with very inadequate technique and contradicting his own previous "subjective" attitude, to base the doctrine on a labor-value theory,[76] influenced, as most of the early labor-value theorists on the Continent were, probably more by Destutt de Tracy than by Ricardo, whose *Principles* was not even familiar to most of them. But on the whole, the supply-demand analysis prevailed with an additional emphasis on the subjective factor (Hufeland and Lotz stressed the subjective character of the whole price-making process, ultimately confusing the value and welfare concepts of Smith) and with closer approach than in the works of the classical writers to modern price-equilibrium concepts. It culminated in F. B. W. Hermann's *Staatswirtschaftliche Untersuchungen* (Munich, 1832). Hermann, starting out from Say's concept of mutual relations between supply, demand, and prices, gave the most realistic analysis of the price-making mechanism available before John Stuart Mill, analyzing individually the elements ruling each side (supply and demand); his presentation, which is still very incompletely appreciated in

[75] In the first volume of his *Revision der Grundbegriffe der Nationalwirthschaftslehre in Beziehung auf Theuerung und Wohlfeilheit und angemessene Preise und ihre Bedingungen* (1811).

[76] *Handbuch*, I, 54, 124.

the standard histories of economic thought, was certainly the best approach of his time toward a sound interpretation of the interrelations between "real" and "nominal" (pecuniary) aspects of economic life, stressing the difference between "technical" and "economic" viewpoints. His approach in price theory, emphasizing the rôle of consumers' desires and income, developed later as the starting-point of Menger's utility-analysis; and after decades of disrepute it is again in high esteem for its fundamental criticism of the wage-fund theory, for its rent-concept, and for its analysis of capital-accumulation as not based on any saving-process.[77]

On the whole, however, the German literature previous to 1830 differed from the English and even from the French by its lack of theoretical originality, its overwhelming interest in fruitless questions of definitions, its trend toward middle-class (peasant and artisan) interests and toward state interference on their behalf, and by greater scholarship in the form of skilful collecting of historical details and of descriptive stuff. As to the middle-class attitude, it was a conscious compromise of free-trade ideals with the actual cameralistic practice and with the guild system persisting partly until 1848. German Smithianism, as a matter of fact, after flourishing for ten or fifteen years, gradually assimilated in the reactionary period of Vormärz a growing amount of cameralistic "wisdom." Professor Rau, in his academic lectures from 1812 on, made the combination official by dividing the lectures into a theoretical and an applied part;[78] the latter was, partly at least, the old cameralistic stuff with a liberal accent superimposed on a completely different economic philosophy. His textbook (1826 ff.) elaborated further the division into an *allgemeiner* and a *politischer* part which became the standard organ-

[77] On Hermann's theory of value and distribution cf. Böhm-Bawerk, *Geschichte der Kapitalzinstheorien* (3d ed.) and A. Marshall, *Principles of political economy*, *passim*.

[78] Roscher, *op. cit.*, p. 848.

ization to be found in almost every German "system."[79] But even Fichte's labor-value socialism was fundamentally orientated on the handicraft system and on the interests of the so-called "middle-class" of independent artisans, on the "right to work," as has been shown recently;[80] it bears closer relationship to Proudhon than to the so-called "Ricardian socialists" of the early nineteenth century.

The "ethical" attitude of Sartorius and Lotz has been mentioned before. The ethicism of Lotz, as also the reasonings of Soden, Hufeland, Jakob, Rotteck, Oberndorfer, and F. G. Schulze, tends in the direction of partial restrictions of free competition in internal trade.[81] But these were just concessions and compromises which did not seriously alter the main liberal structure of their system. The economists mentioned, and many others in Germany,[82] as well as the leading contemporary (mostly German-born) economists in Russia (Christian von Schlözer, Heinrich Storch, etc.), accepted the *Wealth of Nations* as a whole and on most of the important issues.[83] With and without

[79] He called the second part *Polizei;* the term *Politik* came in the 1860's to replace *Polizei.* Another classificatory work of the same time, done by Soden and Jakob, was the separation of *Finanzwissenschaft* ("public finance") as a special field from economics. Consequently, the standard textbooks of public finance (Adolf Wagner, Heckel, Eheberg, etc.) until recently took their field rather for a branch of public law and administration, almost disregarding the underlying value problems. On Smith's influence in the German literature on public finance cf. Walter Lotz, *Finanzwissenschaft* (Tübingen, 1917), Part I.

[80] Cf. Marianne Weber, *Fichte's Sozialismus* . . . . (Tübingen, 1900).

[81] Cf. R. Keibel, "Ansichten über Freiheit und Beschränkung des inneren Handelsverkehrs," *Schmoller-Festschrift,* II, 10–26. With the exception of a few writers (W. J. Behr, Friedrich Bühen, K. S. Zachariae) there was general agreement as to the undesirableness of "unlimited" internal competition.

[82] E.g., von Ehrenthal, *Staatswirtschaft nach Naturgesetzen* (1819); K. H. L. Pölitz, the most-read popularizer of the school in the 1820's (Roscher, *op. cit.,* p. 841, called him the exponent of *Liberalismus vulgaris*); von Mohl; etc.

[83] It is a misrepresentation of the whole group under consideration, usual in recent German literature, to emphasize the differences of its doctrines as com-

restrictions, the idea of competitive society as expressed by Adam Smith deeply influenced also the economic policies of Middle and Eastern Europe. More so probably than in France, where there was, practically speaking, less need for it. The French Revolution had genuinely accomplished the greatest part of the reform of economic policies in the liberal sense; the greatest problem which remained to be solved was the one of external commercial policy. But in this respect, even after Napoleon's end and during the very "liberal" régime of Louis-Philippe, protectionism ruled. The Italian-born Rossi, Say's successor in the chair of the Collège de France, remarked in the forties that the doctrine of economic freedom of Adam Smith was enthusiastically accepted by the French bourgeoisie until they became the rulers of the state, but from then on they seemed to be interested only in protection and in state interference. And even the same Rossi, closely attached to the government of the bourgeois king, replaced Say's vigorous criticism of bureaucratic administration and interference by mild attacks on *centralisme* and argued even for direct state participation in production.[84] Furthermore, the other leader of the school, Dunoyer, formerly the most vigorous critic of bureaucratism among the collaborators of the *Censeur*, turned as a high employee of the state into a *panégyriste de l'autorité*,[85] largely contributing toward the disrepute of economic liberalism in the eyes of the workers. In France, after the Revo-

pared with those of Smith. A typical instance of this misinterpretation is offered in Judith Grünfeld's study on *Die leitenden sozial- und wirtschaftsphilosophischen Ideen in der deutschen Nationalökonomie und die Überwindung des Smithianismus bis auf Mohl und Hermann* (Wien, 1913).

[84] Cf. his *Cours,* IV, 211. On Rossi's development, cf. Gustave de Puynode, *Études sur les principaux économistes* (Paris, 1868), pp. 410–849; Augusto Graziani, *op. cit.,* pp. 229–79; G. Ruffoni, *P. Rossi* (Ferrara, 1897).

[85] Cf. *Allix,* "La déformation de l'économie politique libérale aprés J. B. Say: Charles Dunoyer," *Revue d' hist. des doctrines écon. et sociales,* 1911, pp. 115 ff.

lution, Smith had, on the whole, great scientific and political success but little direct influence on economic policies; whereas in Germany, while the early scientific outcome was much poorer, his practical influence was enormous. This influence of Smith on German policies was a manifold one; there are at least four directions in which the stream of the practical teachings of the *Wealth of Nations* fertilized the economic practices.

First, they helped substantially to create a social atmosphere in which merchants and industrialists became equal in rank to the upper classes of society. In Western Europe this evolution has been already achieved; even in France since the Revolution. In Germany where the traditional organization of society remained almost untouched after 1815, it was certainly the influence of Adam Smith, although supported by such democratic thinkers as Kant and Wilhelm von Humboldt, which worked in this direction. As Professor Cannan has pointed out,[86] the moral and economic justification of the business man was one of the most characteristic features of the *Wealth of Nations*. This influence clearly prevails in quite a number of German works during the first half of the century which in the main argue for the productivity of commerce and for the social importance of the merchant. Lueder, e.g., started out in 1808 with an essay on the influence of industrial progress on ethics and general culture.[87] There may also be mentioned in this connection the *System of European Politics and Commerce* of Stutzmann (1806), the book on *Commerce and its Influence on the Evolution of Civil, Spiritual and Moral Culture* by the Baron von Mylius (1828), and the *Theory and Policy of Commerce* by Charles Murhard (1831).[88] They show a practical application of the new doctrine

[86] "Adam Smith as an Economist," *Economica*, 1926, pp. 123–34.

[87] *Die Nationalindustrie und ihre Wirkungen* . . . . (1808).

[88] Johann Josua Stutzmann in *System der Politik und des Handels von Europa* (Nürnberg, 1806), pp. 103 f., claims commerce to be an ultimate source of

by emphasizing commerce rather than industry. Indeed, this did not mean in Germany, as it did in France, a question of economic or political supremacy; it was a simple question of equal rights for the new bourgeoisie, which was, at the beginning, a purely commercial rather than an industrial class. Even much later, members of the so-called German "Manchester School" of the sixties and seventies, men like Bamberger, Prince-Smith, and Michaelis, were still struggling for the same end and using the same arguments derived from Adam Smith.[89] The full success of the campaign for equal rights, of course, was not due to any one philosopher or to any particular set of ideas, but was rather the neccessary outcome of the industrial evolution of Germany during the last two generations.

Second, Adam Smith had a distinct influence on the development of German agriculture in addition to his influence on agricultural policy. Agriculture as an industry was very backward at the beginning of the century. The men who initiated the technical progress in German agriculture secured their standards of sound agricultural management from the English and derived their main suggestions from Adam Smith. I am referring to A. L. von Seutter[90] and especially to Albrecht von Thaer (1752–1828) whose work it was to reform and modernize agriculture by the propagation of new methods and, generally speaking, of rational techniques. It is interesting to note that Thaer joined

---

happiness and culture, etc.; Anton von Mylius, *Der Handel, betrachtet in seinem Einflusse auf die Entwicklung der bürgerlichen, geistigen und sittlichen Kultur* (Cöln, 1828); Karl Murhard, *Theorie und Politik des Handels* (Göttingen, 1831). Cf., also, G. F. Niemeyer, *Über den Einfluss des Handels und der Handelssysteme auf National- Glück und -Unglück* (Bremen, 1805).

[89] For an able presentation, cf. Julius Becker, *Das deutsche Manchestertum* (Karlsruhe, 1907).

[90] *Versuch einer Darstellung der höheren Landwirtschaftswissenschaft . . .* (Leipzig, 1800).

politically the feudal class and opposed temporarily the program of land reform to strengthen small holdings; and yet, he called Adam Smith "the immortal inventor of economic science." Indeed, in the first half of the century, the political conservatives are probably not less numerous among the disciples of Smith than the radicals.[91] The instance of Thaer, whose fundamental emphasis was on economic freedom as the basis of technical progress,[92] is a very instructive one. It shows a special kind of influence of Adam Smith which historians often disregard. The *Wealth of Nations* offered for the Continent not only a general economic philosophy and a program of governmental policy, it contained at the same time the very elements of a scientific inquiry into the principles of what we would call today "business economics." For most of its Continental readers it revealed for the first time the significance of technical progress through division of labor and businesslike attitude in agriculture as well as in public administration and even in cultural policy. And many of them were more impressed by the technical or production aspects of the *Wealth of Nations,* recently emphasized by American, "Institutionalists,"[93] than by his utterances on the value problem, although the first often served Smith only as illustrations for the second. It was at any rate in this technical sense more than in any other that he appealed to agricultural writers in Italy as well as in Prussia. Here, Thaer was the most important man of the type in question; Thünen started out from him rather

[91] Cf. Keibel, *op. cit.;* for England in the 1830's and '40's: E. Laskine, "La démocratie conservatrice en Angleterre," *Revue d'hist. écon. et sociale,* 1920, pp. 129–78.

[92] *Einleitung zur Kenntnis der englischen Landwirtschaft und ihrer neueren praktischen und theoretischen Fortschritte* . . . . , 3 vols. (1798 ff.); *Leitfaden zur allgemeinen landwirthschaftlichen Gewerbslehre* (1815). Cf. W. Wygodzinski, "Die volkswirtschaftlichen Grundlagen der landwirtschaftlichen Betriebslehre," *Schmoller-Festschrift,* II, 3 ff.

[93] W. H. Hamilton, "The Place of Value Theory in Economics," *Journal of Political Economy,* 1918, pp. 222 ff.

than direct from Ricardo.[94] In Italy, the first volume of Melchiore Gioja's *Nuovo prospetto delle scienze economiche* (Milano, 1815) mainly elaborated the economic and technical aspects of the division of labor. In both countries agriculture was the leading industry; and for this reason, and also because of the prevalence of great estates, it was agriculture to which the contemporary "business economist" was likely to turn in the first place.[95]

Furthermore, and this is especially important, Adam Smith must be credited to a large extent with having inspired the great economic reforms of Prussia during the Napoleonic wars (the so-called "Stein-Hardenberg reforms") which became the foundations of modern Prussia, of modern Germany. The leading men of the reform movement, mostly men of noble families, were chiefly educated for the civil service in the law and philosophy departments of Göttingen, Halle and Königsberg, the universities which at the time were the strongest fortresses of liberal thought in Germany. Of course it was not only Adam Smith's influence which led to these reforms, and German historians are sometimes inclined to overemphasize the influence of Kantian liberalism.[96] So far as the reform of Prussian civil service and

[94] Thünen (*Isolierter Staat,* II, Part II, 8 f.) called Adam Smith and Thaer his masters. In spite of sharp controversy in technical matters, the main trend of Thaer's doctrines was followed by all the important agrarian writers of the period; thus by J. G. Koppe, *Unterricht in Ackerbau und in der Viehzucht* (1812) and by J. N. von Schwerz.

[95] All German Smithians advocated "rational," i.e., capitalistic, methods in agriculture, most of them at the beginning (Kraus, *Staatswirtschaft,* Vol. V.; Thaer before 1809) on the basis of the great (baronial) estates, but after the abolition of serfdom on the basis of a medium-sized proprietorship (Soden, Lotz, Jacob, Buquoi, Schwerz, Rau, etc.). Cf. K. Grünberg, "Agrarpolitik," *Schmoller-Festschrift,* Vol. II, and Else Cronbach, *Das landwirtschaftliche Betriebsproblem in der deutschen Nationalökonomie bis zur Mitte des 19. Jahrhunderts* (Wien, 1907), pp. 20 ff. A similar pro-peasant attitude was characteristic of most of the contemporary French liberals too.

[96] F. Meinecke, *Das Zeitalter der deutschen Erhebung* (Bielefeld, 1906), p. 22, finds Kant more influential than Smith.

the introduction of municipal autonomy are concerned, the ideas of the French Revolution and other factors had certainly a more direct bearing than Adam Smith. An American scholar who recently wrote a study on *The Introduction of Adam Smith's Doctrines into Germany* properly emphasizes how difficult it is to trace specific influences in the great Prussian reform work:

> The Revolution of France, physiocratic views, the great war, as well as Smithian doctrines, all left their impress on the statesmen of this period. Only a preponderance of evidence can be adduced to show that Smith through his German expositors was often of great importance in the formulation of legal change. . . . . Many of the important statesmen of the reforms were filled with his ideas, and the economic changes which were occurring in this troubled period were in part largely favorable to his theories. . . . .[97]

The two main reforms in question were the abolition of serfdom by the so-called "Stein Edict of Emancipation" of 1807 and the reform of the industrial guilds. The first measure, which really created the institutional basis of the modern agricultural system of Prussia, had been prepared many years before by leading officials in the civil service, notably by Schroetter and the two brothers von Schoen; and the minister von Stein found it fully prepared when he took office. Similarly the dissolution of the guild system by Hardenberg as Chancellor of the State (1810–11) was prepared by his predecessors Altenstein and Count Dohna. Nevertheless the reforms as a whole are rightly connected with the names of the two statesmen Stein and Hardenberg. An analysis of their work and of their sources shows that they were actually conscious of adapting Smithian ideas to their policies. Their main collaborators—besides those mentioned before, J. von Auerswald, a pupil and roommate of Kraus in Königsberg; R. F. Friese; J. G. Frey; etc.—also refer mostly to Smith and use his arguments against both agrarian serfdom and the industrial guild system. They may have been

[97] Hasek, *op. cit.*, p. 126.

mistaken to some extent about their own sources; but the mere fact that they emphasized their own dependence on the *Wealth of Nations* and that indeed their policies as their arguments were mostly borrowed from that book, justify us in attributing to Adam Smith's influence a large share of the credit for those very significant developments in Central Europe.

Even after 1815 the German bureaucracy, although less enthusiastic than before for Adam Smith, remained under his influence. Nearly every important German state had at this time at least some liberal men among its high officials; there may be mentioned the Secret Counsel K. Kröncke (1771–1843) in Hessen, von Malchus and the Minister of Finance H. W. Crome in Wuerttemberg, not to speak of the large number of Smithians in the Prussian service.[98] Nevertheless, the general trend of reaction which characterized the period from 1815 to 1848 not only checked the actual application of the reform laws but even caused rather backward steps in internal economic policy.[99] But in one line Adam Smith still remained the idol of Prussian bureaucracy: namely that of foreign trade. Of course here his ideas and the interest of the ruling agrarian landlords were closely related.[100] Prussia was still an agrarian export country

[98] Besides those mentioned in the text and Thaer who co-operated on the agrarian reform-law of 1807, the government statistician J. G. Hoffmann (originally [1803] a radical disciple of Smith, but who became responsible for the reactionary Gewerbeordnung of 1845, which once more sanctioned the guilds), L. Krug, J. F. Benzenberg (1777–1846), and the free-trader Kunth, were more or less known by their publications.

[99] Cf. K. von Rohrscheidt, *Vom Zunftzwange zur Gewerbefreiheit,* (Berlin, 1898); Lehmenn, *Freiherr vom Stein,* Vol. II.

[100] Even on questions of industrial protectionism, the Prussian bureaucracy (Kunth, Maassen, von Humboldt, Hoffmann) took a decided free-trade attitude, although the representatives of the industrial interests in the economically advanced Rhine province (D. Hansemann, L. Camphausen) had fought for protection since the early 1820's. Cf. K. Rathgen, "Ansichten über Freihandel und Schutzzoll in der deutschen Staatspraxis des 19. Jahrhunderts," *Schmoller-Festschrift,* Vol. II.

with few modern industrial developments; for even as late as 1877 Bismarck, who represented agrarian Junker interests rather than any other economic ideas, declared that protectionism would have been a foolish policy for Germany. Two years later, of course, when the competition of the American grain caused the prices of Prussian rye to fall, he introduced the first agrarian import duties.[101] This, however, is a later development. For the fifty years or more which followed the peace of Vienna, the free-trade interests of the Prussian agrarians completely prevailed and led in alliance with the Smithian training of the leading bureaucrats to the policy of the Zollverein (tariff union) of the German states.[102]

V

It is a very significant fact in European history that in the leading western countries the *Wealth of Nations*, in some form or other, became a fundamental factor in popular thought; while in Germany it was accepted by public opinion only with important qualifications and never (except perhaps for a very few years, around 1800 and then again in the 1860's) became really popular. Early in the century the leading German Smithians stood, in every important respect—in originality of thought, in systematic presentation and in literary form—far behind Say. The great German liberal economists Hermann and Thünen came somewhat later; their difficult analysis however, could appeal only to the small minority of technically equipped readers. On the whole, Adam Smith had not found early enough outside of France either his Say or his Bastiat; either the systematic genius to whom he is largely indebted on the Continent for

[101] Cf. J. B. Esslen, *Die Politik des auswärtigen Handels* (Stuttgart, 1926), *passim.*

[102] Cf. Treitschke's *Deutsche Geschichte,* Vol. II; and Walter Lotz, *Die Ideen der deutschen Handelspolitik von 1860 bis 1891* (Leipzig, 1892).

the scientific glory which brought him fame, or the great popular writer who by the simplicity of his style and the clearness of his logical presentation secured for him a really great amount of publicity.

Yet, it is the German professor Kraus of Königsberg who has committed himself to the comparison of the *Wealth of Nations* with the Bible. It would be unjust to ridicule the enthusiasm expressed in this somewhat naïve way. Everybody knows today that all over the world the name of Adam Smith, for three generations at least, became synonymous with economic liberalism in its fundamental aspects. And his work had this great merit (or incompleteness) that anyone who agreed upon its basic liberal philosophy could interpret it on practically all significant issues in his own sense. It was, similar in this respect to the Gospel, the synthesis of many different intellectual movements of its time; and it was sufficiently ambiguous, therefore, to permit such widely different interpretations to be taken.

In the theory of value for example, three trends directly tied to the "classical" one, and a fourth group at least did not feel itself in opposition to the same. The pure and simple labor-value theory in Fichte's *Geschlossener Handelsstaat,* in the *Idéologie* of Destutt de Tracy, in Sismondi's *Nouveaux principes d'économie politique* (Paris, 1819), and in the socialistic writings of Nicolas Massias[103] and Joseph Auguste Rey[104] rightly claimed the authority of Adam Smith for its own viewpoint. But the same was done for the supply-demand analysis, whether it laid its emphasis on the labor cost (like Canard, Sismondi's *De la richesse,* partly also J. B. Say, and J. F. E. Lotz) as determining ultimately some kind of a normal price; or with the trend toward an equilibrium between utility and cost (Gioja, Hufeland, Her-

[103] *Principes de littérature, de philosophie, de politique et de morale* (Paris, 1827), III, 161 ff.

[104] *Théorie et pratique de la science sociale,* 2 vols. (Paris, 1842).

mann, and Rau). And was it not the same Adam Smith who taught that interest, wages, and rent are constituent elements of the price of products? This did not mean much of course for a handicraft-capitalism and an agrarian society based mainly on the traditional exploitation of the soil; yet it could be used, as J. B. Say and Hermann did use it for an interpretation of cost as including all kinds of "real costs." And even such "outsiders" as the industrialist Louis Say,[105] the brother of the famous economist, and later, August Walras[106]—the one emphasizing in a rather confused way, consumers' desires and their dependence on consumers' income; the other basing value-theory on the concept of rarity as the ratio between subjective wants and objective quantities—actually looked upon their own work as further developments of the doctrine of Adam Smith.

Jean Baptiste Say and his immediate Continental followers understood or interpreted him in the sense of industrialism; as the exponent of capitalistic industrial progress. But as has already been pointed out, the physiocrats also claimed him because of his argument that agriculture was more productive than other occupations.[107] Furthermore, Sismondi and most of the early German Smithians understood the doctrine mainly as ex-

[105] *Principales causes de la richesse ou de la misère des peuples et des particuliers* (Paris, 1818); *Considérations sur l'industrie et la législation . . . .* (Paris, 1822); *Traité elémentaire de la richesse individuelle et de la richesse publique . . . .* (Paris, 1827). In the first and third of these books, Louis Say stresses also the differences between private and public welfare, in opposition to the "harmony" assumed to prevail, under free competition, by his brother. Cf. the thesis of A. Desmazières, *Louis Say (1774–1840)* (Lille, 1911).

[106] *De la nature de la richesse et de l'origine de la valeur* (Paris, 1831). Cf. The biography by L. M. Leroy (*Auguste Walras, économiste* [Paris, 1923]) and the remarks of E. Antonelli in *Revue d'hist. écon. et sociale,* 1923, pp. 516–38.

[107] *Wealth of Nations,* Bk. II, chap. v: "No equal capital puts into motion a greater quantity of productive labour than that of the farmer." This is the first phrase of a lengthy paragraph in which Smith elaborates the higher productivity of agriculture and which closes with the words: "Of all the ways in which capital can be employed, it [agriculture] is by far the most advantageous to society."

pounding the interests of the consumer.[108] And they could for this interpretation find just as much support in the *Wealth of Nations* as did Say's followers, especially Dunoyer and Rossi, for their expansion of Smith's occasional remarks on savings as the only source of wealth,[109] to an identification almost of Smith's economics with a theory of production.[110] There was general agreement as to Smith's glorification of private saving and public economy; but his social sympathies were also sufficiently pronounced to attract even radicals; as late as about 1900 both the Manchesterian Leroy-Beaulieu[111] and the *Sozialpolitiker* Lujo Brentano felt themselves apparently closer to Adam Smith than to any other of the "classics." This social interest pervades his discussion of the economic struggle between the classes of society; and Sismondi, laying the foundations of the socialistic analysis of class struggle, followed this line. Yet his book was just as likely to become the literary repertoire of arguments for the ultimate "harmony" of interests, so natural for a son of the

[108] The theoretical difficulties of the later ones (until Hermann) arose partly out of the fact that they confused Smith's "objective" value theory and his "subjective" welfare doctrine. For a clear juxtaposition of the two, cf. Sismondi's footnote to the *Richesse des Nations* (ed. Blanqui, I [1843], 2): *Nous professons avec Adam Smith, que le travail est la seul origine de la richesse, que l'économie est le seul moyen de l'accumuler; mais nous ajoutons que la jouissance est le seul but de cette accumulation....*

[109] *Wealth of Nations,* Bk. IV, chap. ix.

[110] Cf. e.g., Rossi, *Cours,* IV, 7 f.; Charles Dunoyer's principal work, *L'Industrie et la morale considérées dans leur rapports avec la liberté* (Paris, 1825) (1845 new ed. under the title *De la liberté du travail*) almost wholly ignores the problem of distribution; his uncritical biographer Edmond Villey (*L'Oeuvre économique de Charles Dunoyer* [Paris, 1899]), who does not even object (pp. 314 ff.) to his complete confusion of description of facts and their appraisal, is highly surprised (p. 324) to find in his writings *one* reference to unequal distribution as a source of social problems.

[111] Cf. his remarks in a discussion of the *Académie des sciences morales et politiques,* reprinted in E. Levasseur, *Aperçu sur l'évolution des doctrines économiques et socialistes en France sous la troisième république* (Paris, 1906), pp. 103 ff.

eighteenth century. Statements of that kind are certainly not rare in the *Wealth of Nations,* which, furthermore, as Böhm-Bawerk criticized it, sometimes almost in the same phrase explains interest as the reward for capital's services and as a part of the wage taken away from the wage-earner.

Again, in monetary theory and in the theory of international trade, Smith was strongly influenced by his friend David Hume; but his exposition shows also a number of features familiar to the reader of Sir James Steuart's anti-quantitative arguments. Consequently, his early followers in France, especially Canard and Sismondi, were strict quantity-theorists, while most of the Germans (Hufeland, Soden, Jakob) took the opposite position. Even on the issue of commercial policies, the classical master of free trade, was, as everybody knows, ready on occasions to compromise. The first generation of Smithians, of course, saw the master only as the radical free-trader; still in the 1840's, he was the to-be-beheaded adversary of Friedrich List who really did nothing but develop one argument occasionally and disparagingly used by Smith. Half a century later, at any rate, "scientific" protectionism uses Smith's name,[112] which serves in England also to cover a kind of liberal nationalism;[113] and "Back to Adam Smith" did even actually become, strange as it looks, the motto of a method and spirit of inquiry underlying an imperialistic attitude.[114]

The social philosophy of Adam Smith was a fundamentally economic one. Professor William E. Rappard's brilliant essay on

[112] Richard Schüller, *Schutzzoll und Freihandel* (Leipzig and Vienna, 1905), *passim.*

[113] E.g., in J. S. Nicholson's *Project of empire* (London, 1909), chap. xiv.

[114] With W. Cunningham, *The Rise and Decline of the Free Trade Movement* (2d ed.; Cambridge, 1912), pp. 190 ff. On P. Leroy-Beaulieu's partial protectionism, based on Smith's argument for the Navigation Act, *vide* G. Pirou, *Les doctrines économiques en France depuis 1870* (Paris, 1925), pp. 116 ff.

L'économisme historique d'Adam Smith[115] has uncovered an intellectual attitude of the master which can hardly be described otherwise than by the adjective "materialistic." All manifestations of social life, the development of the whole social organism and of every part of it, according to some page or other of the *Wealth of Nations,* can be explained in terms of the underlying economic necessities and interests. It was this aspect of the doctrine which was adopted by the French, underlying the liberal *historicisme* since de Tocqueville as well as the historical philosophy of Saint-Simonisme and the sociology of August Comte; with Dunoyer and Bastiat this pure *économisme* became ethically glorified. On the other hand, the author of the *Wealth of Nations* was—superfluous to say—an ethicist himself, bitterly opposed to the "corruptive" influence of groups and their particular interests on the government,[116] to the politics of a "nation of shopkeepers." The egoism of his *homo oeconomicus* (the figure was actually constructed later) was certainly not a boundless one and not an a priori conceived dogma; the individualism of Adam Smith was—in spite of the occasional "invisible hand" entering the discussion—offered "only as a rule of practice," to use the expression of Lord Haldane,[117] as a description of the "usual" behavior of men rather than as an abstract *maxime* based on alleged natural laws of the physiocrat type. It was a "reasonable" egoism ultimately based on moral standards. Here, the later Sismondi started out with his conservative philosophy, just as Fichte, Sartorius, and Lotz did with their inclination toward state interference to protect the weak against the misfortunes of competition (which however was and remained for all of them the basic foundation of economic society). August Oncken and other historians have sufficiently emphasized the mod-

[115] In the symposium *Les sciences économiques et sociales à l'Université de Genève* (Genève, 1916), pp. 123–61.

[116] Rappard, *op. cit.,* p. 152.

[117] R. B. Haldane, *Life of Adam Smith* (London, 1887).

erate character of Smith's attitude in commercial as well as in social matters. Before the middle of the last century, until after the classical school on the Continent, struggling against the opposition of the socialists, became doctrinaire and dogmatic, it was perfectly possible on the one hand to combine Smithianism with the exposition of capitalistic interests; and on the other, to use it for basic arguments in the opposite direction, assuming only an agreement on the broad outlines of a liberal system.

The eclecticism of the *Wealth of Nations,* the amazing facility it shows in using the "sound" elements of every contemporary doctrine, and the appearance of unprejudiced preparedness to accept facts suitable or unsuitable for its own theories, have indeed largely contributed to the success of the book. It is hardly an exaggeration to say that the history of the interpretations of Adam Smith which filled economic literature in the first half of the century is the history of economic thought itself during that period. This is certainly true in regard to the basic issue of scientific work: the problem of method. The issue starts, in the modern sense, at the end of the eighteenth century and runs like a red thread throughout the whole succeeding century. Its early disciples used to present the system of Smith as a purely empirical one, confronting it with the "deductive" *physiocratie;* that the *physicisme* of this latter one was far from free of strong empirical and sensualistic elements could not be realized by a generation with only slight historical but the keenest practical interest.[118] Sartorius found it worth while to stress the fact that Smith had been connected with the administration of duties, as an argument for the scientific value of his book.[119] Sismondi and Say both started out in 1803 to preach the new gospel which was not based either *sur des calculs arides* or *sur un en-*

[118] V. Edgar Allix, "Le physicisme des Physiocrates," *Revue d'Économie politique,* 1911, pp. 563–86.

[119] Sartorius, *Handbuch,* pp. xxxxv f.

çhainement mathématique de théorèmes, déduites d'axiomes obscurs, donnés pour des vérités incontestables: it was based, they thought, on the empirical study of human "nature" as it appears *en différens temps et en différens lieux.*[120] Nothing but facts, they thought, observed by the author himself or registered in the historical and descriptive sources, were the contents of the *Wealth of Nations!* This mental attitude ought to be realized indeed, to understand the coming reaction of the historical school. But the success of Smith had here, at the time of the rising glory of the descriptive natural sciences and of the historic-philological research, one of its important roots. It was in this sense, too, that even opponents of Adam Smith agreed upon the alleged fact of the sudden foundation of economics as a science through his book.[121]

For longer than a generation, there was almost unanimous agreement on this inductive character of the *Wealth of Nations*, most often stressed, obviously enough, by the German followers. For the Germans, of course, it was a decisive argument against cameralism, which, as a pure description of policies, was at the time obviously closer to "reality" than any competing doctrine. In France the philosophical spirit of *idéologie* was still dominant, in spite of the revolutionary disillusions and of Napoleon's positivist attitude; there, empiricism got a particular meaning, starting out of the interpretation of induction in physics. Condillac and later Destutt de Tracy found for this attitude the methodological formula applied by J. B. Say to economics. Say's economics deals mainly with general facts (*faits généraux*) and uses arguments based on the *nature des choses,* which itself, he thought, is a fact. This last term served to cover the deductive

[120] Sismondi, *De la richesse,* I, xiv ff. Similarly, Say in the introduction to the *Traité* (pp. xiii, xxix, etc. of the 5th ed.)

[121] So Ganilh, who however did not find Smith empirical enough (*Théorie,* I, 35, 243); later Kautz, Roscher, Espinas, etc.

implications of the doctrine;[122] it meant the natural inclination of men to follow their own interests on the one hand, and the technical necessities underlying production on the other. Say's general facts again, as the alleged basis of the theory, were in reality very general indeed; for practical purposes, at least, they were identical with the economic laws of the English school;[123] they have become very popular recently in German methodology in the form of the *Idealtypes* introduced by Max Weber. Say stressed that *les faits généraux sont toujours les mêmes dans tous les cas semblables,* whereas the *faits particuliers* are cases complicated by the effects of *plusieurs lois* reacting on each other. This interpretation of method, however, could have been offered in the main by Adam Smith himself and shows once more the essentially synthetic character of his work, appealing to the empiricist as well as to the theoretical. Indeed, in spite of all its weaknesses, it was the outstanding essay of this type, combining theoretical analysis and historical verification, for almost a whole century.[124]

One of its greatest scientific merits, of course, was the separation of economics and politics, stressed by Say; but in spite of the explicit formulation of the separation of "science" and "art" in economics by Rossi (*Cours, 2e lesson*), this passed almost without notice by the contemporary economists.[125]

It has been mentioned already that there was unanimous agreement among the followers of Smith as to a greater or lesser

[122] A suggestive discussion of the argument by *la nature des choses* as used in Say's works is offered in E. Allix's article "La méthode et la conception de l'économie politique dans l'oeuvre de J. B Say," *Revue d'hist. des doctrines écon. et sociales,* 1911, pp. 321 ff.

[123] Cf. Aftalion, *Sismondi,* pp. 55 f.

[124] H. Denis, *op. cit.,* I, 245 f., gives a fair statement of this combined use of the "opposed" methods by Smith.

[125] Cf. Maurice Block, *Les progrès de la science économique depuis Adam Smith* (2d ed.; Paris, 1897), I 6 ff., 293 f.; Gide-Rist, *op. cit.,* pp. 129 f.

amount of fundamental "liberalism." This basic agreement went even farther. Even the greatest adversaries of the capitalistic organization of society, the socialists as well as the conservatives of the first half of the nineteenth century, agreed upon the fact that "capitalism" was the kind of control of production described by Adam Smith. The presentation of the capitalistic system as a unit; the rôle of division of labor; the rule by the consumer through the market; the significance of risk-bearing, of distribution of income resulting from and, at the same time, regulating the whole system, which was based, instead of on the obsolete artificial mechanism of the physiocrats, on a simple and obvious psychology and was apparently verified by historical data—this "theory of control" more than his doctrines of value or welfare, or any other of his particular theories, was the aspect of the *Wealth of Nations* which produced the deepest impression. Thanks to this theory, which was regarded after about 1800 as a "revelation" and which became the outstanding feature in the revolution of social thought, the name of Smith, for two or three generations at least, was the most used and misused one. This is perhaps the underlying basis of his lasting fame on the Continent.[126]

[126] Gide et Rist, *op. cit.* (pp. 80 ff. of the 2d ed.), emphasize the influence of *l'idée* [of Smith] *de la spontanéité des institutions économiques* in some of its aspects.

INDEX

PRINTED IN U·S·A